Psychology and Law

Psychology and Law

Can Justice Survive the Social Sciences?

Daniel N. Robinson

GEORGETOWN UNIVERSITY

New York / Oxford
OXFORD UNIVERSITY PRESS
1980

Copyright © 1980 by Oxford University Press, Inc.

Library of Congress Cataloging in Publication Data

Robinson, Daniel N   1937-
   Psychology and law.

   Bibliography: p.
   Includes index.
   1. Evidence, Expert—United States.   2.
Psychology, Forensic.   3. Insanity—Jurisprudence
—United States.   4. Social sciences.
I. Title.
KF8965.R6   347'.73'66   79-24050
ISBN 0-19-502725-6
ISBN 0-19-502726-4 pbk.

Printed in the United States of America

For
Francine

Chapter 1

The Positive Yet Purifying Role of Creatures in Our Divinization

An element of doctrine rarely emphasized by his commentators, but which explicitly exists in the writings of St. John of the Cross, is the positive and perfective role of creatures in our sanctification.

Indeed, there are passages and expressions of the Mystical Doctor which can be interpreted as demanding a cutting off from creation. Even if, in order to give these texts a more balanced meaning, we attempt to analyze carefully their literary and historical contexts together with their cultural and religious milieus, certain very real difficulties still remain. For example, what does John mean by *la cárcel del cuerpo?*[1] Do phrases like *actos torpes*[2] express a personal contempt for normal sexual movements, or were they simply the usual manner of speaking at his time? And the list goes on: *nada son y menos que nada, humano y bajo,* etc.[3] Both John and Teilhard were quite aware of the problems of interpretation that their writings would surely cause, and each author in his own way cautioned his readers accordingly.[4]

However, our approach in this study will not take the form of a polemical discussion of such particular questions. Rather, we intend to focus solely on basic principles.

1. Some General Observations

In order to discover the profound meaning and providential place of creation in the process of divinization in the theology of St. John of the Cross, we turn our attention to the *Spiritual Canticle*.[5] The poem begins abruptly with the anxious cry of the soul in search of its Beloved:

Where have you hidden yourself,
Oh my Beloved, having left me in anguish?
You fled like the deer,
Having wounded me.
I went forth searching frantically for you, and you were gone.[6]

This first stanza sets the tone for all that follows. When God opens our hearts more deeply to himself, we experience a painful wound of love. This wound becomes manifest in the agonizing realization that the Beloved has suddenly vanished without warning. Thus, we experience ourselves being immersed in an ever more obscure and confusing condition. We set out anxiously searching.

Previously, we had felt quite secure, very self-confident and self-reliant. Divine consolations and abundant perceptible graces were commonplace. We were basking in the pleasure of God's radiance. Then, without warning or apparent reason, this whole world of divine consolation disappears. What we had naively assumed to have been God is not he at all. We experience ourselves lost, abandoned, truly alone with *nada*.

Meditation on these verses of the opening stanza of the *Spiritual Canticle* enables us to experience through a certain empathy some of the sentiments which must have passed through John's heart in his Toledan prison. But also transparent in these verses are the lineaments of the interior journey of each and every one of us in the course of our deification.

"Where have you hidden yourself, oh my Beloved?" That

is: "Oh Word, my Spouse, show me the place where you are hidden." In this prayer we ask God "for the manifestation of his divine essence, because the place where the Son of God is hidden. . . . is the bosom of the Father. . . . which is concealed from mortal eyes and hidden from all human understanding."[7]

In this way, the *transcendence* of God constitutes the first source of the pain of absence. The deeper God draws us into loving communion with himself, the more we are forced to acknowledge that he completely transcends all we can ever know or experience of him. God so surpasses our powers of perceiving, attaining and feeling that we are left in a state of panic. God is experienced as far away. The pain of this realization is intensified because up to this threshold in our interiorization we had felt so intimately close to God. Now, at least on the level of sensory recognition, all has changed, and we fear that the change may be for the worst.

But John does not belabor the fact of God's transcendence here, since it should be evident to any spiritual person. He emphasizes instead the other essential yet rarely accentuated element of doctrine: namely, the paradoxical experience of the absence of God by reason of his *immanence*. "The Word, together with the Father and the Spirit, is hidden in essence and in presence within the intimate being of the soul. Consequently, thc person desiring to find God must go forth from all created things according to affection and will, and enter within him/herself in deepest recollection. . . . God is hidden within the soul. It is there that the true comtemplative must seek him with love" and in faith.[8]

In other words, God is so overwhelmingly yet subtly present within us that we can no longer find him as before. Our search for God is now mistaken on three accounts: (1) We persist in seeking something from him, of him, rather than God in himself. We are still preoccupied with feeling good about our prayer, with being consoled in our spiritual life, with knowing precisely on which rung of the ladder of interior progress we are situated.

19

(2) We continue looking for him everywhere except where he is truly to be found. We are still looking for him in sensory manifestations, in fond memories, in creatures both within and outside ourselves. The true God must henceforth be found in dark faith deep within the intimate being of our person, there abiding in transforming and purifying love. And (3) we insist on searching for God in a manner that can never approach the real him. We are still searching for him by our own efforts, with our own initiative, out of our own system of "should's" and "should not's." In a word, we are still trying to get something out of God, rather than humbly receiving God himself.

What does the Mystical Doctor mean by the expression "all created things" *(todas las cosas)?* Time and again John uses this or an equivalent phrase to refer to absolutely every created being, whether natural or supernatural, whether in heaven or on earth, whether personal or nonpersonal. In other words, the phrase "all created things" denotes every being that is not God himself, whether the creature is capable of being divinized, is an instrument of divinization or is already divinized. We must eventually go forth from them all, even from this earthly existence. There are no exceptions!

"To go forth from all things according to affection and will" is also a constant refrain in the vocabulary of John. Note that he insists that we must *go forth* from all things. He does not speak of *withdrawing* from anything. The accent falls on the positive movement towards God, in God, rather than away from something. Furthermore, there is not the slightest indication—either in John's life or in his writings—suggesting that the contemplative person (and there is truly a contemplative dimension in each of us) should or even can dispense with the normal and providential need of creatures in the process of interiorization. Nonetheless, because of the relationship of creature to Creator and because of the internal laws of movement from scatteredness to transforming union, the way of true spiritualization demands an unqualified detachment of the will with respect to all that is not God himself.

John furnishes an apt example of the need and providential use of created things on the one hand, together with complete renunciation of the will with regard to these same creatures on the other. Citing several authorities from Scripture concerning the mortification of the appetite, he quotes the Vulgate rendition of Luke 14:33: *Qui non renuntiat omnibus quae possidet, non potest meus esse discipulus.* Then he goes on to translate this logion of Jesus for his reader. As he does so, he carefully adds to it his own personal interpretation: "Whosoever does not renounce *with his will* everything he possesses cannot be my disciple."[9]

That is to say: What we must renounce above all is not the creature as such, but rather our will in regard to the creature. Even though in a general sense all creatures do exist to assist us in our quest for God, the actual presence or absence of any particular creature does not of itself directly help or impede that search. Whether it aids or not depends entirely on our inner attitude (our "will") towards the creature. Thus, the will attaching itself to a creature that is present or coveting something or someone that is absent—in other words, stopping itself on any creature whatsoever—can never go all the way to the goal of its search for the one true God.

In another context John had explained why this is so: "What we call 'night' here is the mortification of the will with respect to all created beings. . . . We are not speaking of the privation of created things themselves, since this would not in fact strip the soul if it coveted them. Instead, we are treating of the detachment of the will and appetite for them. It is precisely this which leaves us free and disencumbered of anything created, even though we may actually have that creature in our possession. Nothing created can occupy the soul nor directly cause it harm because none can enter into it. Rather, it is the will and appetite for creature which can do it much harm."[10]

The object of detachment, therefore, is not the creature itself, but rather the *stop of the will* upon the creature—a stop which obstructs our passage all the way through creation to God in himself. For God is God. He is not his creation. Yet he abides within the innermost being of every creature while continuing to transcend it entirely. Consequently, the person who would encounter him truly must pass all the way through creation.

As for the image "to go forth," John explains it this way: "This spiritual departure may be understood first as a going forth from all things through contempt and aversion for them; secondly, as a going out of oneself through forgetfulness of self."[11]

These sayings of the Mystical Doctor have a very negative ring indeed. Taken literally, one must ask how Christian such an attitude really is. Furthermore, the very image of a going forth in this context raises a question: If one must find God within oneself, would it not seem more normal to *enter into* oneself rather than to go out of oneself? This problem does not escape the attention of John either, for earlier he had stated that in order to perfect the union of love already established between the soul and God "it is fitting for the soul. . . to enter within itself in deepest recollection," communing there with God in love.[12]

What then is meant by this analogy of a spiritual departure from all things and from oneself in order to enter more deeply within oneself for the sake of communing there with God? It means this: God is infinitely beyond yet intimately within each creature. The creature is *of* God and *to* God. Given the proper nuances, it is also capable of being divinized. Nonetheless, the creature is not God himself, nor does it contain him, strictly speaking. The privileged place where each of us ultimately finds him is the intimate center of our being. There God dwells in us in love.[13]

This discovery is realized in a positive manner through contemplation and in a negative manner through the complete purification of the person with regard to everything created (him/herself included). The concentration of this *purifying contemplation* is upon the human will in such a way that God communicating himself to us consumes in love every trace of egocentrism and removes every attachment (stop), whatever it may be. Thus, God abiding within our deepest selves breaks the impasse of selfishness, regardless of its form or manifestation. If we have gone out of our egocentrism, this is not in order to shun any of our gifts, but rather with these same gifts to pass on to God through all.

From a practical point of view, one of the most difficult elements of this going forth is that of getting past the defense mechanisms which we have consciously or unconsciously built up over the years. These defenses constitute formidable obstacles to progress in God. And perhaps it is for this reason that John attacks them with such vehemence: "through contempt and aversion for creatures; through forgetfulness of self."

Having made these general observations, we now move on to develop more specifically the positive contribution of creatures in the process of purification.

2. The Positive Role of Creatures in Greater Detail

Several times St. John of the Cross uses the following literary device: He begins with an abrupt and sometimes startling statement which captures the attention of his readers. He then follows this up with a more ample explanation in order to establish the context in which his initial assertions can be more properly understood. The purifying role of creation in our sanctification, as presented in the *Spiritual Canticle,* is an application of just such a methodology.

John begins the *Canticle* very abruptly: "Where have you hidden yourself, oh my Beloved?" In the opening stanza he describes in just twenty-two words of powerful poetry one of the most complex and perplexing experiences on our journey towards union: the apparent absence of God by reason of his overwhelming presence within us. This experience, so concisely expressed by

John, caps a long personal history of divine preparation within each of us and can be correctly appreciated only when situated within a broader mystical and theological context. Having captured the reader's attention, John then proceeds to fill in that context in stanzas 2–7 of the *Spiritual Canticle*.

Throughout these six stanzas (2–7) he specifically treats of the knowledge *(conocimiento)* of creatures. He addresses in successive order self-knowledge, knowledge of nonpersonal creation and knowledge of persons. The meaning that he gives the term "knowledge" is derived from the biblical usage of the word: namely, experience. Thus, John is stressing our providential need for deep and direct personal involvement with the creatures in our life. In the case of knowledge of persons, he is referring to deep and direct interpersonal involvement.

John's first step in constructing the broader theological context of stanza 1 consists in what might be called the beginning of adult spiritual life (stanzas 2–3): the phase of self-knowledge, active purification and discursive prayer.

Undoubtedly, the single most important creature in the life of each of us is our own self, our very personhood. It is there that all transformation and purgation must begin. Our person is the core where God abides in love. It is the matrix of all his salvific activity in our regard.

The basic principle underlying John of the Cross's theology of self-knowledge and mortification is this: The more we come to experience our true self together with God in us, the more we perceive the obvious stops of our will on certain creatures. What positive action can we take in order to get moving again? We mortify our will and appetites with respect to the creature in question. John goes on to spell out the nature of this mortification: Christian renunciation is basically a positive reaction on our part with respect to our own self-knowledge. This reaction should affect our involvement in/with the created in such a way that we become more mature (ie., less attached). This detachment must attain not only the will, but every facet of the human person. All desires, pleasures and enjoyments undergo intense purification. Every attachment must become detached.

Even though this mortification arises from a positive need and awareness within us, we nonetheless experience it quite painfully. The most obvious source of this pain is the realization that nothing created can ever again bring back the Beloved as before, since God is calling us forward into ever deeper mystery. In this condition, the searching soul directly addresses creation with this anxious cry:

> O forests and thickets,
> Planted by the hand of my Beloved,
> O meadows of green
> Adorned with flowers,
> Tell me, has he passed through *[por]* you?[14]

Some translators render the *por* of the Spanish text "by" rather than "through." This is an unfortunate and misleading choice of terms. John is stressing that the Word passed *through* creation in virtue of his incarnation, death and resurrection. He did not just pass it by or pass it up. Therefore, the true follower of Christ must do likewise. In our journey to God, we too must pass all the way through creation, not circumvent it.

The above stanza marks a new threshold (a more intense interiorization) in our quest. Now "the soul begins to journey through the consideration and knowledge of creatures to knowledge of its Beloved, their Creator. Indeed, after the exercise of self-knowledge, this experience of creatures is the next step along this spiritual road to knowledge of God."[15]

In response, creation recognizes the gifts it has received from its Creator as well as their place in his plan:

> Pouring out a thousand graces,
> He passed through *[por]* these groves in haste.

And beholding them as he went,
With his glance alone
Left them all clothed in beauty.[16]

Yes, he passed through creation in haste: that is, without stopping, without getting hung up, without becoming attached to anything or anyone anywhere along the way.

In the next stanza (6), John elaborates in some detail upon his understanding of the role of creation in our divinization. He introduces his remarks in this manner: "In the living contemplation and knowledge of creatures, the soul beholds the immense fullness of graces, virtue and beauty with which God has gifted them."[17]

This observation is not of course particular to St. John of the Cross, since any person of good will should perceive as much. However, building upon this basis, John offers a deeper insight. At a certain threshold in the process of spiritualization, God dwelling and operating from deep within our innermost being intensifies his transforming activity to the point of thrusting us more profoundly into the obscure way of the night. The role of creatures, without shifting direction, then becomes more acutely and decisively purifying. Thus, "the soul—wounded in love by this trace of the beauty of its Beloved, a beauty that it has experienced in creatures, and anxious to see this invisible Beauty—speaks the following verses:

'Who has the power to heal me?
Cease surrendering yourself to me in this manner.
Do not send me
Any other messenger,
Since they cannot bring me what I yearn for.' "[18]

The truths underlying this stanza may be summarized in this manner: Because God is immanent in his creatures, the more we experience creation in its depths, the more we know *of* its Creator. An increase in the knowledge of God through his creatures causes an intensification of love for him. This in turn increases the yearning for the presence of our Beloved in himself and for complete union with him.

But there is even more to this mystery. This deeper experience of God through creation not only brings about an increase in love, but it furthermore effects an increase in suffering. In becoming more conscious of God, we see all the more unmistakably that no creature, however excellent it may be, is the One whom we relentlessly seek. Only the Beloved can fulfill in perfect and consummated love the inexhaustible yearnings of the human heart. In this way we are wounded ever more painfully by our thirst to be possessed completely by God on the one hand, and on the other by the inability of any creature to give him in the plenitude we crave. This wound of love hollows out a painful vacuum within us which only God in himself can fill.

The more we are drawn into transforming union, the more deeply we experience the wound of love. St. John of the Cross speaks of three successive phases of this wounding in relation to ever intensifying spiritualization: *herida* (a surface wound: *Canticle,* 1) *llaga* (a deeper wound: *Canticle,* 7) and *cauterio* (wound by fire: *Flame,* 2).

In other contexts, John treats amply of the wounds we inflict on ourselves by self-love and self-indulgence—the wounds of false love, as it were. But in our present context he is speaking of the wound caused by mature love of God through his creatures. This wound comprises in essence the impossibility of the human person to become completely satisfied by anyone or anything other than God in himself. Thus, the term "wound of love" does not refer to some form of dissatisfaction nor to the result of negative or regressive attitudes or experiences. It refers to the normal and providential consequence of authentic Christian involvement.

Fully conscious of this wound of love, the soul laments: "Who has the power to heal me? Which means: Among all the

27

gratifications of the world, all the satisfactions of the senses, all the pleasures and delights of the spirit, certainly nothing can heal me, nothing is able to satisfy me. . . . Not only do all other things fail to satisfy the soul. . . but rather they increase its hunger and appetite to see him as he is in himself. Thus, the glimpses of the Beloved which are obtained from knowledge, from feeling or from any other communication whatsoever are like messengers which teach something about him, quickening and exciting the appetite more, as do crumbs in an intense hunger."[19] But they cannot ever bring God in himself to us.

The Sanjuanist theology of the cross inherent in this perception of creation is profoundly positive. True Christian appreciation of creatures causes an emptiness, an absence which only God himself can fill. In this manner, the creature as creature accomplishes its role perfectly. It demonstrates experientially that it is entirely from God and to God without ever becoming God. Furthermore, real knowledge of and mature affection for creation are not only tolerable; they are providentially necessary so that we can experience within ourselves even more acutely the positive void which this very knowledge and love produce.

Once God has brought us through the threshold of spiritual adulthood, he takes possession of us even more directly, but always in a manner which enhances our individual freedom. He accomplishes this progressively with our active participation. Thus, to the degree that we seek him, God himself quickens and directs this same search by the loving wound of his absence, which wound derives from his transcendent immanence.

From a certain point of view this absence of God is a sort of optical illusion. In reality he is more present and more directly operative within us than ever before. Yet, from another point of view, this sense of distance is very real. For God is wholly Other. Each deepening encounter with him in faith through creatures intensifies this realization. Thus, deeper awareness of the immanence of God serves only to increase our appreciation of his utter transcendence. The immanence of God always remains transcendent.

Having enabled us to taste the splendors of creation, God then causes us to experience unmistakably through this encounter our inexhaustible yearning to abandon ourselves unreservedly to him, our Creator. In this sense the images of abyss, of hunger, of thirst serve to accentuate the consciousness of our limitless receptivity to God. Only the person who is stopped on some creature is, so to speak, engulfed or imprisoned. The soul who proceeds on its way towards God through creation reaches its goal. Its heart is becoming ever more opened to the One-Thing-Necessary (Luke 10:42). Thus, creatures fulfill their mission: the finite has opened the human heart to the Infinite. The created has made us more consciously receptive to the Uncreated.

The Mystical Doctor summarizes this chapter of the *Canticle* with a moving prayer: "Lord, my Spouse, what you gave of yourself to me in part, give now entirely. And what you show in glimpses, show now in full light. . . . communicating yourself by yourself. It appears at times in your visits that you are going to give me the jewel of possessing you. Then, when I examine myself more carefully, I find myself deprived of you in the manner I crave to have you. . . . Therefore, surrender yourself now giving yourself completely to all my being, so that I may possess you totally. Henceforth, cease sending me messengers who do not know how to tell me what I seek. . . . Nothing in heaven or on earth can give me the experience I so pine to have of you. . . . Instead of these messengers then, Oh Lord, may you yourself be both the Messenger and the Message."[20]

The seventh stanza of the *Spiritual Canticle* both concludes John's presentation on the positive role of creatures in our sanctification and at the same time introduces a deeper phase in the wound of love. In stanzas 4–6, he had been referring principally to nonpersonal creation: what we would call "things." However, in stanza 7, John treats specifically of involvement with persons other than oneself.

Endowed with intelligence, free will and immortality, personhood is the crown of creation. Our mature love for another person, therefore, carries with it much deeper potential for experience of God. This, in turn, causes such an increase in the wound of love that John even changes the word for wound (*herida* in stanzas 1–6) to *llaga* (in stanza 7).

Thus, in the theology of the Mystical Doctor, not only is nonpersonal creation necessary in the process of our gradual transformation in God, but persons together with personal involvements and commitments constitute an even more crucial service in opening us to uncreated grace. Creation, especially personal creation, is essential to the actualization of our receptivity to God in himself.

Obviously the complete teaching of St. John of the Cross concerning creation is not included in this brief presentation. Nonetheless, what we have presented serves to highlight the dynamics and the positive dimension that he emphasizes with respect to the role of creatures in our divinization. This positive accent underlies his many negative expressions and puts them in proper perspective. Thus, the criticism made by Teilhard concerning this element of John's spirituality—criticism expressed in *The Road of the West* (1932)—is not justified.

In order to summarize what has been expressed above and to introduce what follows, we cite a passage from the *Night* (II, 9, 1). These lines explain particularly well the purpose of the dark night of the soul in its relation to everything created: "Even though this blessed night[21] darkens the spirit, it does so only to impart light in all things. And even though it humbles us and reveals our miseries, it does so only to exalt us. And even though it impoverishes us and empties us of all our possessions and natural affections, it does so only that we may reach forward divinely to the enjoyment of everything in heaven and on earth, all the while preserving a general freedom of spirit in them all."

Notes from Chapter 1

1. "The prison of the body" (*Ascent*, II, 8, 4).

2. "Dirty [lascivious, disgraceful, impure] acts" (*Night*, I, 4, 1–8).

3. "They are even less then nothing" (*Ascent*, I, 4,3); "Human and consequently lowly" (*Night*, II, 16, 4).

4. See *Ascent, Prologue*, 1, 8–9; and *Writings*, p. 272; *letter to Valensin*, July 15, 1929.

5. Most of the stanzas of the *Cántico* were composed during his imprisonment in Toledo, Spain (1578). John's commentary on the poem was written in 1584 after the *Ascent (cir.* 1579–81) only to be followed by a second and definitive redaction *cir.* 1587–1588.

6. *Canticle*, stanza 1.

7. *Canticle*, 1, 3.

8. *Canticle*, 1, 5.

9. *Ascent*, I, 5, 2.

10. *Ascent*, I, 3, 1–4.

11. *Canticle*, 1, 20.

12. *Canticle*, 1, 6.

13. The analogy of "center" for John is consistent with Western mysticism: namely, a loving movement towards the Center who is Christ. This is a transforming and unifying concentration: *engolfarse en el centro* (*Night*, II, 20, 6). Thus, "center" is not a spatial or mathematical term, but rather one which denotes the utter open-endedness of pure quality as in the expression: *en el centro de su humilidad* (Ascent, I, 13, 13).

14. *Canticle*, stanza 4.

15. *Canticle*, 4, 1.

16. *Canticle*, stanza 5.

17. *Canticle*, 6, 1.

18. *Canticle*, stanza 6.

19. *Canticle*, 6, 3–4.

20. *Canticle*, 6, 6–7.

21. *Esta dichosa noche*: the *beata nox* of the Easter Vigil proclamation.

Chapter 2

Purification as Essential to Union with God

This chapter examines certain specific aspects of the dark night of the soul according to the Mystical Doctor. Together with the previous chapter, this one will serve as a basis for comparison with Teilhard's theology of receptivity. The presentation also responds indirectly to Teilhard's remarks: a misguided "form of renunciation is that of a cutting off, a rupture with the World, an evacuation pure and simple of the old man. St. John of the Cross read literally seems to conceive of the night in just that way."[1]

When one speaks of John of the Cross and purification, one spontaneously thinks of the dark night. This phrase refers to his eight-stanza poem, *En una noche oscura,* written within several weeks of his prison break. It evokes also the two commentaries he began on that poem, but never completed: *The Ascent of Mt. Carmel* (cir. 1582) and *The Dark Night of the Soul* (cir. 1585). The phrase, furthermore, denotes the doctrine which occupies such a central place in all his works.

The first stanza of the poem *En una noche oscura* reads:

In a dark night,
Burning in love with anguish,
—Oh happy chance!—
I went forth without being seen;
My house being already at rest.

In order to appreciate the fact that John is describing here not only a personal mystical threshold, but also a very specific historical event in his own life—namely, his nocturnal escape from prison—it suffices to stroll along *El Paseo del Carmen* in Toledo, Spain. There one can stand on the approximate spot where John, emaciated from dysentery and nine months of solitary confinement, jumped to freedom on that moonless August night in 1578. One need only see the jagged cliff which rises up from the raging Tajo River at the foot of the ancient wall of Carmel to imagine some of the indescribable terror and relief that must have filled his heart at that moment. But John does not linger on his prison break as such. Using that historical event as a kind of springboard and symbol, he concentrates instead on describing the fundamental breakthrough which results as God takes definitive possession of each of us.

Thus, the Mystical Doctor presents in moving imagery the first of four essential characteristics of purification: (1) It is down-to-earth. (2) It is received in/by the person. (3) It propels us forward. (4) It establishes us in peace.

First, therefore, purgation is always radically *concrete*, down-to-earth, permeating the person even to the most banal details of his/her daily existence. The specific form that purification takes is tailored by God to all the particulars, no matter how seemingly trivial or insignificant, of each individual's life. No one escapes the consuming fire of divine love. We all pass through the dark night, for we all must ultimately die.

A second essential dimension to purification is that we *undergo* the night. Every truly salvific action within us is received. We do not save ourselves or one another. We are saved by God.

John emphasizes this point while commenting on the fourth line of the stanza in question: "the soul goes forth—God wrenching it out—solely because of his love."[2] Our interior situation is described in this sentence by an active verb "to go out": "the soul goes forth." Immediately, however, John adds with insistence: "God wrenching it out." That is, this departure is in reality more passive than active because it is God who makes us go forth. He breaks our shackles so that we can move freely out of self and more deeply into him.

The phrase "oh happy chance" is another indication of this truth. This going forth, this radical tearing out, *happens* to us. And we are indeed fortunate that it does happen! There certainly do exist what are termed "active purifications." These are the voluntary mortifications which we undertake as a result of self-knowledge. But, at best, these attain only the surface of our personhood in our struggle to overcome selfishness. God himself must directly purify us in our depths. It is the Father alone who prunes (John 15:–1). Moreover, this deeper purification happens not as a punishment, but in love: "solely because of his love."[3]

A third characteristic of this night is its underlying *movement*, its inner tension toward something better. The rhythm of the Spanish text reveals an energetic procession. The verb *salir* (to go forth) indicates not only the act of leaving, but above all that of making a leap forward, that of being propelled. We are freed from certain attachments and immaturities in order to advance more directly on the way of Spirit. This is true progress.

A fourth characteristic of this night is its sense of *peace*. Peace exists in the midst and in spite of the intensity of the purification. John stresses this truth in the second and fifth lines of the stanza in question.

In the second line he juxtaposes love and anguish: "burning in love with anguish." Fear, confusion, pain—in a word, anxiety—are very intense during some phases of the night. Yet, all the while this is going on, our innermost being burns with love. Even in the most intense throes of the night of spirit nothing can ever quench the conviction that God is really in control and that he will faithfully bring all this turmoil to a peaceful resolution.

In the fifth line of this stanza John states the characteristic of peace even more directly: "My house [inner self] being already at rest [in peace]." Moreover, this occurs in (during, on, in the course of) the dark night itself.

There will undoubtedly be a profound peace after we have completed our journey through the night. But here the Mystical Doctor is stressing that in the midst of the perplexities of this purification a very deep peace already exists. This has nothing at all to do with the peace which the world might try to give. God's peace does not consist in the satisfaction of the appetites or in relaxation from tension. Rather, it is that of the purifying and transforming presence of God within us. Love, faith and hope are intensified in proportion to the intensity of the night. This is so, not because suffering of itself is capable of causing an increase of the divine presence within us, but rather because total darkness is the necessary condition for complete abandonment to God. Instead of plunging us into sheer nothingness, the night is a "happy chance"—a veritable grace—and as such becomes the most conducive milieu to facilitate the divinizing and pacifying activity of God within us. Not only can the world not bestow this peace, the world finds it impossible even to comprehend.

Thus, by reason of its essential relationship to transforming union, the night is revealed as a fundamentally positive reality. John explains it this way: "This dark night is an influence of God within the soul which purges it. . . . This we call infused contemplation. By it God secretly teaches us and instructs us in the perfection of love, without our doing anything or even understanding how this is taking place. This contemplation, as the loving wisdom of God, causes two principal effects within us: by purifying us and illuminating us, it disposes us for union in love with God."[4]

These considerations raise two important questions which bear directly on our purpose: (1) What are the far-reaching implications of the phrase: "This dark night is an influence of God within the soul"? And (2) what is the process whereby this purification is accomplished?

1. "This Dark Night Is an Influence of God within the Soul"[5]

Who/what are the causes of the night? Scholastic theology, in which St. John of the Cross was thoroughly schooled at Salamanca, distinguishes four causes: *efficient* (the agent who does something); *final* (the reason why something is done); *material* (that which is acted upon); and *formal* (that which makes something be what it is). Without posing the question in a strictly scholastic fashion, the Mystical Doctor does nevertheless treat the four causes of purification.

John's writings leave no doubt that God himself is the agent (efficient cause) of the night and that transforming union with him in love is its goal (final cause). It is also clear that the human person in all his/her concrete condition—weaknesses as well as potentialities—is, so to speak, the matter which is transformed. But, according to Sanjuanist theology, what can be ascribed as the formal or specifying cause of purgation?

The answer is not really very difficult. If the dark night is an essential element of the process of divinization, and if divinization means allowing oneself to be transformed in God by God, then his influence within us is the formal cause of our purification, just as all his activity within us is also the formal cause of the whole divinizing process. It is God himself who completely permeates the human person. We cooperate maximally by receiving God and letting him be.

Let us examine this "influence of God within the soul" more closely.

First of all, to influence means to act upon. So, if one must use a preposition to express this grammatically, one should normally use "upon" (*sobre* in Spanish). One exerts influence upon another. Notwithstanding, John chooses the preposition *en* to accentuate the interiority of the source of this purgation. This is a purifying influence of God from deep within the human person.

How does John envisage this activity of God? In explaining the signs for discerning the authenticity of the night of sense, he specifically addresses this question. While proposing the first sign in which we find neither satisfaction nor consolation in the things of God or in anything else created, the Mystical Doctor ascribes our aridity to this truth: God himself puts us in the dark night in order to dry up and purify our sensory appetite. Therefore, God does not allow us to find attraction or delight in any thing whatsoever. The causality described here is primarily efficient. However, John gives another sign which subtly effects the transition to a sort of formal causality: When we can no longer meditate or discourse despite our persistent effort to do so, this fact may indicate that God is already "beginning to communicate himself to us by pure spirit."[6] From the context it is clear that God communicating himself to us purifies us. This communication is purgative contemplation.

John sheds further light on this mystery by interweaving two analogies: (1) to consume and (2) to assimilate.

(1) *To consume:* "God accomplished the purgation of the soul by means of this dark contemplation. In it we suffer not only from emptiness and suspension of our natural supports and acquisitions. . . but also this dark contemplation purifies us, annihilating and emptying, or consuming as does fire. . . all the affections and imperfect habits which we have contracted throughout a lifetime."[7]

In this text, John chooses three terms to express the purifying activity of contemplation: to annihilate *and* to empty, *or* (better) to consume like fire. His arrangement of the contrasting conjunctions "and. . . or" implies that he recognizes that to annihilate can mean to destroy completely and that to empty may be taken in an entirely negative sense. So, lest he be misunderstood, John attempts to give a positive interpretation to his thought by introducing the analogy of consuming. This analogy evokes the suffering which arises out of transformation. Whatever is being consumed, as in the case of fire, is being transformed. For this reason, among the three expressions cited, John himself indicates a certain preference for the verb "to consume" precisely because of its positive connotation: "This purifying and loving divine light operates within us as does fire upon wood which transforms the wood into itself."[8]

(2) *To assimilate:* In our passage to eternal life, everything is revealed to us "because of our total assimilation to God. . . . Yet, however highly the soul is exalted before reaching this light something always remains hidden from it. This persists in proportion to what we lack for complete assimilation to divine Wisdom. . . . Love is like a fire which ever ascends upwards with a tendency towards being absorbed in the center of its sphere."[9]

All these notions—transforming union, assimilation in God, fire which ascends and consumes—converge on what the scholastics call formal causality. Yet, that in which God is causing us to be transformed infinitely transcends any classical ideas of causality. For "that in which" is really "him in whom": God himself.

At this point, an important question arises concerning the interdependence of contemplation and purification. Is it more correct to say that contemplation itself purifies, or to say that purification gives way in the end to contemplation? In other words, do we first have to be purified so that afterwards God can communicate himself to us in contemplation, or is it rather the communication itself of God to us which effects the purgation? Which really comes first: contemplation or purgation?

Obviously there is reciprocal influence. But here as always the true Sanjuanist insight is clearly more positive than negative. John explains himself with a comparison which is dear to him: that of light which paradoxically darkens. "The purer and simpler this divine light is in itself the more it darkens, empties and annihilates the soul in all its acquisitions and particular affections. . . . Yet, to say that supernatural and divine light darkens inasmuch as we receive more light and purity seems incredible. . . . Yet, this is understandable if we consider that the clearer and more manifest supernatural things are in themselves, the more obscure they appear to our understanding."[10]

How then does contemplation purify? "This divine ray of contemplation, assailing the soul with its divine light, surpasses our natural light. It darkens us and deprives us of every natural affection and acquisition which we had previously obtained by means of natural light. It leaves us not only dark, but also empty in our faculties and desires, both spiritual and natural. Leaving us thus empty and in darkness, this contemplation purifies and illumines us with divine spiritual light. All this transpires while we think that we have no light and believe ourselves to be in darkness."[11]

In this manner, God, welling up from deep within the human person, really is the cause (formal, efficient and final) of the night. Yet, the actual source of the pain which emanates from the purgation is the human condition as such in all its weakness, immaturity and selfishness. Contemplation (ie., God's direct, loving activity within us) itself purges what cannot be transformed in him. In all transformation there exist both continuity and discontinuity. Something endures beyond, while something else is broken off and left behind. God directly effects all dimensions of this mystery: the forging ahead, the breaking loose and the letting go. Nothing befalls us—not even sin—that God does not somehow make serve our metamorphosis in love (Rom. 8:28–39).

John furnishes three examples of how concretely this mystery translates into the human condition. (1) "The spirit of fornication is given to some to buffet their senses with strong and abominable temptations. . . . (2) Sometimes in this night the spirit of blashphemy is added. It commingles intolerable blasphemies with all their ideas. . . . (3) At other times the spirit of dizziness is given to them, not for their downfall, but to exercise them. This spirit darkens their senses in such a way that it fills them with a thousand scruples and perplexities."[12]

Moreover, it really is "God who sends these storms and trials in this night and purification of senses." He does this "so that having been chastened and buffeted in this way, their senses and faculties may be exercised, disposed and prepared for divine union."[13]

It is not enough, therefore, to assert that the night itself is an essentially positive reality. We must also recognize that the storms integral to the night play an equally constructive role in our divinization. How can this be? How can something so potentially harmful also be so good?

Under different aspects, we experience one and the same event, both as a good and as an evil. These storms are evil inasmuch as they are painful onslaughts of sin truly living within us. Yet, they are also an incomparable good to the degree that they exercise us. Thus, when bombarded by these storms we must simultaneously resist the evil and foster the good in them. This is not only not to succumb to temptation (Matt. 6:13; Luke 11:4), but it is especially to cooperate with God in love (Rom. 8:28). In this manner, the transforming power of God is encountered through the storms and beyond the pain they cause. We can accomplish this, however, only by naked abandonment to God in faith.

Note also that God does not tempt us in the strict sense (James 1:13–14). He exercises us. These temptations and sufferings flow from ourselves. They arise from our inner being inasmuch as we have come with all our poverty and sinfulness into direct contact with the divine, transforming activity within us. Thus, the darkness of the night does not, strictly speaking, proceed from God, but from the human condition: that is, from our inability to receive God as he is in himself. We remain innately powerless in the presence of the all-loving-transcendent-immanent One. We experience our basic weakness in proportion to the force of God within us. God's transforming love systematically annihilates every trace of self-centeredness.

Therefore, the phrase "God sends these storms" indicates that the divine action within us is basically positive because it is divinizing. This phrase, furthermore, accentuates the fact that the disproportion between creature and Creator is so immense that his divine light darkens the soul; that the loving influence of God is so foreign to our egocentrism that it agitates us no end; that the power of the divine presence is so intense that it leaves us with the impression that our Beloved is absent.

How do these general principles affect individual persons in concrete life situations? The compassionate love of the Father sees to all these particulars in a way best suited to the transformation of each one. In other words, the divine will determines the duration, the intensity and the form of this "fast and penance" for each of us "in accordance with the degree of union of love to which God intends to raise us," and in accordance with the greater or lesser amount of egocentrism to be eradicated.[14]

2. The Dark Night as a Perfective Process

Under this heading we shall succinctly group four other aspects of the night according to St. John of the Cross which bear on our study: (A) the place of detachment in our purification; (B) the purpose of renunciation; (C) the role of faith in this process; and (D) the manner in which John envisages receptivity.

A. Detachment of the Will and Desire

At the beginning of the *Ascent* (I, 3, 1–4), John states the problem very precisely: "What we call 'night' in this context is the privation of *gusto* in the appetite regarding all things. . . . We are not treating here of the mere absence of things, since that of itself would not strip the soul as long as it still coveted them. Instead, we are speaking of the detachment of the will and desire *(desnudez del gusto y apetito)* for them. Only in this way are we left free and empty, even if we have them in our possession."

Outside influences do not directly attain our innermost being. Consequently, they cannot directly cause us harm. It is rather our *attitude* with regard to a particular creature which fosters or hinders our interior progress. It is not our immersion in the world which prevents us from progressing spiritually, but only the stop of our will and desire upon the created that impedes this progress.

What then does John really mean by: (1) detachment, and (2), in particular, by detachment from *gozo* and *gusto?*

(1) The Meaning of Detachment (Desnudez)

John uses a variety of words to express the attachment which must be eradicated: *gozos, gustos, apetitos, afecciones de la voluntad, asimientos,* etc. In the context of *desnudez* (detachment, renunciation, mortification, stripping, spiritual nudity) he employs these terms in a nontechnical, yet precise, manner. There is obviously no question here of denying our power to will; or of negating our natural appetite; or of destroying our ability to consent, to enjoy or to be happy. The point is rather the renunciation of all attachment with regard to all that is not God, even if the creature in question is from God and to him.

Once again we find the insightful moderation of the Mystical Doctor. This moderation is evident in the desire to make use of everything that comes from God in order to return to him without, however, stopping anywhere along the way. Yet it remains just as difficult for John as for anyone else to express with all the required nuances the complexities of the detachment process.

The texts which contain these nuances—the "and's," the

"but's," the "however's"—are numerous. For our purpose we shall examine only two key expressions. In each of these texts John qualifies his idea of renunciation by a carefully chosen word: (1) "the *spiritual* detachment in all things both sensory and spiritual." (2) Concerning Christ, whose example we must follow, "he died *spiritually* to what was of sense in his life, whereas he died naturally to it in his death."[15]

According to the contexts, the terms "sensory. . . . of sense" carry no pejorative connotation whatsoever. John is simply making reference to the sensory part of the soul.[16] The accent is placed on "spiritual(ly)." This nuance implies much more than nonmaterial. In effect, John emphasizes the intangible, the inexpressible, the mysterious; ultimately the "I-don't-know-what" of the *Spiritual Canticle* (stanza 7).

In short, it is a question on the one hand of a most subtle balance between love of creatures and quest for God in and through them, and on the other hand of complete renunciation of the will with respect to them all. This balance is literally a personal mystery in the life and vocation of each and every one of us.

This sense of mystery guides us from day to day, enabling us to discern whether a particular affection is in reality a loving search for God in and through his creation, or a stop on some false god. In actual fact there is always a certain mingling of these two elements every step along the way. Hence, there must be just as much detachment regarding a particular creature as there is will to love it, if we are to maintain our ascent. Moreover, true discernment as to exactly what requires detaching and in what measure remains extremely delicate. Therefore, lest we cut off something vital, we very quickly find ourselves obliged to let ourselves be purified passively by God (John 15:1–2). For we can never completely sort out the intricacies of all our wills and desires, of all our pleasures and enjoyments, of all our affections and gratifications.

This is why, in the ultimate analysis, detachment can only

mean letting oneself be carried forward by God, in God, as he unstops all stops and strips all attachments.

But the question still remains: Why is it particularly necessary to renounce *gozo* and *gusto*?

(2) The Necessity of Renouncing Gozo and Gusto in All Things

John's study of *gozo-gozar* is long and complex. For example, in the *Ascent,* the subject is treated in book III from chapters 17 to 45. What does *gozo* mean, and what principles govern it?

El gozo usually denotes spiritual joy or enjoyment. But it can also mean sensory pleasure, satisfaction or gratification. It can even designate all the above without distinction. "The first of the passions of the soul and of the affections of the will is *el gozo,* which is none other than a certain contentment of the will together with esteem for something that it considers desirable."[17]

John's fundamental principle is this: "The will must not *gozar (se)* save in what is for the honor and glory of God. Now, the greatest honor that we can give him is to serve him according to evangelical perfection. Outside this nothing is of value or profit to anyone."[18] We are called to *gozar* or not a particular creature according to the concrete circumstances of our personal vocation.

The problem of *gusto* is similar to that of *gozo,* but only more complex. *Gusto* can mean everything that *gozo* does. But *gusto,* like the English word "gusto," usually accentuates sensory excitement and exhilaration. Translators of St. John of the Cross often render *gusto* "will" in the sense that we have been using the term throughout these two chapters.

Gusto-gustar is found on almost every page of John's writings. He uses it both in a positive sense[19] and in a negative sense.[20] And there are instances where he plays on both.[21] *El gusto* in its perjorative usage is more directly related to our purpose, since it is in this context that John insists upon its complete renunciation. In this pejorative usage, he employs *gusto* not only in the sense of attached will, but also very frequently as denoting sensory pleasure and gratification. We shall examine four assertions of the Mystical Doctor:

(1) *El gusto,* like *el sabor* and *el deleite,* by its very nature tends to entrap us, turn us inward and concentrate us on self.[22]

(2) Those who by their *gusto* are still attached to their prayers, their oratories or their religious customs (such as the habit, solemnities, devotions) have not yet abandoned themselves entirely to God and are resisting the divine influence within them.[23]

(3) We "must not be attached to anything: neither to the exercise of meditation, nor to any *sabor* whether sensory or spiritual. . . for it is necessary that the spirit remain free and annihilated with regard to all things. If we desire to fix ourselves upon any manner of thought, discourse or *gusto* whatsoever, that attachment impedes us, disquiets us and makes noise, thereby breaking the deep silence that should rightfully exist within us."[24]

(4) God "strips our faculties, our affections and our senses, both spiritual and sensory. . . leaving us in deepest affliction. Thus, we are deprived of the feeling and *gusto* which we had previously experienced in spiritual blessings. This privation is one of the principles required in order to reach union of love. . . . The Lord works all this in us through a pure and dark contemplation."[25]

What is there in the nature of pleasure, delight or enjoyment that blinds us? The second and third references furnish a response: namely, attachment to any creature whatsoever. In other words, a particular satisfaction derived from a certain creature captivates us. The fourth reference gives the reason attachment causes such a problem: If we are fixated on anything—even something sacred—we are stopped in our journey to God in himself. This attitude toward a particular creature impedes the creature from fulfilling its providential role in our life. By attaching ourselves to a creature, we turn that being into a god. What then must we do to resume our forward movement? We must become detached. Or more precisely, we must let ourselves be detached by God.

John frequently uses the verb *desnudar* when speaking of detachment. In Spanish this verb can be used to express both the reflexive sense (to detach oneself) and the passive voice (to be detached). The exact meaning intended by the author has to be determined from the context. Translating *desnudar* as used by John in the context of detachment by the reflexive form only can give the false impression that we are expected to *detach ourselves* from all our attachments. Certainly we must make whatever positive contribution that is indicated by divine inspiration and common sense. But at best such actions attain only the surface of the real problem. All truly salvific purging is effected by God. We receive this interior cleansing of ourselves. It happens to us. Thus, although we may indeed *attach ourselves* to a creature, we do not in effect detach ourselves. For *desnudar* means to let oneself be detached by God: in his way, at his time. Moreover, his pruning will be infinitely more effective than anything we could ever accomplish or even imagine.

As for the question of pleasure in particular—and by pleasure we mean the sensory exultation for which joy is the spiritual counterpart—the Sanjuanist explanation for the necessity of its renunciation is this: In accordance with our ontological and psychological structure, what is sensory in the human person is necessary for the development of spirit. However, beyond a certain point, which is variable according to individuals and circumstances, whatever is of sense in a given situation tends to obstruct further interiorization.

The Mystical Doctor insists, nevertheless, that the obstacle does not proceed from *gozo* or *gusto* as creatures (any more than it flows from any other creature). There is nothing intrinsically wrong with either enjoyment or pleasure. Rather the obstacle emanates from *gozo* and *gusto* inasmuch as we are stopped on them and refuse to pass on through them to God in and beyond them.

Therefore, it is necessary to be stripped of and to renounce *gozo* (to the degree that it constitutes a stop) and *gusto* (in the sense of attachment) in everything created. To reach the Goal, we must mortify our *gozo* and our *gusto* regarding each creature without ever rejecting or despising the created as such. Yet, John does point out that pleasure is particularly entrapping since we all spontaneously tend to hold on to it for as long as possible. This is simply human nature. For this reason, the sincerely searching person must be especially honest, circumspect and objective— that is, mortified—where *gozo* and *gusto* are concerned.

In short, in order to reach the Goal, we must pass on through creatures. In order to pass through them, we cannot be stopped on any of them. This renunciation is concretized "actively" by mortification and is ultimately brought to completion in the "passive" night. Thus, we arrive at the peace and interior spiritual joy which the world could never give (John 14:27; 15:11).

To renounce pleasure in its most evangelical sense means this: Enjoy both that which gives pleasure and the pleasure itself. But enjoy them as from God and to him—provided of course they really are—without, however, stopping on either in any way. Examples of such pleasure may include good health (Mark 1:30–31; Luke 7:21); the intimacy of friendship (Luke 10:38–42; John 13:23); a fine wine (John 2:10). A very practical test of this honest enjoyment is our ability to delight in pleasure and to accept its loss with the same equanimity, as did Job (1:21): "Yahweh has given. Yahweh has taken away. Praised be the name of Yahweh!"

Renunciation comes about by undergoing in faith and love the diminishments which occur quite normally in the course of living (e.g., restrictions of diet, bereavements, the aging process). At God's prompting, detachment may also be accomplished by voluntarily sacrificing something, or by cutting down—even abstaining altogether from—certain goods which cause pleasure. Ultimately however, *desnudez* is effected by allowing ourselves to be penetrated "passively" by the purifying action of God in contemplation. This last form of mortification is unmistakably the most efficacious. Yet, each of the others remains necessary throughout life.

To strip, to renounce, to deny, to mortify, to detach our will and desire mean, therefore, to be led by a will and desire for God which is so intense that we simply cannot stop until we rest entirely in him. This truth is a necessary result of increasing receptivity to God in himself.

B. The Purpose of Renunciation

What is the raison d'être of purification according to St. John of the Cross? Is it primarily expiation, or is it rather the exigencies of transforming love?

John responds this way: "Even though this blessed night darkens the spirit, it does so only to impart light in all things. And even though it humbles us and reveals our miseries, it does so only to exalt us. And even though it impoverishes us and empties us of all our possessions and natural affections, it does so only that we may reach forward divinely to *gozar* and *gustar* everything in heaven and on earth, all the while preserving a general freedom of spirit in them all."[26]

The person whom God is calling to himself is a sinner. Sin and its consequences enter deeply into the mystery of our need for purification. However, the basic purpose of the night goes much deeper than expiation as such. Even though other reasons may also be ascribed,[27] the raison d'être of our purification is our existential situation vis-à-vis the uncompromising demands of our passage to transforming union.

In other words, God's loving design for us is really the primary source of our purgation as well as of the intensity of our night. If God had not called us to such an incomparable destiny—to be transformed in himself, to enjoy supreme happiness and freedom in him—there surely would be no need for such purification. Transformation always means dying at least partially in what one loves. But if this dying in another must be all the more perfect the more we give ourselves to one greater than ourselves, then there can be no limits to the uprooting required on our journey in God.[28] We do not just pass from one phase of development to another (as from adolescence to adulthood). Rather we are completely and radically transformed not only to a new life, but to God's very own life and love.

This same doctrine appears even where John accentuates the specifically expiatory aspect of purgation. For instance, after citing Job 19:21 ("have pity on me. . . because the hand of the Lord has touched me"), John comments: "How amazing and pitiful it is that the weakness and impurity of the soul are such that it experiences the gentle and light hand of God so heavy and contrary to it. He only touches it, and does so mercifully without pressing it down or weighing upon it. God does this in order to pour out his graces upon us, not to punish us."[29]

C. Faith and the Dark Night

The role of faith in the process of transforming union remains without doubt one of St. John of the Cross's greatest contributions to the spiritual theology of the Church. With regard to this vast and complex subject, we shall limit our remarks to only one aspect: faith in relation to the process of purification.

At the beginning of the *Ascent* (I, 2, 1), John presents an overview of the process of spiritualization which he compares to a journey: "This passage of the soul to divine union is called night for three reasons. First, because of its point of departure" which is the innate poverty of the soul itself. "Second, because of faith which is the means or road which we must travel to reach this union. Third, because of the point of arrival, namely God" himself.

Faith is that which links together all the diverse elements of the night. Faith is that by which, in which, through which the pilgrim advances, reaches the Goal and is transformed.

In a passage of the *Night* (I, 11, 4) where he alludes to Matt. 7:14, John explains: "The narrow gate is this night of sense in which the soul is stripped so that it may enter therein being united to God in faith. . . . Afterwards, the soul continues on the straight way of the night of spirit. . . so as to journey to God in pure faith, which is the means whereby it is united to him."

Faith is furthermore the principle of union with God. Faith and love unite us to God. Nonetheless, faith in the Sanjuanist perspective is dark and purifying even as it transforms. Moreover, the darker it is, the more completely it unifies. We shall never really appreciate the inner dynamics of the night until we grasp the purifying role of faith in this process. Faith as a purifying and unifying principle is a myriad of paradoxes.

Faith is the fundamental cause of the night, while remaining our only guide through the same night. Stanzas 3, 4 and 5 of the poem, *In a Dark Night,* illustrate especially well this mystery:

> In this blessed night,
> In secret, when no one saw me
> And I could see nothing,
> Without other light or guide
> Than that which burned in my heart.
> —Stanza 3

There comes a point in the night when literally everything goes dark. Not even reason can serve as a guide any more. All that we have at this time is the flame of faith, hope, and love which burns unremittingly in the innermost recesses of our being. These virtues are truly "like a fire burning in my heart, imprisoned in my bones" (Jer. 20:9).

> This guided me
> More surely than the light of noonday
> To a place where he awaited me

—He whom I knew so well—
A place where no one appeared.
                    —Stanza 4

This intensely obscure faith guides us through the perplexities
and anxieties of the night with a deeper peace than the certitudes
of reason could ever furnish. Yet, assuming that our Beloved is
just around the next corner, we discover on arriving there that
he is still further up ahead. Moreover, each experience of being
drawn closer to Christ is always different from the previous one.
Each encounter is more mysterious, more faith-laden, more
obscure to our mental faculties and senses. This is so true that
he whom we thought we knew so well is simply no longer there.
The true God is always beyond. . . .

O night that guides me!
O night more lovely than the dawn!
O night that united
Beloved with lover,
Lover transformed in Beloved!
                    —Stanza 5

The overpowering darkness of faith becomes itself the source of
incomparable peace and strength. Faith is both the guide to and
the ultimate principle of transforming union.

Faith is also both light and night. It darkens by virtue of its
overwhelming brilliance (like being blinded by looking directly
at the sun).[30] As divine light, faith simultaneously illumines and
purifies us. In fact, it purifies us by illuminating us, since it
illumines by way of kenosis (Phil. 2:7). That is, it reveals who
God is not, and it enlightens us regarding our own inner poverty
together with the innate limitation of every other created being.
Faith as divine light is not of itself obscure, even though its
overwhelming force necessarily produces an obscuring effect
within us mortals. Thus, nothing created can adequately convey

51

it: The eye has not seen, the ear has not heard—it has not even so much as entered our imagination who God is in himself (1 Cor. 2:9).

As the night of faith intensifies, it progressively eradicates every attachment. In this way, by a process of elimination the true face of God is made manifest. In letting go all that he is not, we experience him more deeply face to face and thereby live more fully (Gen. 32:31). Nevertheless, this mystical communion between God and the soul in faith causes an even more intense darkness, for he is unmistakably experienced as nothing *(nada)* that can be grasped, held on to, comprehended in any human fashion. God is truly the Ineffable, the Inexpressible, the "I-don't-know-what" of the *Spiritual Canticle* (stanza 7).

This darkness of faith is the necessary and providential condition in the progression of our total abandonment to God. Ultimately, this condition wrenches every trace of egocentrism from us. Obviously, the darkness as such does not cause the abandonment of faith. God alone is the cause of faith and of its intensification. Yet, the obscurity resulting from our poverty vis-à-vis the divine force within us is the condition *sine qua non* in which true surrender takes place.

In other words, to the degree that a given creature is not affected by obscure faith, we try spontaneously to cling on to it. It is as if that particular creature were a ray of sensory light in an otherwise dark and mysterious tunnel. This phenomenon is so for reasons profoundly entrenched within the human psyche. The human person spontaneously resists obscurity and seeks out what s/he considers certitude, clarity and order. This darkness, however, elicits a most positive response on our part. For the less we can see, cling to, attach ourselves to, the more we necessarily plunge into the mystery of the divine Person up ahead. To cling is to reach behind, to hold on to something or someone for dear life. Faith is sheer leap forward; pure risk in God. Thus, faith increases in proportion to the intensity of the darkness of the night, up to and including death itself. Death is our final leap into total darkness. And yet in death we end up in total Light.

In this manner, faith conceals God, while uniting us with him.[31] Faith is the very lifeblood of purgative contemplation.[32]

Faith is God's gift. It is that which he bestows on us, enabling us to respond to his initiative. The most salvific response that we can give is commitment: the return-gift of ourselves to God.

The logia of Jesus and the writings of St. Paul are replete with declarations that faith is the commitment of that which is deepest and most ineffable in our person to that which is deepest and most mysterious in the personhood of God (Father, Son and Spirit). The Gospel consistently requires that the true disciple not only believe *what* Jesus proclaims, but especially that s/he believe *in* Christ Jesus himself: "Do you believe in the Son of Man?" (John 9:35). The difference is that of believing someone or of believing *in* someone. It is the difference between merely accepting the veracity of another and fully committing oneself to the other's person. In this sense, faith and love constitute the basis of all interpersonal relationships, transformation and union. In this sense too, faith is necessarily obscure since it is commitment to that which is truly most *mysterious* in the Other. In this sense, finally, faith is loving response, rather than intellectual assent.

In short, faith is gift; faith is commitment. Faith is both light and night. Faith guides and conceals, illumines and darkens. Faith strips us while uniting us to God. He wells up from within gently drawing us forward. God gives himself, communicating himself without ever being exhausted. Faith empties us in such a way that nothing precise or particular remains to which we can cling. What is left is *Todo,* who completely possesses us without himself ever being totally possessed. God does not come to fill a void. He was always there. Everything that is not God has become, in/by faith, *nada*.

D. The Meaning of Receptivity in St. John of the Cross

Teilhard consistently uses the noun *passivité(s)* to denote our attitude of receptivity toward God's transforming activity within us. Although the corresponding noun *pasividad* does exist in Spanish, the Mystical Doctor does not ordinarily use it. He does, however, employ the adjective *pasivo(a)* and the adverb *pasivamente* in the traditional Christian mystical sense of loving receptivity. Yet, whatever the actual expression, the leitmotif of all John's teaching remains this: Everything that is done within us in order to divinize us is done by God. We, in turn, receive all this in love, letting it be done while actively contributing to the process whatever God indicates should be done.

To illustrate this truth we shall examine four passages. Each contains its own particular nuance.

(1) The first passage is situated in the context of contemplation: "Often the soul finds itself in this loving and peaceful presence. It does not work actively at all with its faculties. . . . It simply receives" God. "Nonetheless, it will sometimes need to make quiet and moderate use of discourse in order to be better disposed" for contemplation.[33]

This last sentence reveals a subtle dialectic between activity and receptivity within the person. Before purifying contemplation definitively takes over, considerable effort is usually necessary in the realm of discursive prayer. This activity proceeds from God's initiative within us, and also precedes his more intense operation within us. In a subsequent phase, when we are more passive, we must sometimes return to a limited activity in order to become more receptive.

John continues: "But when the soul is led into contemplation, it must no longer work with its faculties, because at this time. . . understanding and delight are produced in the soul, not by its activity, but by its loving attentiveness to God and by its remaining without any desire to feel or to see anything."

This last sentence stresses the attitude of deep, mystical receptivity which we maintain in contemplation. This has absolutely nothing to do with laziness, idleness or inertia. Moreover, once we are drawn into receptivity of a superior order, we must make every effort not to make any effort at all. All we have to do is to wait, remaining as open as possible to the divine activity within us. This is required because "God is now communicating himself passively to the soul just as light is communicated to a person who has his/her eyes open."

In this communication of God to us, our effort to remain attentive is the spiritual, receptive effort of making no physical or mental effort at all. It is simply letting go, really abandoning ourselves to God. What God does within us is so penetrating and so transcendent that the best we can do is to do nothing, surrendering ourselves lovingly to him who dwells within.

(2) The second passage is in reference to *padecer* which means to suffer, to endure, to undergo in love. John uses this word very frequently to stress the transcendent excellence of the way of utter receptivity: "Another reason why we walk securely through the night is this: we advance *padeciendo*. The way of *padecer* is more secure and more profitable than that of enjoyment and activity. First, because in *el padecer* God supplies the strength, while in our enjoying and our activities we exercise our weaknesses and imperfections. Secondly, in *el padecer* we are exercised and acquire virtues. We are purified, made wiser and more prudent."[34]

(3) The third text accentuates the intense and consistent receptivity necessary in a contemplative vocation: "When the soul desires to remain in interior peace and leisure *(ocio),* every act, affection or desire wherein it may then seek to indulge will distract it, disquiet it and make it feel aridity and emptiness of sense. The more we attempt to find support in affection or knowledge, the more we experience the void which can no longer be filled in that way." John then adds: "Contemplation is nothing other

than a secret, peaceful and loving infusion of God" himself within us, "which, if we allow it, enflames us in the spirit of love."[35]

(4) Finally, the dynamics of love pertain par excellence to the mystery of receptivity: "The spirit experiences itself intensely and passionately in love. . . for since this love is infused, it is more passive than active. Thus, it generates in the soul a strong passion of love. This love, because it already possesses something of union with God, participates to some extent in those properties which make it more the actions of God than of us. These properties are received in us passively. Here we simply give our consent."[36]

For St. John of the Cross, the notion of passivity (receptivity) is used in opposition to activity. This is true when John is speaking of passivity both in the sense of remaining receptive to the divine activity within us and in the sense of remaining passive in relation to any created action which we ourselves could perform. But passivity especially derives its meaning from passion/passionate. In the context of contemplation, the word "passive" (receptive) means being enflamed with love, becoming fully alive in Christ: "I live now, no longer I, but Christ lives in me" (Gal. 2:20). To receive passively, not to work actively, to love passionately all mean, therefore, to allow God to open us in order to permeate us completely. It is God himself who does all. We let it be done (Luke 1:38). By doing nothing we are in actual fact doing our very best. For by abandoning ourselves wholly to God, we cooperate fully.

Thus, everything that is done within us in order to divinize us is done by God. We in turn receive all this in love, letting it be done while actively contributing to the process whatever God indicates should be done.

3. Summary

Throughout these two chapters we have examined two essential aspects of Sanjuanist mysticism: (1) the positive role of creatures in the process of sanctification, and (2) the positive thrust of the night, which consists in its necessary relationship to the process of transforming union. Two basic conclusions flow from these considerations.

First, this truth: God is revealed and communicated to us only in an actual kenosis of ourselves and of everything created. This is true in virtue of our personal incorporation into the integral mystery of Christ: his incarnation, death and resurrection. In light of this mystery, the positive role of creation is to open our hearts to the Uncreated. The finite is meant to point us beyond itself to the Infinite. This opening is effected by way of *nada*, which consists in essence in this mystical experience: God is nothing created.

Second, kenosis is truly a process, a development. We do not, strictly speaking, enter into it. Rather we are permeated and swept along by it. The most efficacious way for us to cooperate with this movement is, therefore, to let ourselves go in order to let ourselves be united to God, by him.

Notes from Chapter 2

1. *Cor.*, p. 31.
2. *Ascent*, I, 1, 4. "—*Sacándola Dios*—": *sacar* means to extricate, to force out with determination, to tear out.
3. *Solo por amor de él (Ascent*, I, 1, 4). John intends both senses of *de él*: God's love for us and our love for him.
4. *Night*, II, 5, 1.
5. Some translations unfortunately render *una influencia de Dios en el alma* by "an inflow(ing) of God into the soul." John is stressing the activity of God from *within* the person, a welling up (John 4:14); not an "inflow" from the outside.
6. *Night*, I, 9, 4–8. See *Contemplation*, pp. 60–71.
7. *Night*, II, 6, 5.
8. *Night*, II, 10, 1.
9. *Night*, II, 20, 6. In a context where he is accentuating the mystical dimension of the Omega Point, Teilhard twice evokes the model of John of the Cross and uses the following terms to describe what he and John have in common in contrast to Oriental mysticism: "Pantheism of union (and hence of love). Spirit of 'tension.' Unification by concentration and hyper-centration to the center of the Sphere," "My Fundamental Vision," 1948, in *TF*, p. 201).
10. *Night*, II, 8, 2. Ibid., II, 10, 1–10.

11. *Night,* II, 8, 4. Ibid., II, 16, 10–12.

12. *Night,* I, 14, 1–3. See *Contemplation,* pp. 85–89.

13. *Night,* I, 14, 4. See *Contemplation,* pp. 89–96.

14. *Night,* I, 14, 5.

15. *Ascent,* II, 1, 1 and II, 7, 10. The stress is mine.

16. John consistently speaks of *la parte sensitiva del alma (Ascent,* I, 1, 2) rather than the sensory part of the body: *la noche y purgación del sentido en el alma (Night,* I, 14, 1).

17. *Ascent,* III, 17, 1.

18. *Ascent,* III, 17, 2. By "evangelical perfection" John means living the Gospel deeply, whether in religious profession or not. The verb *gozar* can be translated by: to enjoy, to take pleasure in, to derive satisfaction from, etc.

19. E.g., as in the interchange between the Beloved and his spouse: *gustándolo El, lo da a gustar a ella, y gustándolo ella lo vuelve a dar a gustar a El, y así es el gusto común de entrambos (Canticle,* 37, 8).

20. E.g., *Flame,* 3, 73.

21. E.g., "In order to be able to *gustarlo* all, you must desire to have *gusto* in nothing" (*Ascent,* I, 13, 11).

22. See *Ascent,* III, 10, 2–3. *Sabor* means: savor, taste, pleasure. *Deleite* means: delight, joy, satisfaction.

23. See *Ascent,* III, 24 and 38; *Night,* I, 6.

24. *Flame,* 3, 34.

25. *Night,* II, 3, 3.

26. *Night,* II, 9, 1. Ibid., II, 16, 7.

27. E.g., so that the appetites themselves may attain their proper perfection and accomplishment (*Ascent,* I, 4—10); "according to the degree of union in love willed by God's mercy" (*Night,* II, 7, 3; ibid., I, 14, 5).

28. See *DM,* p. 88.

29. *Night,* II, 5, 7.

30. See *Ascent,* II, 3, 1–6.

31. *Ascent,* II, 4, 1–8; *Night,* I, 11, 4.

32. See *Ascent,* II, 10, 4.

33. *Ascent,* II, 15, 2–5. (The same for the subsequent quotations.) See *Contemplation,* pp. 27–52, 72–75.

34. *Night,* II, 16, 9. See *Contemplation,* p. 113.

35. *Night,* I, 10, 5–6. See *Contemplation,* pp. 97–109.

36. *Night,* II, 11, 2.

Phase II

Père Teilhard de Chardin

Preliminary Remarks

In responding indirectly to certain criticisms of Teilhard regarding the writings of St. John of the Cross, we have indicated in the previous two chapters that the work of the Mystical Doctor does explicitly contain a most positive teaching concerning the role of creatures in our divinization. Moreover, he explains how the purification essential to this process is fundamentally dynamic and unitive. These two elements of his spirituality are perennially valid. Hence, they are also of the utmost importance to every Christian in our time.

In these same chapters we have also set forth certain points that can serve as a basis of comparison between the doctrine of receptivity in Teilhard's spirituality and the basic elements of the Sanjuanist night. This comparison will not be made in the form of a synopsis of more or less parallel passages or vocabulary. Instead, our comparison will highlight the fundamental points of convergence and divergence between Teilhard and John of the Cross. Since their respective theologies are formulated independently, we set forth their teaching on the subject independently of each other. We have already discussed John's position. We now move on to Teilhard's. The comparison itself will be presented in the conclusion of this study.

Teilhard approached the question of *les passivités* in a manner consonant with Christian mystical tradition: namely, to designate our receptive attitude towards God as we undergo his transforming and purifying activity within us. In *The Divine Milieu* (p. 75),

Teilhard expresses his understanding of receptivity in its broadest terms: "That which is not done by us is by definition received in us." He connects the noun "passivity" with the verb "to pass into," as in: "The power of Christ has passed into me"; and with the adverb "passionately," as in: being more passionately in love with Christ Jesus.[1] This understanding of receptivity is in continuity with a theme which goes back to his earliest writings: "Christ had overwhelmed both me and my Cosmos."[2] Thus, Teilhard's theology of receptivity is profoundly linked with his Christology, especially with the mystery of the passion of Jesus: "When we suffer: (1) We suffer Christ, and (2) Christ suffers in us. We suffer together [com-patimur]."[3]

The term *passivité(s)* is found most frequently in his essays and correspondence between the time of his tour of duty during World War I and the composition of *The Divine Milieu* (1927). It occurs principally in contexts which treat one or other aspect of the mystery of interior detachment or which involve some other painful experience. Often Teilhard employs the expression *les passivités* without any qualifying word. In certain contexts, however, he does specify a particular form of receptivity. I shall arrange my treatment of this mystery according to the three basic forms which Teilhard designates and which I develop in chapters 3, 4 and 5.

Notes from Preliminary Remarks

1. See for example *DM*, pp. 111 and 127.
2. "The Priest" (1918), in *Writings*, p. 216.
3. *Journal*, Feb. 28, 1919.

Chapter 3

Passivities of Existence

Teilhard uses the expression *les passivités de l'existence* for the first time in a letter to his cousin Marguerite.[1] In this letter he discerns two essential components of our contribution to "the Real:" (1) That "effort without which a certain portion of being would never be realized," and (2) those "powerful energies which force even our staunchest resistances to bend before them and acknowledge their mastery." The efficacy of these energies arises from the fact that they make us undergo "the creative and formative action of God who alone has the power to detach us from ourselves." These passivities "establish in us something that is not of us." They are *"in nobis, sine nobis."* Teilhard epitomizes his sentiments this way: "Oh, the joy of experiencing the action of the Other within us! That is precisely what makes the passivities of existence so delicate and so worthy of adoration, since through them God asserts his primacy over us."

In other words, there are two essential and complementary components of our contribution to reality (i.e., to the actual world into which God has purposely brought us): personal effort and the passivities of existence. These passivities are energies—a whole complex of influences—which overwhelm us, forcing us, contrary to some of our innate tendencies, to yield to Someone who completely surpasses us. These passivities constitute an essential element of the creative and re-creative action of God, since they form the only force powerful enough to detach us from our egocentrism. They impart to us something of the Real, which otherwise we could not attain.

The phrase "passivities of existence" refers to the transforming and purifying action of God deep within the human person. This phrase accentuates the purgative aspect of that activity, for in undergoing God more intensely we necessarily also suffer more acutely than ever our inner poverty. The word *passivité* denotes our fundamental disposition of receptivity and availability with respect to the divine presence within us and all around us. Because God asserts his primacy over us through these passivities, they are worthy of adoration. Furthermore, they produce profound joy even though we undergo intense suffering proportionate to our resistance, imperfection and selfishness.

Teilhard's views, expressed above, accord remarkably well with those of St. John of the Cross which were treated in the previous chapters. But there is this notable difference: Teilhard formulates his teaching within a vocation which is decidedly active. He is conscious of a call to build up the Earth. John, on the other hand, expresses his doctrine within a way of life that is decidedly contemplative. His was a call into ever increasing solitude. This difference of concrete milieu and of personal charism explains perhaps one of the nuances that Teilhard gives to the prepositional qualification "of existence" in the expression "passivities of existence." This qualifying phrase is equivalent to another phrase which he frequently employs: "of the Real."

Teilhard explains what he means by "Real" in the essay *The Mystical Milieu* (1917:[2] "In the initial phase of the mystic's movement in God, the experience of him present in all things presupposed an intense *zest for the Real*. A little later, immersion in God operative in all things forced him/her to develop as broad a consciousness as possible, *again of the Real*. And now that s/he is progressing further into the immanent God, s/he is committed as a person to an unremitting fulfillment, *always of the Real*. This can mean only one thing: we are inexorably forced by our passion for union with God to give all things their *highest possible degree of Reality*, of existence, whether it be in our knowledge and love for them, or in our proper being. Thus, from the depths of his/her rapture in God, the true mystic is ever *a supreme Realist!"*

During the months it took to write *The Mystical Milieu,* Teilhard reflected many times on his own interior life and on his particular gifts. In his *Journal* (March–August 1917), he expresses the belief that God had given him mystical graces. Teilhard entertained no illusions at all about the role of such mystical phenomena as visions, levitations and locutions in the process of spiritualization. Nor did he give the slightest indication of ever having experienced any of these during his life. But he was convinced that he had received the sober mystical gift of being an indefatigable searcher for the Real; for the One-Thing-Necessary; for the Universal; for the Consistent; for the Absolute: for God in himself. "My lifeblood is to live and help others live the mysticism of God in all." A couple of years later, again in his *Journal* (February 19, 1919), he becomes even more explicit: "My inner strength, my sole force is to be 'mystic.' "

The determinative "of existence" (in the phrase *passivités de l'existence*) evokes still another meaning: The human person actually exists in order to become more. We are in tension becoming. In view of the Christ-event, this becoming is not just towards a vague, nondescript "more." It denotes transforming union in God himself. For this to be effected, we must fully undergo Christ. The very fact that we exist then carries with it the call to be in a way which completely transcends whatever we could become of ourselves. Thus, we receive not only our initial act of existence, but also the entire complexity of re-creative energies which comprise transforming union.

The expression "passivities of existence," therefore, refers to all the creative and formative graces which constitute the core of the purifying action of God within us. They are called "passivities" because of our receptive attitude towards them. They are in us, in spite of us. These passivities are qualified by the phrase "of existence," since without them we could neither attain the fullness of our own being-becoming, nor efficaciously foster the highest possible degree of the Real in them.

Every true mysticism is above all a lived experience, a living mystery. In the case of Teilhard, this truth is especially obvious. The unfolding of his interior life not only comes through in his writings, but also his spiritual journey remains their best interpreter. For these reasons, and also to illuminate the origins of the receptive element in his spirituality, we shall examine certain turning points in the early and mid-life of Teilhard, wherein he experienced the passivities of existence in a particularly intense manner. These turning points are grouped under two headings: (1) certain thresholds in the genesis of his interior vision, and (2) his spiritual crisis during the battle of Verdun.

1. Certain Thresholds in the Genesis of Teilhard's Interior Vision

At the age of thirty-six, in *My Universe* (1918), Teilhard made a concise first attempt to trace the genesis of his "interior vision." This vision comprises "the earliest and most essential characteristics of my 'view of the World' together with the successive stages of my complex interior attitude." Reflecting on this, he observes: "As far back as I can remember (even before the age of ten), I can distinguish clearly within myself the presence of a dominant passion: the passion for the Absolute. . . . This expressed itself in an insatiable need to rest unceasingly in Something tangible and definitive. And I sought everywhere for this blissful object. In fact, the history of my interior life can be said to revolve around the development of this search directed as it was upon realities ever more universal and perfect."[3]

Then, at the age of sixty-nine, Teilhard tried again to synthesize the major components of his interior vision. This time, in *The Heart of Matter* (1950), he identifies the axis of continuity of his life as "the Sense of Fullness" or "Pleromic Sense," thus coining a term derived from a New Testament expression used in reference to Christ (John 1:16; Eph. 1:23; Col. 2:9). These phrases delineate his quest and irresistible need for "the unique, all-sufficing and necessary Reality" (Luke 10:42). This need is born of the conviction that within him, but without him, something essential exists to which everything else is only accessory. This grace can rightly be called mystical, and it impressed itself upon his consciousness in unmistakable fashion: "Once it has been experienced, it is impossible to confuse it even in the least degree with any other passion of the soul. . . . For it is of a superior order." Thus, what Teilhard calls successively "Sense of Consistency, Cosmic Sense, Human Sense, Christic Sense," is merely the account of a gradual explication which evolved within him of this essential element expressed in ever richer and more refined ways.[4]

What exactly were some of these ever richer and more refined ways?

They revolve around what he termed in later life "the call of Matter," or more precisely, "the call of Something burning at the heart of Matter."[5] Reminiscing back to the age of six or seven, Teilhard notices that he was already a searcher. Whereas most children of that age would be lost in a world of make-believe, he found himself seeking out a solitary corner of the family property in order to "contemplate the savored existence" of his "God of Iron." Curious behavior for such a little boy, wouldn't you say? And why iron, of all things? Teilhard himself smiles as he recalls these events. But he was dead serious at the time. It was not just any piece of iron either. It had to be massive and heavy—like a plow or a statue or a column—in order to attract his "adoration." Thus, in his childish perspective, through the symbol of iron he sought that which must be lasting and durable: in a word, immortal. Nonetheless, to the child's despair, he realized one day that iron rusts and corrodes. It was not he whom his heart sought with such ardor.

The setback, however, was only momentary. For it had the effect of a catalyst, forcing him to search further and elsewhere for something more consistent. This time rocks attracted his attention. But not just any rocks. They too had to be massive, huge, indestructible, like the immense boulders in the mountains of his native central France. But alas! Even these boulders occasionally broke loose and came crashing down into the valleys below, shattering into a thousand pieces. So he had to search ever further. This time Teilhard was thrust in the direction of the planetary, which in turn progressively brought him "towards the vision of the Universal and the discovery of Evolution," and finally to the "inner awakening to Cosmic Life" (i.e., to a divine call emanating from the Heart of Matter; to a divine Person transforming Matter from within).

Thus, from iron to rocks to the cosmic, Teilhard's quest produced in the end "the awakening and development of a dominant and victorious Sense of All." *Todo*.[6]

In this brief summary of certain thresholds in the genesis of Teilhard's interior vision, several features of the passivities of existence are striking. First, there is his irresistible and progressive quest for more and more. This need always to search further is within him, without being of him. Yet it remains intimately linked to his own voluntary cooperation with this inner Force.

Second, each threshold crossed towards the more and more is effected within a painful detachment of self. This detachment proceeds from two interrelated sources: (1) from the progressive intensity of the action of God within him (i.e., God exerting his primacy over him), and (2) from the purification emanating from that transforming presence. In this manner, Teilhard is placed directly on the road towards true fullness of being-becoming.

This last point deserves a more detailed examination. Two examples from Teilhard's early adult life serve to illustrate how adversity brought him directly into contact with deeper values: (A) the death of his older brother Alberic; and (B) a dead end: the cult of inert passivities.

A. The Death of Alberic

In *My Universe* (1918), and in *The Heart of Matter* (1950), we discover several passages which reveal Teilhard's personal horror in the face of corruptibility: "As a child, the flesh of Our Lord appeared to me as something too fragile and too corruptible." "Pathetic despairs of a child! To find one fine day that iron corrodes, that steel rusts. . . . As a consequence of their apparent frailty, living beings greatly disquieted and disconcerted my childhood. . . . The physical-chemical instability of organic substances, and more particularly of the human body, shocked my need for consistency in spite of intellectual evidence to the contrary."[7]

In the eyes of young Pierre, everything which corrupted seemed to cease existing. Corruption (mortality) was equivalent to disappearance of being. This attitude is easily understandable from the perspective of a youth enthralled with nature. However, the setbacks caused by the decomposition of his cherished matter incited Teilhard to go through and beyond the appearances. He continued to search for the Incorruptible not exactly in matter, but rather at the *Heart* of Matter.

It is difficult to reconstruct exactly the interior upheavals of a young boy, but the thread which at that time ran through all this restlessness is undoubtedly the mystery of death. Teilhard had seen death at close range several times during his formative years, but one death in particular wrenched him to the very core of his being: the passing of his eldest brother Alberic on September 27, 1902.

Teilhard's reflections on this death reach us from Cairo in 1905. In a dozen or so letters to his parents (1905–1908), he mentions Alberic. There is nostalgia and pain, but no sign of moroseness in his correspondence. Pierre speaks of the passing of his brother with deep feeling and tenderness, as if this death had a direct and lasting effect upon his life. Instead of diminishing with time, his memories seem only to increase with fondness and depth during his years of theology at Hastings (1908–1912).

Just who was Alberic for Teilhard? Alberic embodied for him the ideal older brother: handsome, intelligent, courageous, the type of man that the younger Pierre spontaneously desired to imitate. He was a unique model of that consistency which Teilhard so craved. But alas! At the very apex of his manhood, Alberic was struck by a slow and pitiful emaciation that ended in death.

Such a soul-wrenching experience in Pierre's impressionable youth must have shattered a host of idols within his world. At the age of twenty-one, on the occasion of this heartrending ordeal, he was forced to face with particular acuity these critical questions of life: What is death? Does it have a positive meaning? Does incorruptibility exist even where we are apparently most corruptible?

A meditative reflection on the death of Alberic in its relation to the interior maturation of Teilhard helps us to appreciate a little more the following sentiments addressed to Marguerite in 1916: "I really liked Blondel's lines on suffering which you sent me. Through every word shone the creative, formative action of God whose influence alone has the power to detach us from ourselves. . . . That is precisely what makes the passivities of existence seem so delicate and worthy of adoration since through them God asserts his primacy over us. . . . The more I think of it, the more I find that death, by the great invasion and intrusion of everything new that it represents in our individual development, is a liberation and a solace—even in spite of the fact that it is essentially painful (because it is essentially regenerating and detaching)."[8]

The death of Alberic as well as the passing away of others whom he loved so much both within and outside the family certainly constitute painful intrusions upon his individual development. These intrusions are without him, in spite of him. Yet, beyond their appearances these detachments efficaciously bear witness to the creative, formative influence of God: an influence which detaches him, freeing and regenerating him in God.

B. A Dead End: The Cult of Inert Passivities

In the letter to Marguerite cited above, Teilhard had introduced his remarks regarding the passivities of existence by referring to his "cult" of them. By cult in this context he means an attitude of joyous, voluntary submission arising from personal conviction. This he distinguishes vigorously from the "cult of passivity" which he sees so prevalent in Oriental mysticism. The cult of passivity consists in succumbing to "the temptation of matter" (small "m"), thus giving in to the inclination towards least effort. This latter is a false cult wrongly pursued by certain putative mystics, especially those favoring a pantheism of fusion and dissolution.[9]

Teilhard knows by personal experience whereof he speaks, for he found himself locked into *a dead end (un point mort)* in this regard. It came about this way: Teilhard had grown up in a familial and religious milieu which was staunchly dualistic and thoroughly imbued with Jansenism. There was his Christian self and his pagan self; his love of God and his love of the World. He wanted desperately to dedicate his service both to the Church and to science. The same passion was going in two apparently irreconcilable directions at the same time. He firmly believed that they could be—indeed, must be—capable of being integrated, but he was powerless to do so himself. Nor could he find much help in seeking spiritual guidance other than the sound advice that somehow he must continue to pursue both as far as they might take him.

In his late twenties, Teilhard became deeply frustrated with the inability of the asceticism in which he had been reared to bring about a peaceful resolution of this seemingly interminable, interior conflict. So, without clearly adverting to what was happening during his regency in Egypt (1905–1908), he began to drift further and further into the cult of inert passivity. This cult consisted in a sliding back and down into the multiple (scatteredness, dissipation), rather than struggling forward and upward towards true union in love.

"In order to be All, I must be fused with all. . . . Such was the mystical movement to which, following so many Hindu poets and mystics, I was logically being driven by an innate, ungovernable need to attain self-fulfillment. . . by becoming one with the Other." Teilhard might really have succumbed to this temptation "had it not been that just in the nick of time the idea of Evolution sprouted up within me, like a seed: whence it came I cannot say."[10]

Thus, it was actually the notion of Evolution—ultimately that of Christogenesis—which constituted the resolution of his interior dilemma. Like a presence welling up within him, the realization came to Teilhard that the detachment inherent in the process of transforming union is not a question of Matter *versus* Spirit, nor even of Matter *and* Spirit, but rather of Matter *becoming* Spirit. Spirit is that which being is becoming. In this way, spiritualization is not accomplished by dematerializing oneself, but instead by letting Christ christify one's self, by letting his Spirit spiritualize one's Matter (Rom. 7–8; 1 Cor. 15). This truth is at the core of the passivities of existence. This is what makes them so worthy of adoration. This is authentic Christian receptivity.

In *The Road of the West: Towards a New Mysticism* (1932) as well as in other essays,[11] Teilhard contrasts Oriental mysticism with Christian mysticism. Using terminology common to both, he describes mysticism in general as the teaching and the practice of attaining both the Universal and the Spiritual simultaneously and through each other. Thus, at the same time and by the same act, we become one with the All *(Todo)* by a Power abiding within us, but which is not of us. This Power (i.e., the transforming activity of God) frees us from multiplicity, scatteredness and dissipation. In this manner, the mystic attains all things in God in their ultimate degree of purification and transformation.

The *Road of the East* is characterized by a movement towards spiritual union through return to a common divine basis. This élan would attain oneness by suppression of the multiple (hence, by negation and withdrawal) and by retreating from the interior forward propensity of evolutionary effort towards individuation and personalization. Thus, absorption of self into the mass would replace differentiation of self and of others. Oriental mysticism is a pantheism of identification in which one becomes coextensive with the sphere through dissolution of self and others. Everything and everyone are engulfed in one huge mass. The human person would then exist in a complacent rest which would be the result of withdrawal from the tension inherent in straining forward.

The *Road of the West,* on the other hand, is characterized by a movement towards spiritual union through convergence forward *(en Avant)* and upward *(en Haut)* towards the ultimate point of consummation, the Omega Point. This is accomplished by becoming one with the All through consummate differentiation of self and by convergence with all other persons and things in Christ. "True union ascending towards Spirit is accomplished by establishing in their own perfection the elements which it dominates. Union differentiates."[12] Thus, there is a sense in which the term "pantheism" may be applied to Christian mysticism: "God all in all" (1 Cor. 15:28; Eph. 1:23; Col. 1:19). This refers to transforming union with God in love and in him with all creation. Unification transpires by concentration and transformation at the Center of the Sphere, together with sublimation and metamorphosis of Matter and of the Multiple in the Spirit. In this way, a very real tension and restlessness (Rom. 8:24–25; Phil. 3:13–14) are necessarily integral to the whole process of transforming love.

Thus, in his search for true Consistency and in his quest to be united with Truth, Teilhard was tempted to indulge in the cult of false passivity. He was saved, however, by a true passivity: the intervention of a force, a new light which sprang forth from within him permeating his interior like a Presence. This influence within him, yet not of him, manifested itself in proportion to his own effort: the spiritual effort of receptivity to Truth, of letting himself be corrected, of letting himself be reformed by the creative, formative action of God.

In this way, the dead end of the pantheism of fusion and dissolution did not cause a lapse into nothing-nothingness (which is certainly not the *nada* of St. John of the Cross). Rather it worked like a catalyst prodding Teilhard to encounter grace (which is indeed true *nada*). This grace did not arise from the dead end as such. It emanated from God. But it was manifested through this temptation even though the source of the grace was beyond it. God does not tempt the soul. This is entirely a question of a temptation of matter. God exercises the soul. He tests it, and causes it to pass on.

In this way, God used this situation to teach Teilhard an invaluable lesson: namely, the One who seeks him and whom he seeks can never be found in the direction of matter, but only in the direction of Spirit. In fact, "the sense of Plenitude was turned upside down in me. And I have followed this new direction ever since without ever looking back. . . . It literally spun me around in my fundamental quest for Consistency."[13]

The death of Alberic and the ordeal of the temptation of

matter constituted painful, salutary experiences which Teilhard underwent in faith. Through them, God asserted his primacy over him, and deepened his search for the Absolute. However, the passivity of existence which was perhaps the most detaching (at least up to the age of thirty-six) occurred during his involvement in the battle of Verdun.

2. Teilhard's Interior Crisis of May–June 1916

At this period of his life Teilhard was corresponding with his cousin Marguerite two or three times a week and writing in his *Journal* almost daily. Then, all of a sudden, we discover complete silence with regard to both. There are no letters to Marguerite between April 9 and June 18 and no entries in his *Journal* from May 14 to June 26. Consequently, we possess no direct references concerning the conflict which was coming to a head within him. However, immediately after passing through the most intense part of the trial, Teilhard does name certain specific elements of his interior crisis.[14]

A first aspect he calls a "sort of numbness," a certain personal difficulty with regard to his military duties. Teilhard was a stretcher-bearer for an infantry regiment. "I've been very down of late. I don't seem to be able to muster any effort. . . . Perhaps it is something physical, a kind of lethargy that is making me so listless. One thing though is sure: my natural energies have been depleted. I'm near exhaustion." To Marguerite he confesses: "I no longer feel like myself: the individual monad full of plans for personal activity. Rather I feel lost in this gigantic clash of nations and brutal energies. This has left me drained and depersonalized."

A second dimension to his trial is linked intimately with the first: Christ seems hidden from him. "Add to this my being deprived of the celebration of the Eucharist. This is somewhat compensated for, since I am carrying the Blessed Sacrament on me."

Yet, this privation pierced through to the very core of his being: "How distant Our Lord seems to me now!"

Reflecting on Teilhard's pain, one cannot but recall the lines of the opening stanza of the *Spiritual Canticle*: "Where have you hidden youself, oh my Beloved, and have left me in anguish. . . . I went out searching frantically for you, and you were gone."

Teilhard indicates two other characteristics of his crisis in this prayer which he addresses to Jesus: "My soul is weighed down and unsettled. My mind and my heart are captivated by ideals which I sometimes fear may be neither heavenly enough nor sufficiently orthodox. O Master, preserve in me and in those whom I love so much—whatever the cost!—the light of your purity and of your truth."

Teilhard's prayer regarding his heart and purity is in reference to his vow of celibacy. A glance at his *Journal* entries immediately preceding this event reveals just how preoccupied he was with sexuality and chastity: February 8, 10, 14, 20; March 9, 12; April 27, 29; May 3–6, 8–10, (1916). He was certainly struggling in his effort to integrate his love for a particular woman with his commitment to Christ.

Teilhard's prayer regarding his mind and truth is in reference to the intense conflict arising within him between certain cries of unorthodoxy coming from some of his confreres and the authenticity of what he considered to be a personal charism: the reconciliation of God and the World. Or, as he was to put it the following year: "My vocation is to be the apostle of the Communion with God through the Cosmos."[15]

Of the three trials which St. John of the Cross singles out as most characteristic of the deepest throes of the night of sense—spirit of fornication, spirit of blasphemy and spirit of dizziness[16]—Teilhard gives indication of having undergone all three. The spirit of fornication: his struggle with his consecrated celibacy and chastity. The spirit of blasphemy: his questioning God for depriving him of Mass and for seeming to be so far away. The spirit of dizziness: doubts about his own orthodoxy and personal charism—fears, scruples, perplexities for which he can find no solution.

Teilhard reveals still another aspect of this crisis of May–June 1916: "What has been going on in me this month is a loss of my will to live. The very source of my strength has gone out from me. 'If salt becomes insipid, how can it be made salty again [Matt. 5:13]?' In a very real sense I seem to have lost all confidence and interest in myself."

In this condition he asks himself what should be his proper interior attitude: "What is one to do in this case where one can find no support of any kind? I must cling fast to Our Lord without feeling anything, and pray. . . . For if I succeed in doing this, what joy and peace I will discover in humbling myself without limit before Our Lord, in losing myself by letting go all confidence in myself. . . until I am completely united with his divine will!"

On the feast of the Sacred Heart (June 30 that year), Teilhard synthesized for himself the various elements of this trial as well as their profound meaning: "I can see more clearly now what was so disconcerting for me at Verdun. It was the concrete and immediate sight of possible destruction." He really believed that he would be killed. "I experienced in every fiber of my being what it means to be utterly lost, and to have to give up every cherished hope, every meaningful plan. . . . This threat overshadowed me, chilling and freezing in some way all my ardor. My will to live and to act was wiped out. . . . The sources of my life withered." He prays: "Jesus, grant me true, sincere and courageous renunciation founded on absolute faith in him who is stronger than death" (Song of Sol. 8:6; Phil. 3:9). Teilhard concludes: "The heart of Our Lord is the source of all the passivities which exert mastery over me and of all the activities which awaken me and sweep me along."[17]

Two years later, Teilhard expressed the above conclusion in

a formula which became very dear to him: *"Quidquid patimur, Christum patimur"* (Whatever we suffer, we suffer Christ). *"Quidquid agimus, Christus agitur"* (Whatever we do, Christ is done).[18] In effect, these complementary aspects of the mystery of Christ in our personal, daily lives constitute the principal subject matter of *The Divine Milieu* (1927).

The events of May–June 1916 are among the most significant in the interior genesis of Teilhard de Chardin. Before attaining this breakthrough, he underwent a long and painstaking maturation under God's guidance. This spiritual threshold constitutes for him a real personal conversion, a veritable fundamental option, a true spiritual death and resurrection. It was as if the old Teilhard had died somewhere in the wild countryside near Verdun in order to allow the new Teilhard to be reborn out of the depths of human despair. Four months later, as a matter of fact, he composed *Christ in Matter* (October 1916) to capture the significance of those events. This essay comprises three stories in the style of Robert Hugh Benson, a very symbolic and unique literary form for Teilhard. The first story—that of the picture of the Sacred Heart—recaptures his thirty-five years of struggle to see the reconciliation of Christ and Matter. The second account—that of the monstrance—expresses the intensely transforming and purifying events of May–June 1916. The third story—that of the pyx—brings out the realization that even though a fundamental breakthrough had been accomplished, there still remained a barrier between Christ and himself. That barrier consisted of all the years and of all that he had yet to do and to suffer before his death.[19]

With these passivities in mind, we appreciate all the more those poignant lines he wrote to Marguerite on December 18, 1916: "I remain faithful to my cult of the other component of the Real: that is, to the powerful energies which force our staunchest resistances to bend before them and acknowledge their mastery. I really liked Blondel's lines on suffering which you sent me.

Through every word shone the creative, formative action of God whose influence alone has the power to detach us from ourselves 'in order to place in us something that is not of us'—'Oh, the joy of experiencing the action of the Other within us!' That is precisely what makes the passivities of existence seem so delicate and so worthy of adoration (since through them God asserts his primacy over us)." Teilhard concludes: "The more I think of it, the more I find that death, by the great invasion and intrusion of everything new that it represents in our individual development, is a liberation and a solace—even in spite of the fact that it is essentially painful (because it is essentially regenerating and detaching)."

3. Promoting the Passivities of Existence

What must be not only our attitude towards, but also our voluntary collaboration with, all that we undergo throughout life? Teilhard responds: "I do not give way passively to these blessed passivities, Lord. Rather, I offer myself actively to them, and I do all in my power to promote them."[20]

We can understand without too much difficulty what is meant by offering ourselves to these passivities. It means to be open to them, to leave ourselves open before them, and above all to let ourselves be opened by them. It means persisting in an attitude of true Christian resignation which invites and promotes the action of the Other in us. This resignation is active in two senses: (1) Together with God we must energetically resist evil. And (2) true abandonment to God is itself a positive and affirmative act on our part. We must say "yes" to these passivities and honestly mean it. Therefore, if we are really to commune with God operating within us and all around us, it is not enough to simply let come what may, but we must positively give ourselves to him who comes in and through the very act of receptivity.

Teilhard explains: "My God, in order to promote and foster your activity within me through all things, I must do even more than open myself and offer myself to the passivities of existence. I must voluntarily associate myself with the work you effect in my body and in my soul. I must strive to obey and to anticipate your slightest impulses. My cherished wish, O Lord, is that I might offer so little resistance to you that you could no longer distinguish me from yourself—so perfectly would we be united in the communion of one Will!"[21]

We must offer ourselves and remain receptive even to the point of striving to obey and anticipate the least promptings of the divine Presence within us. This is what is meant by not giving way to them passively, in the sense of inert passivity. It is necessary to make the effort—the terribly demanding spiritual effort—of being and of remaining Christianly passive, receptive.[22] The mystical act par excellence is that of unreserved, passionate abandonment of the soul in sheer faith to ineffable Love: the *no-sé-qué*.[23] This personal, spiritual effort; this total, passionate surrender; this positive resignation constitute the apex of our voluntary cooperation with the transforming and purifying activity of God within us. This is the quality and the intensity of receptivity that Teilhard designates by the expression, "promoting and fostering the passivities of existence."

However, this receptivity, as comprehensive and intense as it may be, still does not exhaust all the positive richness of our collaboration with Christ. The complete offering of self to God attains its fullness only when accompanied by a maximum personal effort to collaborate actively in producing the best possible *opus* (work, labor, task, product). In the faithful accomplishment of our daily chores—even down to the most minute details—we bring to Christ a little more fulfillment. Thus, we not only make up for what is lacking in the passion of Christ (Col. 1:24), but we also contribute our share in making up what is lacking in his activity.[24]

By both receptivity and activity then, we do our best qualitatively and quantitatively to promote as fully as possible the creative, formative action of God within us and around us. In this twofold way, we contribute positively to the transformation of all things through him, with him, in him. For in whatever we suffer, undergo, endure, we receive Christ. And in whatever we do, foster, promote—not only in terms of good intention *(operatio)*, but also down to the most material aspect of the activity *(opus)*—we collaborate with Christ in building up his Body.

Teilhard perceives activity as related to the passivities of existence in four complementary ways. First, the power to act is itself gratuitously received in the primordial gift of existence: "What do you have [what are you] that you have not received?" (1 Cor. 4:7). The very first passivity for each person is his/her gift of being-becoming. This is the very first fruit of the Spirit (Rom. 8:23). Second, maximum effort and maximum fidelity in every undertaking serve as an essential sign of authenticity regarding true receptivity. This effort prunes and discerns authentic passivities from lassitude, laziness and the temptation of matter. Third, the daily accomplishment of one's tasks with uncompromising honesty and fidelity for Christ constitutes a formidable asceticism. Detachment through action! If I really do exactly what God wants of me minute-by-minute, hour-by-hour—as his providence reveals it to me through all the converging circumstances of the moment—then he will purge me of self-centeredness through my fidelity to this activity. Fourth, an active and vigorous resistance against all evil is necessary in order to arrive at true Christian resignation.[25]

Our considerations in this chapter pertain to the passivities of existence, of life, of just living, being, becoming. After World War I, however, Teilhard ceases using the expression "passivities of existence" in preference for a more precise designation based on the perspective of the person receiving them. Henceforth he distinguishes the passivities of growth and the passivities of diminishment.

Notes from Chapter 3

1. *MM*, Dec. 28, 1916, pp. 156–158. (The same for the quotations which follow.)
2. *Writings*, p. 139.
3. *HM*, pp. 196–208.
4. *HM*, pp. 15–17. The French word *sens* means both "sense" or intuition (as in sense of mystery) and "direction" (as in *sens unique*: one-way street). Teilhard intends both senses.
5. *Hm*, pp.. 17–29, 197–198.
6. *Hm*, pp. 29–58, 82–99, 199–208.
7. *HM*, pp. 17-44; 197.
8. *MM*, Dec. 28, 1916, p. 158.
9. *HM*, pp. 23–24; *CE*, pp. 56–75.
10. *HM*, pp. 24–29, 45–49.
11. *TF*, pp. 40–59, 134–147, 199–205, 209–211, etc.
12. *HE*, p. 144.
13. *HM*, pp. 26–28.
14. The following quotations are taken from his *Journal*, June 26–30, 1916, and from *MM*, pp. 100–101 (letter of June 18, 1916).
15. *Journal*, Dec. 22, 1917.
16. *Night*, I, 14, 2–3. See *Contemplation*, p. 85–96.
17. *Journal*, June 30, 1916. See *MM*, pp. 106–108.
18. *Writings*, p. 259; *Journal*, Feb. 28, 1919; *HM*, p. 204; *DM*, p. 123.
19. *HU*, pp. 41–55; *HM*, pp. 61–67.
20. "The Priest" (1918), in *Writings*, p. 215.
21. *Writing*, p. 216.
22. "There is nothing more crucifying. . . . than spiritual effort" (*SC*, p. 69).
23. The "I-don't-know-what" (*Canticle*, stanza 7).
24. *DM*, pp. 49–62.
25. *DM*, pp. 62–73, 90–93.

Chapter 4

Passivities of Growth and of Diminishment

Teilhard composed his first book, *The Divine Milieu* (1927), to serve as testimony to his deepest convictions regarding the spiritual life. He dedicated it to those who love the World, since God has so loved the World (John 3:16). This book comprises three sections: (1) the divinization of our activities, (2) the divinization of our passivities, and (3) the Divine Milieu proper. *Les passivités de croissance* and *les passivités de diminution* constitute the subject matter of the second section.[1]

1. Human Passivities in General

After a lengthly development of our powers, energies and capacities, we eventually arrive at the stark recognition of the influence of passivities within our lives. Little by little we become conscious that we receive immeasurably more than we give, and we gradually realize that we are dominated by the objects of our conquests. "Like Jacob wrestling with the angel, the soul faithful to life and to grace ends up by adoring the One whom it was struggling against" (Gen. 32:26–31).

Paradoxically, "the soul has hardly arrived at the heart of things, when it finds itself ready to be detached from them. Having taken its fill of the Universe and of itself, the soul one day discovers that it is possessed by an intense need to die to self and to be led beyond itself. Moreover, this is not the result of disillusionment, but rather issues forth as a logical development of its own effort."[2] One cannot but see the baptismal symbol underlying the truth which Teilhard is expressing: namely, that immersion in the World with Christ, which is the first phase of our incorporation in him, is necessarily followed by a second phase, that of our emergence from the World in Christ. Or, to paraphrase John the Baptizer: initially I must increase so that Christ may increase, but eventually I must decrease so that he can further increase (John 3:30).

Immersion and emergence are like breathing in and breathing out; like the arsis and thesis of a musical measure. The more you take in, the more you let out (let go); the greater the upbeat, the more meaningful the downbeat. That is, the more realistic is our incarnation in the World with Christ, the more complete is our renunciation of the World for him. These are not two movements, but one movement in two phases. Each phase is characterized by its own type of receptivity. The passivities of growth pertain mainly to the sphere of immersion, whereas the passivities of diminishment are associated principally with emergence. As a matter of fact, our activities are sandwiched in between these two genres of passivities. We receive the ability to act. We then activate that capacity, which activity leads us ultimately to total abandonment to God in love.

In its most general sense, therefore, the term "passivities" refers to everything that is received by and within the human person. What is not done by us, is by definition undergone in us. Thus, our passivities embrace the immense complex of everything within us and around us, without us and in spite of us. This complex is as vast, as intricate and as incomprehensible as the totality of the World's past and present.

From the point of view of the person receiving these passivities, we distinguish two groups. Our destination stems from our surface perception of them as being amicable or painful to us. Those friendly and favorable forces that sustain our effort and point the way towards what we ordinarily consider success, we call passivities of growth. Those hostile powers which laboriously obstruct our innate tendencies, hampering or impeding what we normally consider progress towards heightened being are termed passivities of diminishment.

2. Passivities of Growth

"We undergo Life at least as much as, if not more than, we undergo Death."

This truth eventually impresses itself upon the consciousness of every thinking person. Living and dying—are they something we do, or are they done to us? In their most profound sense, both life and death are actively received in us, by us. Obviously they are primarily passive. Yet there is surely something we must do about each of them. In the case of life, we have to correspond to it, cooperate with it. Otherwise the gift is squandered. In the case of death, we must accept it, become resigned to God through it and beyond it. Not only do we have to say *amen,* but we must especially be *amen.*

So natural to us are living and growing that we do not usually pause long enough to distinguish our activities from the host of passivities which nourish that action or from the given circumstances which favor its success. Generally we take for granted our health, our self, our life, until of course something happens: illness, contradiction, death.

How, then, do we get in touch with this immense wealth of

reality which Teilhard calls our passivities of growth? We must penetrate prayerfully the depths of our most elusive selves and there try to perceive the ocean of forces to which we are subjected and in which our personal as well as collective development is steeped. We have to enter into ourselves in deepest recollection to imbibe the depth and universality of our dependence on so much which remains altogether outside our control and which goes to make up the intimacy of our communion with the World to which we belong.

So, with the light of faith and intuition, I leave behind the zone of everyday preoccupations and relationships where everything has a name and a place and a number, to search and to listen with my heart to those depths whence I feel dimly that my power of action emanates. But as I move further and further away from the conventional certainties on which social life thrives, I discover that I am losing contact with myself. At each step of the descent a new aspect of person is disclosed within me, the name of which I am no longer certain and which no longer obeys me. And, when I stop my exploration because the path fades from beneath my steps, I find a fathomless abyss at my feet, out of which comes—I know not whence—the stream which I dare call *my* life. My life: *vita mea!* My life is not really mine *(mei)* as if it were of me, rather it is to me *(mihi)*. What is mine that I have not received (1 Cor. 4:7)?

What human endeavor will ever be able to reveal to me the unfathomable origins of my being? Certainly not my own effort or that of anyone else around me. Nor can I or anyone else effectively change who I truly am and who I am truly becoming. Oh, I may be able of course to trace my roots back several generations. By means of certain ascetical and physical disciplines, I might even stabilize or enlarge certain aspects of my ability to receive. But none of these can harness the deepest sources of life. "My self is given to me far more than it is formed by me." My destiny is shaped within me far more than I shape it. "In the ultimate analysis the interior life, life at its source, the nascent life completely eludes our grasp."

That is the firstfruit of my interior journey to discover the passivities of growth. The second flows from the first. Shaken by this realization, I want to return to the light of day and forget this disturbing enigma in comfortable surroundings and familiar things. This temptation of matter would have me forsake my salutary quest and settle instead for lassitude, complacency and mediocrity. But just when I am about to succumb, there—beyond all this darkness and confusion—appears the Unknown, the I-don't-know-what, that I am trying to escape. It (he!) is not only deeper than the abyss, but also intimately intertwined among the innumerable strands of the web of providence: the very stuff of which the universe and my own individuality are woven. He infinitely transcends my life and my world, yet he remains the immanent, vital force not only at the Alpha and Omega of my being, but also all the way through my becoming.

A third effect also results from my interior journey to search out the passivities of growth. The third flows from the first and the second. I begin to reel even more when I try to contemplate, much less number, the myriad of favorable influences which must have converged to produce me. I could go out of my mind trying to analyze the supreme improbability, the incalculable unlikelihood of finding myself existing at all in a world that has actually survived and succeeded in being a world. Thus, having come to the realization that my life is not really mine, but to me, and that I am called infinitely beyond myself, I discover the indescribable poverty of my spirit and the ultimate meaning of the first beatitude: Blessed are those who know their true need, for God is theirs and they are God's (Matt. 5:3).

But there is still a fourth dimension of my interior journey. The fourth recapitulates the previous three. As anyone else will find who dares make the same pilgrimage, I felt the anxiety characteristic of a person lost, adrift, floundering, when I encoun-

tered the fathomlessness of my own personhood, the utter trans-
cendency of the God for whom my soul pines and the seeming
endlessness of my inner poverty. And, if something—Someone—
saved me from my distress, it was the gentle and unmistakable
voice of Jesus coming across the lake and "from out of the depth
of the night: 'I am. Be not afraid' " (John 6:20). Faith in the Son
of God is the culminating effect of my quest to encounter the
passivities of growth.

This faith, however, must be translated into daily life, into
actual attitudes and action. In the Life that wells up in me (John
4:14) and in the Matter which sustains me, I find much more
than God's gift. I encounter God himself: he who makes me
participate in his being and molds me in his likeness (2 Cor.
3:18). I discover, as it were, the two hands of the Father. One
hand holds me so firmly, yet so tenderly, that it coincides with
all the sources of my life. In it I experience the Father's immanence. His other hand stretches beyond my wildest imagination
in all-embracive coherence, holding together the immensity of
the cosmos. In it I encounter his omnipresence, his transcendence.

We must respond to this discovery in twofold fashion: on
the one hand, by our personal will to be and to become more and
more; and on the other hand, by making our contribution to the
being and ultimate becoming of all the created realities which
providence brings into our lives. That is, we must take care, first
of all, that we never stifle, distort or waste our power to love,
to do or to become. Then, we must strive never to miss an
opportunity to direct others towards Spirit.

The life of each of us is woven of these two threads. There
is the thread of interior development and the thread of outward
achievement: our within *(le dedans)* and our without *(le dehors)*.
In the former are gradually molded our ideas, our affections, our
human and religious attitudes. In the latter "we always find ourselves at the exact point where the whole sum of the energies of
the universe converge to effect in us the work which God desires."

"May I never break this double thread of my life."

3. Passivities of Diminishment

To be open to God within the internal and external forces which animate our being and sustain its development means basically to be open to and to trust all the influences of life. In responding to the passivities of growth by our fidelilty to action, we commune with God. Thus, the desire to undergo God leads us to the very fulfilling task of promoting our own personal growth and that of others.

However, "the soul faithful to Life and to Grace cannot proceed indefinitely in the direction of building up a strong self. . . . It gradually becomes aware of the emergence from the very operation of its impulse toward self-fulfillment of a hostile component that grows more dominant: the predilection for renunciation."[3]

How amazing! The zest for being and the quest for the fullness of life have within their own inner dynamics the predilection for detachment, for death to self. Moreover, this is a logical and necessary outcome of this development. All true growth, all real development—in short, all Progress towards Spirit, towards the qualitative, towards the interior—is accomplished ultimately only through a *metanoia* (conversion): "The World cannot attain consummate fulfillment except through a death, a 'night.'. . . . The Earth does not take cognizance of its destiny except through the crisis of a conversion."[4]

To encounter God as the animator of the passivities of growth is truly awesome. It is terrifying, freeing and hope-filled—all at the same time. But what is this predilection for renunciation? We can understand something of the meaning of the zest for life, the zest for being and becoming. But how can anyone develop a taste for detachment? The fact that God is discovered in and through life we readily accept. But can God be found not only also, but above all in and through death? And yet, the incontestable lesson of every living creature and of all interior progress has always been that one must die in order to rise transformed: "Unless the grain of wheat falls into the ground and dies. . . . " (John 12:24–25). Resurrection not only follows death, in the sense of coming after it, but resurrection occurs especially in death, through it and out of it.

The passivities of growth develop us. These friendly and favorable forces which sustain our effort and direct us towards Progress really foster growth. Nonetheless, in an extremely paradoxical manner the passivities of diminishment cause us to grow even more. These hostile powers which in one way reduce and even destroy our capacities for development constitute in another way the passivities par excellence by which we commune with God. Of all the passivities we are subject to in this life, the passivities of diminishment remain those most charged with power to divinize.

The expressions "of growth" and "of diminishment" designate, then, a division of the passivities of existence into two general categories. These qualifying words denote that aspect which at first sight strikes the observer. Some passivities appear friendly, others seem hostile. However, beyond their appearances both genres exercise a truly positive and interacting influence on our interior progress: "Even though physically we may be falling into decay, our inner selves are being renewed day by day" (2 Cor. 4:16).

How is this possible? The response of Teilhard is that of St. Paul: "For those who love God, everything is transformed into good" (Rom. 8:28). And they do mean absolutely everything (Rom. 8:31–39).

"The forces of diminishment are, nonetheless, our real passivities," for not only do we suffer them, but also we suffer immensely from them. "The ways they affect us are innumerable, their forms infinitely varied, their influence constant. In order to understand them better, we shall divide them into two groups. . . those diminishments which originate within us and those which originate outside us."

Generally speaking, the external passivities of diminishment comprise all our experiences of ill fortune. They spring up from all sides. They may be the microbe which infects the body or the inopportune word that wounds the heart. They are the incidents and the accidents of varying importance and diverse kinds which crush us, hurt us, anger and frustrate us. They are the barriers that block our way, the walls that hem us in, the defeats that bring us down.

All these passivities are diminishing enough, but the ones whose origin is within us "constitute the darkest element and the most despairingly useless years of our lives." They are represented by all kinds of natural defects. They are all the physical, intellectual and moral limitations that plague us, restrict us, humiliate us from birth to death. They are the temperamental, nervous, personality and emotional disorders which overtake us all sooner or later, one way or another. They are our moodiness, our sinfulness, our innumerable manifestations of selfishness. In the end, old age itself gradually robs us of all vigor, pushing us irreversibly towards death. Even the passage of time *(la durée)* is a formidable passivity. It is either too long or too short. It is either too cluttered or too empty, too much or not enough. But in any case it moves us inevitably towards death.

Death. "Death is the apex and the consummation of all our diminishments. Death is the epitome itself of all evil." It epitomizes physical evil inasmuch as it results organically from the complete disintegration of matter to which we are all subject. It epitomizes moral evil inasmuch as it is immeasurably compounded by the abuse of freedom and by the sin of the world (John 1:29). Yet, death surrenders us totally to God. Through it we pass over to him by losing ourselves in Someone greater than ourselves.

Thus, death is also supreme good. But how? How can that which is the epitome of evil *(le Mal)* be transformed into the greatest good?

A. The Struggle with God against Evil

The first question that must be posed regarding the transformation of evil into good is this: Just what is the relationship of God to evil? In response to this question, we shall summarize the points of view (1) of the scholastics, (2) of St. John of the Cross and (3) of Teilhard.

(1) The classical scholastic view is formulated according to these distinctions: God wills good directly. He wills physical evil only indirectly. He merely permits moral evil.

(2) The Sanjuanist perspective introduces into this tripartite framework certain subtle nuances. Even during the most trying temptations of the night of sense, the influence of God within us remains constant and positive. In fact, it is the loving, transforming activity of God in direct contact with our inner poverty that produces all the pain and darkness which John calls night. God himself sends these storms and trials in order that, having been chastised and buffeted, we may advance more securely in our search for absolute good. These storms exercise us, disposing us and accommodating our senses and faculties for union with God in love. "If the soul is not tempted, exercised and proved by these trials and temptations, its senses cannot be strengthened in preparation for Wisdom."[5] Even Jesus "was led by the Spirit out into the desert in order to be tempted" (Matt. 4:1).

(3) Teilhard adds a complementary insight to the two preceding views. When suffering befalls him/her, the Christian says with Job (19:21), "The Lord has touched me." This, of course, is profoundly true. But, this affirmation, so tersely formulated, summarizes a whole complex of influences: some very good and divine, others very evil and painful. Thus, only when we have passed all the way through these influences, do those words attain their full truth.

If we retrace the beginning of our encounters with a given evil situation, we realize that we prayed at that moment—and continually thereafter—as did Jesus in Gethsemane (Luke 22:41–44): Lord, free me from this diminishment. I want with all my being to assist you in removing this chalice from me. However, not my will, but yours be done!

These words express the first will, so to speak, of our Father: namely, that every evil—even physical evil—be reduced to a minimum. Indeed, the Father wills that it be done away with entirely whenever possible. The Father wants each of us to struggle together with him against every evil. Therefore, at the approach of these diminishments, we are called upon to utilize all our resources in order to struggle against whatever is of evil in them. This resistance is absolutely necessary if we are to adhere as faithfully as possible to the creative action of God within us and all around us.

However, even if we wrestle with God against evil, despite all our effort we shall sooner or later be vanquished by evil. For, in the end, each one of us must die. How, then, do we find God's will in this? What is the significance of defeat?

B. Our Apparent Defeat and Its Transformation

The problem of evil—that is, the reconciliation of our failures with the creative goodness and power of God—remains one of the most disturbing mysteries of the universe for both our hearts and our minds. This is all the more perplexing when we read in the Gospel "that it is necessary for scandal to occur" (Matt. 18:7). It is difficult enough to have to admit that failure, sin and death do exist. But what is really difficult to admit is that they *must* exist.

Teilhard responds to this enigma in several ways, all of which converge in one manner or another on the providence of God in the actual economy of salvation. He does not indulge in "what-if's" or in "what-might-have-been's."

A first response stems from the evolutionary process itself.

Everything that becomes suffers and commits its own faults. One cannot get through the first of the three phases of the dialectic of evolution (divergence, convergence, emergence) without experiencing many blind alleys, dead-ends and explorations incompatible with self-fulfillment. In the ultimate analysis, we all learn and grow by experience. And experience is gained only at the price of much suffering, failure and after many mistakes. Just ask the son of the prodigal father (Luke 15:13–17). In every aspect of evolution there is both continuity and discontinuity. In the process of becoming, something endures and something is necessarily left behind. At every step of the way something must be relinquished. Advancement always costs. Nature abounds with examples: the grain of wheat, the caterpillar, the cutting of the apron strings, etc.

A second response flows from the nature of evolution, especially as directed toward a point of ultimate consummation. Evolution (or genesis) is movement from the imperfect to the perfect. It is transition from scatteredness to unification. Evolution is transformation from chaos to accomplished being. This necessitates intense struggle, both interior and exterior. One cannot succeed in becoming more without exerting immense effort at considerable cost of energy and discipline. We have only to think of the endeavors of athletes, scholars and diplomats.

A third response views the laws of statistical necessity latent within evolution. Within the universe there is such a multitude of agents pursuing their own individual and collective progress that some of these energies are bound not only to cross, but to clash head-on. Most of the cycles of nature are predicated upon this principle. What is good for one species is death to another. What is meal for the fox is end for the rabbit. Thus, plants drain minerals from the soil, cattle eat the plants, humans dine on beef, and then they in turn fertilize the ground. Other examples related to the laws of statistical necessity can be given: traffic fatality predictions for the Labor Day weekend, Murphy's Law (whatever can go wrong will sooner or later), etc.

A fourth response considers the inner nature of created being becoming. Within creation as a whole and within each individual creature in particular, there exist two contrary forces: entropy and evolution. Entropy is that innate tendency which turns the creature in upon itself, whereas evolution, especially in the Teilhardian sense of genesis, is that energy within each being driving it beyond its present state to become something more. Translated into the realm of human beings (the Noosphere), entropy becomes self-centeredness, pride, sin; whereas evolution elicits gift of self, commitment, love.

When we understand the above four responses specifically in the light of the Christ-event, the necessity of suffering and death assumes a new significance and a decidedly positive thrust. Not only are we called to become fully human, but also to participate in the very life of God himself, to be united to him in love through transforming union. Thus, "if being united means in every case migrating and dying at least partially in/to what one loves, then this being annihilated in the other must be all the more complete the more we give our attachment to the One who is greater than ourselves. We can set no limits to the uprooting that is involved in our journey in God."

But the myopic person still counters: Couldn't God have made a better world? A universe without pain, failure, death? A journey that would be easier, simpler, more enjoyable? This narcissistic view of the world perceives the cost of progress as good or bad inasmuch as it suits or does not suit one's own likes and dislikes.

Yet, even transcending a self-centered appraisal of divine providence, we can see it at best only upside down and in reverse, as if we were looking at the underneath portion of a tapestry. All we see are loose ends and disjointed patterns. Instead, we must view the world and our lives in faith, from God's loving perspective: looking down from above, as it were. For God did indeed make the best possible world according to his purpose, which is transforming union.

Thus, our defeat only appears as such. We merely seem to fail. In view of Jesus's paschal mystery, no effort is ever wasted, no struggle is ever in vain, no death is without some victory. Everything is transformed into good for those who believe in him (Rom. 8:28). This good may not be apparent to the victim: for example, to the soldier who falls during the assault which leads to peace. Nevertheless, God does bring forth not only some good, but a greater good. He produces something greater than what would otherwise have been. "Like the artist who knows how to use a flaw in the rock he sculptures in order to bring out more exquisite lines, God—provided we abandon ourselves to him in faith and love—transforms everything into our good. For those who seek God, not everything is immediately good, but everything is capable of becoming good." And not only good or even better, but absolutely the best, since the end of it all is transforming communion with God in himself.

Providence can be said to convert evil into good in three general ways. The first is after the manner of Job. A defeat diverts our energies towards more propitious endeavors, but on the same level of human means and ends: for example, the merchant who loses his/her whole business in a fire. This misfortune forces him/her to start the same business all over again, but this time s/he becomes even more prosperous than before.

The second way occurs when a fall, a setback or a failure diverts our energies toward more spiritual pursuits. These are the many *felix culpas* which dot our existence: the knife which prunes, the sin which brings us to our senses, the accident which changes the whole course of our life. This is evident in the lives of many people. They are thereby forced to a deeper level of activity and receptivity.

In each of the first two modes, providence allows us to see some concrete results from our suffering. We can say that at least eventually we come to understand something of why our defeat had to happen in the first place, or why it had to occur in a particular manner. Our minds and hearts are at least partially at rest, for now we see a reason. We are somewhat satisfied. It was a blessing in disguise, a happy chance.

But what about the far more common and much more difficult situations in which our understanding remains completely frustrated and totally in the dark—the situations where we cannot see any good coming out of evil? What about those frequent instances where no profit can be perceived on any material or spiritual level to counterbalance the diminishment? For instance, a crib death, an irreconcilable divorce, ravaging famines, suppression of human rights by brute force, genocide. These pertain to the third way in which providence transfers evil into good. In fact, "this is the most efficacious and the most sanctifying of all ways."

C. Communion with God in Faith through Diminishment

In what concerns the mystery of faith—especially the darkness of faith—Teilhard's convictions accord profoundly with those of St. John of the Cross. Both men imbibe deeply from the Gospel and from Christian tradition. Teilhard's insights on the obscurity of faith in relation to diminishments—particularly on the epitome of all diminishments, death—are especially noteworthy.

First of all, what does he mean by the expression, "the darkness of faith"? "I, as much as anyone, walk in the darkness *[les ombres]* of faith. . . . In order to account for this darkness, which is so contradictory to divine light, some spiritual masters try to explain that the Lord intentionally hides himself from us to test our love. One would have to be irretrievably lost in mental gymnastics or completely insensitive to the agonizing doubts within oneself and in others not to perceive the inveterate inhumanness of such a solution. . . . To my mind, this darkness *[obscurité]* of faith is simply a particular instance of the problem of evil. . . . If God allows us to suffer, to sin and to doubt, it is because he cannot immediately and in one fell swoop heal us and manifest himself completely to us. And if he cannot, it is solely because we are still incapable of letting him do it, since we have not yet passed beyond our pilgrim state."[6]

Concerning the mystery of death, Teilhard considers every diminishment a kind of death. Death, properly speaking, is the definitive detachment of the human person from every experiential point of reference *(tout cadre expérimental); that is, from every framework that is perceptible or tangible in this life. Each detachment is a particular severance from some point of reference in our mortal world. All our daily deaths are recapitulated and consummated in the end by our personal death. Thus, for each of us living in faith (Gal. 2:20), death becomes the only way truly capable of definitively detaching us and wrenching us from all that is not God in himself.

But, in order that faith be unconditional surrender to ineffable love, complete darkness in relation to every experimental framework is necessary. Otherwise, we will not let go. We will irresistibly hang on for dear life.

Therefore, only our loving Father, who knows exactly what we need in its proper measure, can prune us in such a way as to preserve in us all that is transformable in himself, while cutting away all that is not capable of becoming divinized (John 15:1–5).

Teilhard expresses the intensity and all-embraciveness of our abandonment in darkest faith to God through the symbol of the *orans,* or perhaps more precisely of the *adorans.* "To adore. That means to become lost in the Unfathomable, to plunge into the Inexhaustible, to find peace in the Incorruptible. . . . It is to offer oneself to the" all-consuming and transforming "Fire of divine love, to let oneself consciously and voluntarily be annihilated in the measure that one becomes aware" of one's inner poverty. "To adore means to give of one's deepest to him whose depth has no end." In sum, "to adore is to lose oneself unitively in God."[7]

Yet, why can unreserved surrender to God in faith be accomplished only in total darkness? Teilhard's explanation parallels closely that of the Mystical Doctor.

A first response stems from the overpowering nature of faith as divine light. This light, which of itself is so pure and illuminating, has an obscuring effect on our powers of comprehension and understanding. This is so because we are still incapable of going beyond the limitations of this life. Only the complete detachment wrought by death can definitively break through these limitations.

Another response arises from the paradoxically positive role that darkness plays in the intensification of abandonment in faith. Darkness does not cause faith, nor an increase in faith. God alone is its cause (together with our voluntary cooperation). However, darkness is the necessary condition for an increase in faith. The more we walk in darkness, the more we are providentially disposed for true surrender. When darkness is total, abandonment to the Other is perfect. That is, in essence, what death so effectively accomplishes. It is precisely the situation of complete darkness in death which allows us to pass into total Light.

All that is of life in our being spontaneously abhors darkness and letting go. We instinctively reach out for some support, some crutch. If allowed to have its way, this aspect of our humanness would effectively impede our adoration. It is necessary, therefore, that every suppport be taken from us, ultimately even that of our earthly existence. This is exactly what the darkness element of faith accomplishes. It eliminates progressively all the supports we try to cling to. It ultimately removes even the possibility of clinging to anything. Darkness forms the concrete milieu in which we have no one and nothing else to depend on except God himself.

At the outset of our journey in faith, God leaves much of the initiative for our purification to us. Through self-knowledge we perceive certain attachments in our life. We then take calculated measures to remove these obstacles in order to continue our passage through creation. We detach ourselves to the degree that we can. Gradually, however, as we perceive the limitations of our efforts and the preponderant efficacy of God's activity within us, this initiative is tranformed into abandonment to him. God uses all these passivities of existence to actualize our potential. Yet, of all these passivities, those of diminishment are the most sanctifying, since they are also the most detaching. In their darkness they favor most efficaciously the full development of surrender in faith.

In this way, God does not directly darken the soul, and he certainly takes no pleasure in pain or death. Rather, he unites us to himself and divinizes us, but in a manner which respects completely the laws of our mortal being. God permits the normal activity of the interior and exterior forces of growth and of diminishment to ascend towards definitive metamorphosis. These diminishments in themselves represent the destruction of being. Yet, through these same diminishments and beyond the darkness which they cause, God is encountered in faith and love.

Communion with God through death coincides then with his victory (and ours in him) over evil. Nonetheless, true victory over evil is situated in the realm of faith, beyond evil itself. Evil as such is not directly destroyed. It does not have to be. For, left to itself, as we transcend it by faith, evil self-destructs, falling back by its own weight into the multiple (i.e., into what the Gospel calls exterior darkness). This occurs in and through the personal death of each individual. It will happen collectively at the end of the world.

The dying Christ conquered evil not by destroying it directly, but rather by not letting it destroy him, even though it literally killed him. Jesus allowed evil to destroy itself in trying to destroy him. (Deicide is the absolute epitome of all conceivable and actual evil.) In his death, Christ passed through evil to the Father. In death, by his interior act of total submission to the Father as well as by his theandric love for him and for creation, Jesus allowed his divinity to permeate completely his humanity, thereby transforming it in God and detaching it from all the limitations of this mortal existence. Yes, Christ surely resisted evil right up to the point of death in that he did not allow it to vanquish him interiorly. Jesus's submission was to the Father alone. He never capitulated to evil. So too for us in him. By abandonment in faith, we rise with Christ above and beyond every death, leaving evil behind in outer darkness.

Thus, the true Christian prays, "It is not enough, Lord, to die while communing with you. Teach me to commune in the act of dying itself." Not only does communion with God eventually and literally cause each person to pass from this life, but also we experience in faith real communion with God through the darkness of the very act of dying.

D. True Christian Resignation

For Teilhard, our attitude towards diminishments comprises two essential elements: maximum effort against whatever is of evil in them, and maximum receptivity towards God alone through them and beyond them. This is active submission to the Father's will, whether we are speaking of the obedience of Jesus to the Father or of our obedience to him in Christ. Resignation is truly Christian only inasmuch as we make a vigorous resistance with God against evil. This resistance arises from our unlimited abandonment to and trust in him beyond evil.

If we do not do everything within our power to resist a given evil, we do not find ourselves with the particular quality of receptivity willed by God. Consequently, we cannot undergo him as much as we could have otherwise. If our effort is courageous and persevering, we rejoin God through the evil, beyond the evil. In this way, "the optimum of our communion in resignation" indeed "coincides with the maximum of our fidelity to human endeavor."

However, we must not conceive of this effort against evil and this receptivity to God as successive elements, the one following the other. Both coexist concomitantly from the beginning and endure right up to the end. On the one hand, this maximum effort safeguards our receptivity so that it does not become capitulation to evil rather than submission to God beyond evil. On the other hand, our abandonment to God from the beginning ensures that the effort in question is not against God, but is uniquely against evil. Christian resignation is not just something residual, as if it were merely a consequence of all else having failed. Christian resignation is inherently positive, because it is toward God. In this manner, the faithful person is not, properly speaking, resigned either to suffering or to death. We are resigned only to God, deeper than the pain and beyond the death. The faith-filled person must resist all suffering and death with every ounce of his/her strength. And when exterior resistance becomes no longer possible, like that of Christ our interior resistance must continue right up to the very end. The final human act of each one of us in faith is always toward Life beyond death.

True Christian resignation emerges, then, as the point of convergence between the struggle against evil and our receptivity to God alone. It is the point where God exercises his full primacy over us as we abandon ourselves totally to him.

Having resisted evil for God with all our force, we arrive sooner or later at inevitable defeat (defeat, that is, according to our experimental framework). This is the hour par excellence of Christian resignation. For if we accept this diminishment "in faith, without ceasing to struggle against diminishment, the diminishment itself can become for us a loving source of renewal. . . . In the realm of faith a further dimension exists which allows God to effect imperceptibly a mysterious reversal of evil into good. Leaving behind the zone of human successes and failures, the Christian reaches by an effort of trust in the One greater than him/herself the region of supersensible transformations and growths. This resignation is but a movement that transposes the field of his/her activity into a higher realm."

Thus, death is not only *le Mal*, but it coincides especially and in a transcendent manner with the recapitulation and consummation of all Christian resignation. Death is the apex of communion with God in darkest faith. It is the loss of self in One greater than self. Death becomes the place of limitless abandonment to God in himself.

Notes from Chapter 4

1. All quotations unless otherwise identified in this chapter are found in *DM*, pp. 74–94.

2. *Writings*, p. 261. See *Contemplation*, pp. 117–122.

3. *Writings*, p. 260.

4. *Cor.*, p. 31; *HE*, p. 38.

5. *Night*, I, 14, 4. See *Contemplation*, pp. 85–96.

6. *CE*, pp. 131–132. Whether or not Teilhard includes John of the Cross among those spiritual masters *(docteurs)* is conjectural. In any case what Teilhard justifiably criticizes does not represent the Sanjuanist position.

7. *DM*, pp. 127–128; *TF*, p. 65.

Chapter 5

Receptivity of a Superior Order

In *The Mystical Milieu* (1917), Teilhard refers to a certain receptivity of a superior order. "In his/her eagerness to undergo the domination of God, there was a time when the mystic found him/herself forced into action. Now, however, the process is reversed. The very excess of his/her desire for action orientates him/her towards *une passivité d'ordre supérieur.*"[1]

At the end of the same essay, Teilhard goes on to insist that what he had written was only an introduction to mysticism and that he does not believe that he possesses the necessary qualifications to describe the sublime states of transforming union.

Is he too modest, or is he confessing a real incompetency? Neither. At the age of thirty-six, Teilhard was not yet sufficiently qualified to analyze in depth the advanced stages of this mysticism, even though he discerned their existence and situated them quite well in the overall development of interior progress. Later in life, however, he does take up some of the elements which constitute true mystical union. Needless to say, he expresses these elements in his own inimitable way.

Before we take up these expressions, let us examine more closely what Teilhard means in general by the phrase "receptivity of a superior order."

When referring to the passivities of existence, of growth or of diminishment, Teilhard consistently employs the plural, *les passivités*. In the context of a superior order, however, the word *passivité* is used in the singular. This is so because, in the context of a superior order, he is not referring directly to a host of influences. Instead, he is stressing a basic interior attitude, that of remaining receptive before a variety of situations which converge on God's influence within us. It is a question of our fundamental stance towards all passivities. This attitude of receptivity increases in proportion to our christification as God brings us into the advanced states of transforming union. At these thresholds—which St. John of the Cross calls night of spirit, tranquil night, serene night, spiritual espousals, spiritual marriage[2]—our receptivity is permeated by an intensity and a quality which are truly of a superior order. It is indeed "superior" in comparison to whatever we had previously experienced.

In the concluding paragraphs of *The Mystical Milieu*,[3] Teilhard reveals some of his insights concerning the superior quality of this receptivity:

"Already at the earliest dawning of the mystical movement within the soul, God is experienced as the only One who can sustain it and direct it." Authentic mystical experience is received entirely from God. Moreover, it is completely sustained and directed by him alone.

"The zest for life *[le goût de vivre]* which is the source of all our passion and of all our wisdom does not arise from ourselves. . . . It is God himself who must give us even the impulse to seek him." Yes, we undergo life as much as, if not more than, we undergo death. Not only is our individual act of existence received, but also all our potentiality for becoming greater. Moreover, not only the potentiality to become, but also its very actualization is received. "We cannot do other than receive ourselves *[nous ne faisons que nous recevoir]*."

"And even though the soul experiences itself on fire for heaven, it still cannot by itself see what it lacks in order to get there." This expresses the quintessence of passive purifications; namely, even with the assistance of the most competent spiritual direction, we come to know ourselves only up to a certain point. Beyond that point, God alone has the power to penetrate our innermost being so as to detach us from every trace of egocentrism. We let it be done by him.

"And when, finally, the soul has discerned the flaming Center that has been seeking it out, it remains powerless of itself to follow the divine Light all the way. . . . For it is written: 'No one comes to me unless I take him and myself draw him into me' "(John 6:44). Teilhard concludes: "The beatitude of mystical union is consummated in the realization of the absolutely gratuitous act of this supreme dependence on God."

Thus, we understand the simple meaning of *passivité d' ordre supérieur:* Everything which is done in us in order to divinize us is done by God.

Throughout the course of his life, Teilhard affords various concrete examples and specific insights regarding this receptivity of a superior order. Among these we select the most important and group them under the following five headings: (1) the meaning of the Cross; (2) the spiritual power of Matter; (3) Teilhard's third way; (4) detachment by passing all the way through and by sublimation; (5) the saying, "Everything that happens is adorable." Under some of these headings we shall treat the subject in a more or less systematic fashion. In several instances, however, we shall apply this receptive attitude in a concrete manner to the situation at hand.

1. The Meaning of the Cross

By its very nature the Cross has always been a principle of selection and a sign of contradiction. The Cross inherently makes no sense at all (1 Cor. 1:18, 22–24). Yet, in faith it becomes "a sublime goal that we attain in transcending ourselves." The Cross is "the symbol, the way and the act itself of making Progress."[4]

Teilhard calls the Cross the symbol of Progress because it is the Christian sign par excellence of Christ carrying the weight of a World in Progress. Jesus on the Cross symbolizes the blood, sweat and tears of all generations trying to make something better out of their lives and out of their world for themselves, for their progeny and for God. It is the way—indeed the only way (John 14:6)—because true spiritualization is accomplished solely through detachment from every experimental point of reference. "Our daily deaths together with our personal death are but so many thresholds sown along the road to Union."[5] The Cross is the very act of Progress by reason of the principle that Teilhard reiterated in so many different ways. "The more perfect the Union, the more intense must be the suffering."[6] Or, as he expressed it in *The Phenomenon of Man* (1940, pp. 50—51): "Every synthesis costs something. . . . Nothing worthwhile is ever made except at the price of an equivalent destruction of energy. . . . As a matter of fact, from the real evolutionary standpoint, something is necessarily burnt up in the course of every synthesis in order to pay for it."

Thus, the Cross is a sublime goal, but not in the sense of an end in itself. God is our sole End. The Cross is a goal in the sense of a necessary condition in order to attain transforming union in him.

In its most general sense, the reality of the Cross effects the basic separation among men and women. It distinguishes the courageous from the pleasure-seekers. It separates the serious from the frivolous, the sincere from the takers, men from mice. Whether one uses the word "cross," "night," "self-discipline," "asceticism," "mysticism," or any other term, the effect is the same: Each person convinced that true Progress lies up ahead at the cost of intense personal effort and suffering adheres by this very fact to the doctrine of the Cross. Life has but one term, and it imposes only one direction: "Towards the highest possible spiritualization by means of maximum effort." Whoever makes his/her best effort to improve the World has already begun in his/her own way to follow the crucified Jesus, since all conscientious human activity is necessarily an ascesis.[7]

To this general, human disposition Christianity offers certain specific insights. First, the mystery of "the sin of the world" (John 1:29) provides the deepened perception of the moral and physical weaknesses inherent in the evolutionary process. Second, the unfathomable reality of the historical Jesus, especially in his passion and death, reveals without doubt that true growth and goodness "is not to be sought in the temporal zones of our visible world, but that the effect required of our fidelity must be consummated beyond a total metamorphosis of ourselves and of everything around us."

The Cross means "detachment from the sensate World, and even in a certain sense, rupture with this World." The Cross is the way of "a veritable positive 'annihilation' which is born of the very paroxysm of our development."[8] "It is the road of human effort supernaturally rectified and extended."

From a hedonistic point of view, suffering and death (even effort and discipline) constitute the slagheap of nature and particularly of humanity. It is so much waste, futility, rubbish to be done away with, buried or incinerated. But to the person of prayer and faith, the Cross recycles, so to speak, all this debris in the direction of Spirit.

From a purely pragmatic standpoint, long-term and terminal sufferers should be put out of their misery. They are useless drains on society's resources. For whatever reason, they are failures and must not be allowed to obstruct progress. The mystery of the Cross manifests not only the inhumanness of such attitudes, but also the fact that they are absolutely unchristian. For, from the perspective of the Body of Christ, there are many different organs and diverse functions. That charism which is most charged with potential to advance the spiritual Progress of the World is the *adorans,* the contemplative. By circumstance and by providence, sufferers are forced out of the realm of exterior and material development into the realm of interior and spiritual Progress—a veritable contemplative life. Thus, in a most intense manner, sufferers carry the weight of our World in Progress. By a mysterious act of providence, they have paradoxically the capacity to become the most active contributors to the same development that seems to have victimized them.[9]

If the image of the Cross is the sublime goal and the way of spiritual transformation, then Jesus upon his Cross is both the symbol and the reality of the immense labor necessary in order to liberate spirit. The crucified Christ represents and recapitulates all the effort of creation struggling together with God "to ascend the slopes of being, at times holding on to creatures to find support, at other times being detached from them in order to go beyond them. . . . The Cross, consequently, is not something inhuman, but something vastly superhuman. . . . For the Christian, it is not a question of swooning in its shadow, but of ascending in the light of the Cross."

Yes, the Cross is definitely not something inhuman, but superhuman. The receptivity which allows us to accept joyously this truth is indeed *une passivité d'ordre supérieur.*

2. The Spiritual Power of Matter

"Matter is the ensemble of things, energies, creatures which surround us. . . . It is the common, universal, tangible milieu infinitely varied and shifting within which we live."[10]

Matter thus defined presents itself to us to be acted upon in two ways. On the one hand, it is a burden. It fetters. It is the prime source of pain and sin which threaten our lives. It weights us down. It wounds us and tempts us. Matter makes us grow old,

109

paralyzed, vulnerable, guilty. Who will deliver us from this body doomed to death? (Rom. 7:24).

Yet, on the other hand and at the same time, Matter is what nourishes and uplifts us. "It is physical exuberance, ennobling contact, virile effort, the joy of growth. Matter attracts, renews, unites, flowers. By Matter we are linked to everything else." Who will give us an immortal body? (1 Cor. 15:42–53).

Matter is a fundamental principle of both death and life.

In order to illustrate the paradoxes of Matter, Teilhard makes use of two comparisons: (1) that of the diver who wants to surface from the depths of the sea, and (2) that of the mountain climber who, facing a slope enveloped in fog, struggles to climb to the summit bathed in light. These two images have three points in common with our inner selves in regard to Matter. First, space is divided into two zones with opposing characteristics; the one behind appears ever darker, while the one up ahead becomes progressively more luminous. Second, we are the ones who ascend or descend. Matter provides the support necessary for our movement. Third, in the course of our effort, the light ahead increases with each forward advance, while the darkness behind increases.

In itself, therefore, and prior to any position or choice on our part, Matter is simply the slope on which we can just as easily go up or go down. "By nature and as a result of the sin of the world, matter represents. . . a perpetual tendency towards entropy. But, also by nature and as a consequence of the incarnation, it offers us the spur and the allurement to be our accomplice towards heightened being. This counterbalances and eventually dominates the former tendency." Each of us finds ourselves situated, then, at a particular point somewhere on the slope. In order to advance towards light, certain creatures are placed in our path not as obstacles, but as footholds to pass beyond and as intermediaries to be made use of. The concrete possibilities are as numerous as the charisms proper to each individual. There is a St. Peter and a St. Paul as well as a John of the Cross and a Teilhard de Chardin.

Upon the slope, true separation is made not exactly between Matter and Spirit, but rather between carnal and spiritual. As a result of our initial position on the slope and as a result of each position which we thereafter occupy on it, Matter is divided according to our effort and our intention into two zones: "Matter in the material and carnal sense" (that which tends towards entropy), and "Matter in a spiritual sense" (that which we make use of in our spiritualization). Over the long haul, two gifts gradually dominate our movement towards the summit: contemplation and chastity. The first represents what is deepest in the mystical thrust. The second sums up the ascetical effort.[11]

All this describes the general ascent of Matter toward Spirit. In virtue of Christ's incarnation, death and resurrection, all evolution is being directed toward the Parousia. It is in Christogenesis. The movement is one: toward the highest possible degree of being. Its rhythm is twofold: immersion and emergence.

"Matter, in you I find both seduction and strength, caresses and virility. You can enrich me or destroy me. I surrender myself to your mighty layers trusting in the heavenly influences which have penetrated and purified your deep waters. The power of Christ has passed into you. May your allurement draw me forward. May your sap nourish me. May your resistance make me strong. May your detachments free me. And, finally may your whole being become the matrix of my divinization."

The abandonment of oneself to Matter with such deep conviction and determination is extraordinary in the history of spirituality. In order not to succumb to the temptation of matter, Teilhard would surely be in need of a special grace, a grace emanating from a receptivity of a superior order. In fact he expressed just such an awareness in his *Journal* (April 23, 1919): "My life must be a great example of obedience—passively accomplished—to the universal operation of God: a great act of faith in the 'spiritual power of Matter.' "

Toward the end of his life, in *The Heart of Matter* (1950, pp. 46–47), Teilhard leaves us a mature reflection concerning the

111

seriousness of this vocation. "Even at my age [sixty-nine], I am still learning by experience just how risky it is for one to be called to leave behind the well-trodden path of a certain traditional asceticism. . . . Yet, I have been forced by grace and by inner necessity to search in the direction of heaven for a way—one not mediocre, but superior—in which all the dynamics of Matter and of Flesh pass into the genesis of Spirit. . . . Yes, to Christify Matter! That sums up the whole venture of my interior life. Although I am still often frightened by this pursuit, I have never been able to do other than take the required risk."

3. Teilhard's Third Way

Just what is this way that is not mediocre, but superior?

In a certain sense, Teilhard's *via tertia* synthesizes his spirituality. It also sheds considerable light on the meaning he gives to the word "superior" in the phrase "receptivity of a superior order."

In effect, Teilhard's third way is a succinct formulation of a complex and all-embracive reality. He uses it often in the sense of a *via media;* that is, a way between two extremes, a way out of a dilemma, a way through an impasse. This middle or third way, however, is far from compromising, mediocre or neutral. "It is a superior and daring way which recapitulates and corrects the values and characteristics of the other two ways," whatever they may be in a specific situation.[12] This third way is like a synthesis in a dialectic, like a threshold in an evolution, like an emergence in a genesis.

In other words, the mysticism of the *via tertia* can take two opposing factions, digest out of them what is really of Spirit in each, and synthesize this into something superior to either or both. In Teilhard's personal life, the question underlying this *via media* was experienced in an acute form of dualism: either love of Heaven or love of the Earth; either cult of Spirit or cult of Matter. It took him almost half his life to resolve the dilemma

112

for himself: "We must go to Heaven through the Earth. There exists true communion with God through the World. Moreover, to give oneself completely to this truth is not to contradict the Gospel and to try to serve two masters [Matt. 6:24]. . . . No, between the cult of Spirit which requires us to flee Matter and the cult of Matter which forces us to deny Spirit" there is another possibility: namely, "detachment no longer by running away from, but by passing all the way through and by sublimation. Spiritualization is not accomplished by negation of or withdrawal from creatures, but by" convergence with them in Christ and "emergence beyond them in him."[13]

Perhaps nowhere is this truth applied in a more down-to-earth fashion than in the question of celibate love. Teilhard experienced the agony and the ecstasy of this gift as keenly as anyone. In fact, he perceived the ability to love both deeply and celibately at the same time as the ultimate test of his theology of attaining Spirit through Matter. "The living heart of the Tangible is the Flesh," he wrote in 1950, "and for Man, Flesh is Woman. . . . At the term of the spiritual power of Matter lies the spiritual power of the Flesh and of the Feminine."[14]

Teilhard certainly does not intend the above expressions to be taken in any kind of chauvinistic manner. Nor are they pro-feminist, anti-feminist or sexist in any way. On the contrary, he is trying desperately to return to the pristine message of the Gospel and to learn from the incarnation and the resurrection how to grow in/through/with his deep love for a particular woman and his love for Christ in the context of a celibate vocation. He experienced each of these loves as special graces, not to be lived like parallel lines, but as divine gifts converging one upon the other in a deeper synthesis. Moreover, he was convinced that until he could integrate his love in interior peace and joy despite whatever surface turbulence and tension might persist, his convictions about the spiritual power of Matter would remain only a pipe dream.

"Theoretically this transformation of love is quite possible.

All that is needed to effect it is that the pull of the personal divine Center (Christ) be experienced with sufficient force to transform our natural attraction. . . .

"In practice, I must admit the difficulty of such an undertaking. . . . Surely, you say, universal experience has proven conclusively that spiritual loves have always ended up in the mud. Well, you said also that man is meant to walk with his feet firmly on the ground. Who could have ever dreamt that he would fly? [Much less walk on the moon!]

"Yes, I respond, some dreamers have dared. . . . Yet, what paralyzes Life is the lack of faith and the refusal to risk. Life's greatest difficulty does not lie in solving problems [or in answering questions], but rather in posing them correctly. . . .

"Thus, the day will surely come"—indeed it is already here!—"when, after harnessing space, gravity, the winds and the tides, we shall harness for God the energies of love. And on that day, for the second time in the history of the World, man will have discovered fire."[15]

Needless to say, the grace to live day-in and day-out all the formidable exigencies of this *via tertia* does not pertain to any passivity of a compromising, mediocre or half way. It can arise only out of a courageous receptivity to and of a superior order.

4. Detachment by Passing All the Way through and by Sublimation

Throughout this book the question of detachment has recurred in a variety of contexts and from diverse points of view. Here we propose a synthesis of Teilhard's teaching on the subject, stressing some of his particular insights.

From an evolutionary perspective, detachment can no longer be primarily understood as a rupture with the World (although something in that view is valid), but rather as a passing all the way through creation and as a sublimation of it: *détachement par traversée et sublimation*. Let us examine each truth contained in the above affirmation in order to appreciate better Teilhard's unique contributions.

A. Detachment Viewed from an Evolutionary Perspective

In *The Phenomenon of Man* (1940, p. 218), Teilhard expresses not only his personal theories and Christian extrapolations regarding evolution, but also responds emphatically to a frequently asked question: "Is evolution a theory, a system or a hypothesis? It is much more. It is a general condition to which all theories, all hypotheses, all systems must bow and which they must henceforth satisfy if they are to be thinkable and true. Evolution is a light illuminating all facts; a curve that all lines must follow." Even ascetical-mystical theology! There exist innumerable theories and hypotheses regarding the particulars of the evolutionary process (even more today than in Teilhard's time). But development, evolution and genesis as a general condition is an indisputable fact. It has always been integral to the process by which God effects transforming union.

Thus, long before Darwin or Teilhard, true Christian mystics have been caught up and swept along by a dynamic élan emanating from deep within the Gospel. This élan ascends relentlessly toward the Parousia. It has always been at the very soul of Christian mysticism. From the beginning, the person of Jesus has constituted its Alpha, its Way and its Omega (Rev. 22:13; John 14:6). Yet, the scientific discovery of evolution as an all-embracive reality has shed enormous light on the mystery of life, especially interior life. Even though scientific evolution as such has been preoccupied almost exclusively with the outside of things *(le dehors)*, it remains Teilhard's outstanding personal contribution to have uncovered scientifically the within of things *(le dedans)*.

115

So, how does this affect the high school dropout or the illiterate peasant? What does this mean to the humble mendicant of centuries past or to the otherwise sincere person of today who still is skeptical about scientific evolution?

Teilhard responds, "One can be extremely 'cosmic' in affection and in tendency, while at the same time remaining rigorously detached in the narrowest and most austere sense of the term. That is, a Trappist can actually live a truly open interior life, even if he still thinks that the world is flat and that he must be cut off from all its machinations. . . . Stark detachment, such as that practiced by the great contemplative orders, should not be viewed in contrast to or in rupture with the arduous labor of cosmic Evolution. On the contrary, their asceticism is a flourishing and a prolongation of the latter," even if they do not directly advert to the fact.[16]

"It would not only be useless, but also wrong to try to find in the Saints of the past explicit approval or condemnation of what I call cosmic asceticism, since the question of Evolution proper never entered their minds. What we do need to be able to perceive, however, is that, when we translate their quest for holiness into today's terms, we are able to see that indeed their detachment was by beyond-attachment [détachement par surattachement]." That is, that their ascesis of spiritualization was not in effect "anti-Matter or extra-Matter, but trans-Matter."[17]

B. Detachment No Longer Understood Primarily as a Rupture with the World

By reason of the element of discontinuity inherent in the evolutionary process, there is quite literally a leaving behind, a separation, a kind of rupture in every detachment. This is most evident in the case of death. Furthermore, whatever pertains to the machinations, to the self-centeredness, to the self-indulgent

116

elements of the world (John 1:10–11) quite obviously must be cut off and left to fall away (John 15:1–5; Matt. 13:43, 50).

Teilhard's point in this regard, however, is that the negative element is not primary. It flows only as a consequence from the primary positive thrust. It is because conversion is towards God that we turn away from sin. It is because our commitment is to Christ that we consequently give up whatever is holding us back from further christification.

During Teilhard's time the following phrase often recurred in the prayers of the Mass and the Breviary: *Da nobis, Domine, terrena despicere* (Grant us, Oh Lord, to despise everything terrestrial). Needless to say, that phrase used to irritate Teilhard no end. Nonetheless, he did try to give it as favorable an interpretation as possible: "Fortunately, this sentiment can be reconciled with 'cosmic love' if we understand *despicere* in the sense of 'to regard as secondary' and *terrena* as 'things loved for themselves without reference to Christ.' Nevertheless, it seems that there has been an important evolution in Christian thought on this subject. Sanctification is envisaged less as a work of rupture with or withdrawal from creation than as a love of detached involvement *[un amour du travail désintéressé]*." [18]

What is this detached involvement, or, as he expressed it in *The Divine Milieu* (1927, p. 120), a passionate equilibrium regarding all things *(une indifférence passionée)*?

C. Detachment by Passing All the Way through Creation and by Sublimation

Teilhard has his own way of expressing the dialectic of *todo* and *nada: tout m'est Tout, et tout ne m'est rien: tout m'est Dieu, et tout m'est poussière.* [19] That is, everything is both All to me and nothing; it is both God to me and dust. Every creature is from God, to God and, with the proper distinctions, is capable of being transformed in God. But it is still not God, nor will it ever become God in himself.

The above truth constitutes the gist of what Teilhard calls cosmic life, cosmic love, cosmic ascesis, cosmic mysticism. The ability to live this truth peacefully and joyfully is what constitutes a fully integrated Christian.

Teilhard's theology of suffering and mortification sheds considerable light on the above terminology. Most eighteenth- and nineteenth-century interpretations of suffering can be summarized thus: Suffering is first and foremost a punishment, an expiation. Its effectiveness derives from the fact that it hurts. In fact, the more it hurts, the better it is. It is born of sin and makes up for sin. It is good to suffer, to deny oneself, to inflict pain and deprivation upon oneself. This is sacrifice, penance, reparation.

In contrast to that view, an evolutionary perspective sheds a very different light. Suffering and detachment are primarily the consequence of the labor of development and the price that has to be paid for it. Their effectiveness derives from the generosity of the effort, the blood, sweat, tears involved in trying to make a better World for Christ. Physical and moral evil are the by-products of the process of becoming, for everything that develops suffers and commits its own faults. The Cross is the symbol of the arduous task of Evolution. This is how the sin of the World is taken away. This may be called evangelical poverty, Christian asceticism, *détachement par traversée*.

Detachment by going all the way through denotes this: In full discipleship with the Incarnate Word, we become deeply involved not only with creation as the sum total of creatures, but also with creation as the ongoing process of Evolution. We become involved all the way through to its very term—recapitulation of all in Christ (Col. 1:20). If we become so involved with him in his involvement, then we must go all the way and die with him in all so as to rise with him beyond all.

At this point, Teilhard adds a further insight: sublimation.

Detachment not only *par traversée,* but also *par sublimation.*

In true detached involvement there exist not only discontinuity with respect to creatures, but also continuity. Passing through creation, we bring along with us in a purified and transformed manner the quintessence of everything in our World. In this sense, detachment is not exactly the opposite of attachment. In other words, it is "a kind of transformed attachment like spirit is transformed matter and internationalism is transformed patriotism."[20] In this way, we abandon ourselves to creatures with passionate equilibrium. We experience in their regard—with equal truth—that we have need of everything and that we have need of nothing. The One-Thing-Necessary comprises everything.

On the occasion of his interior crisis-conversion during the battle of Verdun, Teilhard expresses in his *Journal* (July 17, 1916) a very personal and insightful integration of all these elements. "We must go to God with all our heart [Matt. 22:37]. This means not only our heart as a capacity for loving, but especially our heart as actually filled with concrete loves. . . . Our conversion to God does not consist in emptying our heart and substituting him for all our loves. No, our conversion rather consists in assimilating in him all our loves in their concrete fullness," letting God purify them and transform them. This is a truly integrated Christian life.

Thus, God is encountered in those we love to the degree that both we and they become more and more spiritualized. Christ is not a substitution for our loves. Rather, these loves must be sublimated in him. They must become integrated in his love. Attachment and detachment—like breathing in and breathing out. That is the true breath of the mystic.

Could anyone seriously doubt that this lived experience in all its day-in and day-out implications must pertain to a receptivity of a superior order?

Yes, you say, that's great for an active person, an active spirituality. But what about the contemplative? Isn't contemplative life one of all renunciation with no involvement? Detachment by withdrawal? Oh, you of little faith! (Not to mention of little understanding!) The true mystic, the real contemplative, is the person most involved in the World, and therefore necessarily also the most detached. For s/he has gone all the way through to the very Heart of Matter, to the very Core of the Universe—there where the Action and Passion really are—sublimating all in All.

5. "Everything that Happens Is Adorable"

Tout ce qui arrive est adorable. "Properly understood," Teilhard adds, "that saying summarizes the core of my religious conviction."[21] It also explains in a very practical way the continual and eventually final dominance of renunciation in God over personal progress. Put another way, ultimate personal progress is achieved only in total surrender of self to God.

Teilhard had used a variation of this saying when he first spoke of the passivities of existence. "Oh, 'the joy of the action of the Other within us!' That is exactly what makes the passivities of existence appear so delicate to me and so worthy of adoration."[22] Moreover, Teilhard charges the French *adorable* with much more force than its English equivalent normally conveys. "To adore means to give of one's deepest to him whose depth has no end. . . . to lose oneself unitively in God."[23]

Gradually, as he became more imbued with a receptivity of a superior order, Teilhard reflected ever more deeply on the significance of all passivities precisely as *adorables*. In his *Retreat Notes* of October 21–29, 1944, he gives that phrase its necessary nuances. In effect he affirms that whatever befalls us, whether good or bad, eventually becomes adorable on the condition that we have done everything within our power "to give Christic energy its full meaning and its full being in the Universe."[24] In other words, on condition that we have done our maximum to bestow on creatures the utmost reality that Christ desires us to give them, and also on condition that we have left ourselves receptive to imbibe the maximum spiritual energy with which they have to endow us, only then in his providence is anything truly *adorable*.

Furthermore, the word *adorable* is not only an adjective. It also has the force of a noun, a proper name: *l'Adorable*. For "Whatever we suffer, we suffer Christ." That is, we undergo Christ himself while he suffers in us, with us. He and I suffer each other together. We suffer each other for one another and on account of each other. *"Com-patimur."*[25]

This is the ultimate in true Christian resignation. This is to commune with God in the deepest way possible this side of the resurrection. To experience *l'Adorable* in everything that happens is unquestionably a receptivity of a superior order.

6. Summary

Some spiritual authors have tried to summarize ascetical-mystical theology in vast syntheses. We think of Rodriguez, Tan-querey, Garrigou-Lagrange and more recently Royo-Aumann. These are almost like textbooks. They offer a relative service, but they lack the personal touch of the lived experience.

Neither St. John of the Cross nor Teilhard attempted a compendium of spirituality. Each described his own communion with God in his way and according to his particular gift. Their words, their sentences, their paragraphs flowed out of a deep, moving faith, and they simply let the pieces fall where they might. Neither was concerned about being published: John, because the possibility never really entered his mind; Teilhard, because the immediate possiblity was removed by ecclesiastical edict. They were not even concerned with polishing their writings, getting imprimaturs or satisfying this critic or that. John and Teilhard were simply themselves, and they let their written expression reflect their uniqueness in Christ Jesus.

In this vein, therefore, let us summarize all that we have been considering regarding the mystery of receptivity in Teilhard with a very homespun confession of his written in 1924. "Spiritual authors dispute whether activity should precede contemplation as a preparation for it, or whether it should flow from contemplation as a divine superabundance of it. I must confess that such pseudo-problems mean absolutely nothing to me. Whether I am active or whether I am praying, whether I laboriously open my soul to God through work or whether he assails my soul with passivities from within or from without, I am equally conscious in all instances of being united to/in Christ Jesus. . . . First, foremost and always I am in *Christo Jesu*, and only afterwards do I act, or do I suffer or do I contemplate."[26]

That is the caliber of receptivity proclaimed and lived in the Gospel.

Notes from Chapter 5

1. *Writings*, p. 144.
2. *Canticle*, 8–40.
3. *Writings*, pp. 148–149.
4. *DM*, pp. 101–104 (and the same for all quotations unless otherwise identified in this section); *FM*, p. 98.
5. *HE*, p. 88.
6. *HE*, p. 87.
7. See *Rom* 1:18–25; 8:18–25; *Writings*, pp. 65–68, 71.
8. Teilhard, letter to Jeanne Mortier, Feb. 15, 1940.
9. See "The Significance and Positive Value of Suffering," (1933), in *HE*, pp. 48–52.
10. *DM* pp. 105–111 (and the same for all quotations unless otherwise identified in this section). See *HM*, pp. 67–77, 225–239.
11. See "The Eternal Feminine" (1918), in *Writings*, pp. 191–202; "The Evolution of Chastity" (1934), in *TF*, pp. 60–87; "The Feminine, or the Unitive" (1950), in *HM*, pp. 58–61.
12. *AE*, p. 56.
13. *AE*, pp. 53–57; *CE*, pp. 76–95.
14. *HM*, p. 58; *TF*, p. 70.

15. "The Evolution of Chastity" (1934), in *TF*, pp. 86–87.
16. *Journal*, Oct. 20 and Nov. 5, 1916.
17. "A Note on the Concept of Christian Perfection," (1942) in *TF*, pp. 105–106.
18. *Journal*, May 10, 1916. See *Cor.*, pp. 72–74.
19. *DM*, p. 120; Ibid., pp. 95–101; *Writings*, pp. 70–71, 259–264.
20. *Journal*, May 9, 1921.
21. *LT*, pp. 288–289.
22. *MM*, p. 158.
23. *DM*, pp. 127–128; *TF*, pp. 65.
24. *LT*, p. 294.
25. *Writings*, p. 259; *Journal, Feb. 28, 1919; HM*, p. 204; *DM*, p. 123.
26. *SC*, p. 75.

Phase III

Teilhard de Chardin and
John of the Cross

Preliminary Remarks

In the Introduction to this study of the mystery of receptivity, we posed three questions: (1) According to St. John of the Cross, what is the positive yet purifying role of creatures in our progress toward transforming union? (2) How does Teilhard envisage receptivity vis-à-vis the divine activity within us and all around us? (3) Now, what are the main points of divergence and of convergence between the respective teachings of John and Teilhard? Also, what might be the areas of complementarity and personal contribution of each?

Conclusion

Divergence and Convergence

At the end of his major essay, *The Christic* (March 1955), [1] Teilhard addressed a question which he had often asked himself and which his critics are still posing: namely, how is it that as I look around me I find myself alone? Alone to have seen this immense vision of the World, of the Cosmic Christ, of the Divine Milieu? If I am really the only author in the history of theological reflection to have come up so explicitly with such insights, what objective basis do I have to substantiate my convictions?

Teilhard himself responds with what he calls a threefold evidence:

First, there is the evidence of coherence. Despite certain obvious lacunae, disputable tenets and unanswered questions, the substance of his spirituality is radically in accord with the Gospel. The person of Christ is really at the source of both his theology and his life. Moreover, Teilhard firmly believed that his teachings were grounded on what is most authentic in Christian tradition.

Second, there is the evidence deriving from a certain contagious power of his theology. Although he cannot quote a single author who sees the world exactly the way he does, he nevertheless perceived during his lifetime that countless persons were beginning to sense reality basically as he described it. He was, as it were, merely the spokesman of an idea whose time had finally come. He was articulating a realization that was universally beginning to take root.

Third, there is the evidence of a certain superiority to, yet identity with, what he had been taught. This is the area which pertains more directly to our study of receptivity in Teilhard and John of the Cross. Even though one can readily understand in the context of *The Christic* what Teilhard means by *supériorité* and *identité,* we prefer to use the words complementarity and convergence.

Thus, the question remains: Regarding the mystery of receptivity, is there convergence between Teilhard's spirituality and that of St. John of the Cross? And does Teilhard make a personal and complementary contribution in comparison to the Mystical Doctor?

Numerous factors differentiate John and Teilhard: historical and cultural milieus, particular vocations and personalities, world views and interior experiences. Yet, each experienced a very real coherence with the Gospel as lived in the tradition of the Church. Each experienced the prodigious, contagious power of his insights, even within his own lifetime. And each is recognized for his particular contributions to the mystical élan of Christianity.

Furthermore, each derived much profit from the teachings of previous spiritual masters while remaining remarkably unique and personal in his own perceptions and presentation. In the case of John of the Cross, he imbibed deeply from the Carmelite tradition, notably St. Teresa of Jesus; from the pseudo-Dionysius; from St. Augustine, St. Thomas, the Rheno-Flemish mystics; and from the author of the *Cloud of Unknowing.* As for Teilhard, he received a great deal from St. Augustine, St. Francis of Assisi, the Ignatian tradition, St. Teresa of Jesus, St. John of the Cross, Rodriguez, Lallement, Surin, Newman and St. Therese of the Child Jesus. Nonetheless, with the exception of sacred Scripture, direct references or quotations from any of these past masters by either John or Teilhard are comparatively rare.

130

Their mystical expression arose out of a profound, intimate experience of God within them; a personal, loving encounter with Father, Son and Spirit. Their respective mysticisms grew out of their unshakeable faith in Christ Jesus and out of their participation in the living tradition of the Church. Their communion in the one God, in the one faith in his Son, and in the one tradition constitutes the fundamental basis of their convergence. That is, John and Teilhard do not converge directly one upon the other, but rather both upon the Other. This truth is also the focal point for authenticating their respective spiritualities.

We might summarize the quintessence of St. John of the Cross's mysticism in these terms: Although he possesses a very intimate and balanced teaching on the immanence of God, he consistently accentuates the divine transcendence and the *nada* of everything created. God's immanence is itself transcendent. John explicitly recognizes the necessity of our involvement in creation and our consequent passing all the way through, but he stresses what lies beyond the passage. To encounter God in himself is infinitely superior to attaining his presence within creation. The quest for God through creatures must lead ultimately to direct and immediate communion with him beyond them all. The Christ of St. John of the Cross is the Jesus of St. Paul and of the Gospel, but John accentuates his kenosis. John's asceticism is founded almost entirely on *desnudez*. Its thrust is positive and dynamic, at the same time straight and narrow. He is the co-reformer of Carmel, the apostle of direct and loving transformation in the Beloved in contemplation.

The quintessence of Teilhard's mysticism can be summarized thus: Although the transcendence of God always remains the beginning and the end of his immanent presence, Teilhard stresses his Diaphany: God all in all (1 Cor. 15:28; Eph. 1:23), God through all. The Christ of Teilhard is the personal Jesus of St. Paul and of the Gospel, but he tends to stress the Cosmic Christ: the Universal Christ, Christ the Evolver. Teilhard's asceticism is also cosmic. It is situated in a renewed World vision. Its transversal movement (going all the way through) is constituted by an immersion into the World for Christ, followed by an emergence through the World with him, with a continual and eventually final dominance of the second over the first. This élan comprises both the vertical and the horizontal in such a way that the *En-Haut* and the *En-Avant* converge towards the Christic. Detachment is accomplished by *surattachement*. Spiritualization is effected not by becoming anti-matter or extra-matter, but by being drawn trans-Matter. Teilhard is the apostle of communion with God through the Earth.

Thus, the mystical theology of Teilhard is obviously not identical with that of John of the Cross (any more than the spirituality of St. Paul is identical with that of the Beloved Disciple). Yet, these two points of views are reconcilable. They do converge in their depths upon the same ineffable mystery of God's transforming love. Each contains its own personal contribution to Christian mysticism. Moreover, each complements the other within the vast theological and mystical pluralism of the Church. Nonetheless, there remains considerable difference of emphasis and tone between Teilhard and St. John of the Cross.

The movement of John is towards the transcendent, towards what Teilhard calls God-on-high *(Dieu-en-Haut)*. Except for a few notable passages at the beginning of the *Spiritual Canticle,* the positive role of creatures in our sanctification remains obscure. The historical perspective of God-up-ahead *(Dieu-en-Avant)*—in other words, the God of Evolution—never crossed his mind. Nonetheless, neither in his personal life nor in his writings does John scorn what Teilhard calls the Divine Milieu or Matter. Even though John stresses the transcendent and *nada,* the reality of a Diaphany is not foreign to our quest for our Spouse in and through creatures.

In comparing their respective spiritualities, we find that on the whole Teilhard contributes more to a better understanding of God's immanence, his presence within the World. In some respects, he situates and explains the ascetical dimension of the spiritual life more positively and constructively than does John. Nevertheless, no one can touch the Mystical Doctor in what pertains specifically to the mystical dimension of interior development. Furthermore, no one has ever penetrated more deeply and with such insight into the advanced stages of faith, night and transforming union than St. John of the Cross. Needless to say, these advanced stages constitute par excellence receptivity of a superior order.

Both Teilhard and John first lived all that they later wrote concerning receptivity. The spiritual theology of each derives from intense faith-experiences seeking understanding. Whether it is a question of the purgation sustained during the battle of Verdun (1916) or of the purification endured during nine months of physical and mental anguish in a Toledan dungeon (1578), the mystery experienced by each has the same Agent and the identical Goal: namely, the divine influence within each detaching him in darkest faith from all egocentrism so that he can be united in purest love to God. Reflecting on this mystery with a faith rooted in the Gospel and in the living tradition of the Church, Teilhard and John discern and express substantially the same doctrine of receptivity, yet with all the uniqueness of their individual personalities, gifts and vocations.

The quintessence of that doctrine on receptivity is this:

All that I am and all that I am called to become, I receive from God: my personhood, my individuality, my existence, my self, my gifts, my call to transforming union. I receive all this in the raw, in the rough, in such a way that the process of my personal sanctification is a gradual interior movement from the imperfect to the pluperfect, from immaturity to ultra-maturity, from scattered bits and pieces to actual union with God in himself. I am already in the process of transforming union. The progressive act itself of becoming more and more one with God transforms me into a state of perfection which is totally beyond my self or my capabilities. Thus, everything which is accomplished in me in view of my transformation in God is done by God. I let it be done (Luke 1:38).

This élan, this becoming, this letting-it-be-done follows a general pattern.

First, aware of my self and of my gifts, I plunge into created things and there mingling with them elicit from my personhood and from them as rich a nature as I am capable of and as circumstances permit. I increase so that Christ may increase. This immersion into creation requires a very serious discipline, a veritable ascesis on my part. I perceive certain stops, immaturities, hang-ups, and do something positive to counteract them. This positive action is called mortification, active purification or simply common sense.

My ability to know myself and my real needs, however, is severely handicapped. The intricacies of my inner poverty and the depths of my personhood are so ineffable that beyond a certain relatively superficial point I cannot penetrate myself or anyone else. Here God must take a more directly active and interior role in my spiritualization. Indeed, he must take over entirely. Moreover, I cannot continue in the direction of immersion into creation indefinitely. The very effort of immersion requires an eventual emergence from all that is created. I must decrease so that Christ may further increase (John 3:30). This is the specifically Christian hour—and a grave one at that—but one full of inestimable peace and joy for the man or woman of faith and prayer. Here begins the specifically mystical movement. This threshold marks the beginning of contemplation, the passive night of sense and spirit.

From here on, there is no limit to what God can do in me (Eph. 3:20).

The mystery of receptivity can be epitomized thus: Whatever is effected in me in order to transform me is done by God, and he accomplishes this in a complete kenosis of my entire being. This is the ultimate in Christian receptivity: I let God be done in me.

Sic finis libri, non autem mysterii.

Notes from Conclusion

1. *HM*, pp. 80–102.

Preface

This is a small book on a vast subject. It is scarcely necessary, then, to pause to list all the issues and concepts ignored or only touched on in the following pages. I have not attempted to develop a theory of justice, nor have I set aside space to defend the one that animates judicial practice in the Western democracies. No attempt has been made at an exhaustive review of relevant case law. Indeed, I do not try to provide even a "representative" sample of the jural settings in which psychologists and psychiatrists have come to take a leading part.

What would seem now to be beyond dispute are the many and various influences the psychosocial point of view has come to have on the administration of justice, on the very concept of justice. Usually insensibly, often proudly, and sometimes reluctantly the contemporary courts have adopted this perspective and, in the process, have put their reasonings at odds with traditional formulations and defenses of justice. In part, this is the unavoidable consequence of a theory of judicature which defines the courts as "social" institutions; in part, the result of an all too innocent willingness to accept without challenge the claim that the "social sciences" are, indeed, sciences. The argument of this book is that the first of these tendencies is perilous and that the second is utterly unwarranted.

In articulating this argument, I have chosen a small number but an instructive range of jural matters now rendered contradictory or incoherent by psychosocial thinking. These include the "insanity" defense, challenges to testamentary capacity, the protections afforded voluntarily and involuntarily committed patients, the position of the courts on psychological tests and on the legal standing of the defenseless. Where appropriate, I review the historical developments behind these current tendencies and attempt to show that neither history nor a careful appraisal justifies them. The picture of the modern court that emerges is of an institution increasingly so clouded in its judgment by irrelevant facts and specious theory as to be inaccessible to that body of principle to which it owes its very existence.

Georgetown   D. N. R.
February 1980

Contents

1   Justice, Morals, and Science   3

2   Insanity and Responsibility:
        Understanding *M'Naghten*   32

3   Insanity and Responsibility:
        Testamentary Capacity   75

4   Voluntary and Involuntary Commitments   111

5   Education, Testing, and the Judiciary   143

6   Persons: Their Nature and Their Rights   177

7   Some Modest Proposals   204

    Legal Citations   213
    Bibliography   215
    Index   217

Psychology and Law

1 Justice, Morals, and Science

1. Principles of Justice

The subtitle of this work has a provocative ring, but it is not intended as a veiled polemic against the social sciences. Rather, it might be read as if the question were "Can leopards survive on a vegetarian diet?" or "Can dental health flourish in the presence of sweets?" To ask whether justice can survive the social sciences is merely to acknowledge certain incompatibilities between the sorts of things produced by the social sciences and the sorts of considerations that have served historically as the foundation of systems of justice. The question is a serious one and is not by any means rhetorical, for in the balance of this book I will attempt to defend what finally is a negative answer. But before the effects psychology, psychiatry, and related disciplines have had on the processes of justice can be considered, it is necessary to examine, if only briefly, those traditional principles of justice now threatened by the social sciences.

The literature devoted to justice as an abstract principle is so vast and vexed that no brief treatment can even pose as a summary. It is, therefore, not my purpose here to review the history of the subject or to provide an exhaustive list of arguments favoring this or that theory of justice. Instead, I will note only those relatively persistent ideas that surface throughout the history of thought when writers come to grips with both the idea and the problem of justice. The subject is particularly vulnerable to useless and confusing pedantries, but to strip discussion of all philosophical elements is to reduce it to nothing more than a wrangle over opinions. The balance between scholarly purity and appeals to the general intelligence is not easy to strike where fundamental issues are involved, so I begin with apologies to both the specialist and the layman.

If we examine periods unburdened by developed and reasoned systems of justice, we find one or another version of the so-called law of the jungle. Such an expression immediately excites images of brutality and callousness and usually evokes pity and contempt from the civilized quarters of the modern world. Yet we must remain mindful that the essential nature of an animal is not completely determined by the environment in which that animal is found. Thus, in placing man in the setting of a jungle, we do not by that fact convert him into a beast. Indeed, with strikingly few exceptions, every record we have of man in society—including the most primitive societies—establishes what can only be called a basic *moral* nature. I do not suggest here that this nature expresses itself invariantly such that anywhere we find human aggregates we will discover the workings of exactly the same moral dictates. This, I believe, is a defensible claim, but it is not the one I am making here. I have not referred to *the* basic moral nature, but to *a* basic moral nature, and one that distinguishes all human communities observed to date from all nonhuman communities observed to date.

Perhaps the reader's first reaction on confronting this claim is to offer any number of observations and experiments flowing from "sociobiology" tending to prove that altruism, territorial claims, bartering, maternal care, hierarchic chains of authority within groups, and many other seemingly "moral" phenomena can be found among many species of animals. Of course, we did not need a new science to bring such things to our attention. Thoughtful observers since antiquity have noticed these features of nonhuman societies, and many of them, long before Darwin, proposed that these same features constituted something of a model or fundament or primordium by which to understand the developed moral systems of man. However, when we examine the concept of morality and strive to understand what we ordinarily mean by a "moral nature," we begin to see how irrelevant the ethological data are. We accept that there is a connection between a person's conduct and his moral sense, but we also recognize that the two are not the same. In every instance in which we seek to assign a moral value to an action, we consider not only the consequences of the action but the intentions of the actor. What sets moral actions apart from mere responses is that they are only understandable in terms of ulterior motivations that have "good" or "evil" as a goal. This is what separates the emotional and the moral elements of, for example, "maternal" behavior. The woman who cares for a child merely because she loves it is driven by motives that are exclusively self-regarding. The woman who cares for a child she doesn't love—one she doesn't even know—and is doing so simply on the grounds that she judges such care to be right and the withholding of such care to be wrong is driven by moral considerations which, properly understood, are not motives at all. A motive, from the very etymology of the word, pertains to a condition or state or stimulus that impels one to act. To remove all possibilities for action is to remove the very grounds of moti- vation. It is for this reason that we can distinguish between a desire (or hope) on the one hand and a motive on the other. We can say, for example, that Smith desires to live forever, but it would be a corruption of language to say that he is motivated to live forever. The two become associated only to the extent that some hopes can be realized through action, and it is these hopes that lead to states of motivation. A man watches his house burn- ing to the ground and knows that his terrier is caught within it. There is, in fact, nothing he can do to save her. He wishes that this were not the case, but it is a wish to which no relevant behavior attaches.

When persons are described as having a moral nature, what is usually meant is not merely that they are driven to act or not act in this or that situation, but that they have a certain class of desires or wishes which, in practical terms, may or may not ever be satisfied; desires or wishes for which there may be no possible means of fulfillment; furthermore, these desires or wishes have as their objective a state of affairs which, if brought into being, they would call "good." Still another qualification is required since what I have said thus far could well apply to, for example, the wish to have pudding and the judgment that were such pudding forthcoming, the resulting state of affairs would be "good." The added qualification is that of *universalization*. It is this qualification that adds to the desire, or to the wish, the belief that the state of affairs in question would be good for all persons and for all time, past and present. Again, I am not weighing the moral worth of any given desire or wish, nor am I at this point arguing that any given desire or wish is common to all moral beings—only that all moral desires or wishes must be "universals" as a condition of their being moral. This, however, is not the same as saying that no genuinely moral desire is immune to qualification. To say, for example that

> I wish for all persons that they be wealthy, excepting those who prefer to be poor

is to utter a universal wish, and to qualify it with still another universal, i.e., that universal class of persons "who prefer to be poor." The point is that moral desires are universalized even in their exceptions. The exclusions do not diminish the domain of the goal; they only identify that universal class for which the goal is desired. Thus, the exceptions in moral wishes are not exceptions to the rule but declarations as to the class of entities to which the rule is applicable, and the effect of such declarations is generally to call for a reformulation and simplification of the rule. Thus,

> I wish for all persons that they be wealthy, excepting those who prefer to be poor

is reformulated as

> I wish for all persons that they have the wealth that they would choose for themselves.

These considerations bring before us what has always been treated as the essence of morals, the concept of *ought*. That is, to desire that X prevail or obtain or come into being with respect to all Y's, and to believe that if this were to be the case it would be good, is finally to insist that X ought to be or ought to happen. It is of the utmost importance to recognize the difference between having a wish and believing that it ought to be fulfilled universally. Wishes can spring from emotion and subside as quickly as they appear. There are, after all, rash wishes. In any number of circumstances, persons find themselves wishing for an outcome which, even at the time of the wish, they acknowledge ought not to occur. It is in just such circumstances that the party harboring the desire faces the consequences of the universalization of that desire—a confrontation that quickly converts wish to whim and strips it of its moral dimension.

Perhaps the reader at this point will recognize the absence of an important qualification of the assertion that, "to desire that X prevail . . . is finally to insist that X ought to be or ought to happen." It surely would not follow from Smith's desire that the legions of the dead arise from their crypts that they *ought* to, even if Smith were convinced that such an occurrence would be "good." But as we shall see when we are further into the analysis of morals and in later chapters, the moral realm is an island in that vast sea of non-moral transactions called the physical universe. No one is *morally* responsible for events which are governed completely by the laws of science. No one is obliged to do that which is physically impossible. Thus, it is part of moral sensibility and moral discourse to distinguish between those universalized desiderata accessible to human intervention and those falling beyond the perimeter of possible human involvement. To the extent that human cleverness can neutralize the laws of nature or deflect them, moral discourse may become enlarged by scientific or technological advances. Accordingly, if it became possible to revivify the dead and restore them to human life, the moral dimension would be engaged, for it then would be plausible to claim that such actions *ought* to be taken. But just as it is contradictory to claim that a person "ought" to have done that which physical necessity prevents, it is contradictory to assign moral worth to events proceeding according to nothing but the laws of science. The qualification, then, is this: To insist that X *ought* to happen— that is, that it is morally *right* that X happen—X must be drawn from the domain of occurrences in which human agency is or could be determinative.

At a less practical level, there is something that further differentiates mere wishes from moral "oughts." The entire realm of desire is, in principle, available to our experiences. That is, even those wishes that cannot possibly be satisfied (e.g., that all persons live forever) can be conceived of as experiences. We can imagine living in a world in which no one ever dies, and we can imagine this world in terms of a collection of facts that prove immortality. In principle, therefore, no wish or desire is utterly destitute of empirical or experiential content. A world in which everyone is happy is, among other considerations, a world in which everyone truthfully claims to be happy; in which no one ever says he is unhappy; perhaps in which no one even looks unhappy. In other words, were the world of our universalized wishes to come into being, we would recognize it. But "ought," on the other hand, has none of these properties in principle or in practice. There is nothing of an empirical or experiential nature by which we can distinguish what "ought" to be. The domain of perception is the domain of mere material existence, the domain of "is." But the domain of "ought" has no material reference and cannot, therefore, be confirmed by observation. Nonetheless, we all know what it means when someone says that he wishes for this or that state of affairs because this is the way things ought to be. He is saying, in the ageless language of moral discourse, that it is right that things be this way and wrong that they be some other way. And it is just this consideration that renders the conduct of animals irrelevant to moral discourse, for there is nothing in the conduct of animals that reveals evidence of a universalized desire based upon belief in what ought or ought not to be. A dog will chase another away from a bone. This proves that dog A can chase dog B. We now teach dog A not to tear up newspaper. We then present the spectacle of dogs $B, C, D \ldots K$ chewing newspapers. Has dog A universalized the injunction against such behavior? Is there evidence on the part of dog A to suggest not only that he has learned that he must not chew newspaper but that he ought not? If such questions seem to be unanswerable—and, indeed, they are—then the behavior in question is simply irrelevant to moral discourse, which is discourse not merely about what is but about what ought to be in all instances.

Let there be no confusion between the analysis I have set forth up to this point and that famous "categorical imperative" advanced nearly two centuries ago by Kant. Kant defined the imperative illustratively thus: *So act that the maxim of your action be instituted as a universal law of nature.* This surely addresses an aspect of morality, but not that feature of it that common sense most readily apprehends. J. S. Mill was the most influential of an army of critics judging Kant's categorical imperative to be a justification for acts of unconscionable barbarousness. Examined at a superficial level, the Kantian principle would seem to contend that, were there a malign and misanthropic felon who wished that all persons behaved themselves according to his own felonious maxims, the terms of the categorical imperative would be honored. This, of course, was not Kant's position, nor is it a position that can be validly drawn from Kant's analysis of morals. To read such possibilities into it is akin to interpreting "Do unto others as Ye would have them do unto you" as licensing masochists to cause others to suffer. But of course what Jesus was teaching with his law was rooted in our sense of right and wrong, something that proceeds from that very sense. That is, given that we know what is right and what is wrong, we must treat others rightly and we must not wrong them, just as we would not choose to be wronged by them. The injunction, therefore, pertains to the universalization of desire, not to the content of the desire. This is also true of Kant's "imperative." As a catch phrase or bromide, all the categorical imperative asserts is that moral propositions are universal in their extension. It does not attempt to classify all behaviors according to their moral worth. But I am persuaded that at the level of actual persons coming to grips with the problems of social life, it is just this classification that forms an inextricable element of genuinely moral wishes. Such wishes proceed from a classification of right and wrong, good and evil. And since nothing in perception qua perception can provide grounds for such classifications, it would appear doubtful to the point of impossibility that the moral categories are learned.

Is morality, then, an "instinct"? Let us recall those genial moralists of eighteenth-century England who would base all morals on our "native sentiments" and would thus root all moral sanctions in our feelings. On this account, moral desires are universal only to the extent that all human beings become possessed of very much the same sentiments when they confront, for example, suffering in others, the torture of animals, an insult to their own character, and the like. But apart from the fact that it would be hazardous to propose a biological mechanism by which such "instincts" might come into being, we have the more difficult, indeed the insuperable, problem of being unable to account for just what we set out to explain: our sense of right and wrong. There is nothing in the mere sight of blood that makes the causal element "wrong," for some blood is shed in surgery. As has been noted, the moral weight attaching to any outcome is assigned only after the intentions of the actor have been assessed. Accordingly, the data of perception are never sufficient to establish moral judgments or even to elicit them. Nor would it help much to increase our instinctual baggage by adding "an instinct toward good intentions," for what is salient about moral nature is the ingredient of desire in company with the belief that the object of desire is good. Since our genetic composition is constant and our scheme of desires changing, it would appear that we do not have a gene for every wish. Alas, we cannot have a gene for any wish! But if our moral nature is not the gift of instinct and, as has been shown, cannot be provided by perception, what other source is there? Do not learning and heredity exhaust the possibilities?

Even if these two processes exhausted all the possibilities we have conjured up, they would not, of course, necessarily exhaust all the possibilities. After all, it is really enough to show that there cannot be a gene for wishes and to show further that "right" and "wrong" cannot be conveyed by the evidence of the senses to show that both an environmentalistic and a hereditarian account are insufficient. We do not have as an added burden the task of settling the matter once and for all in order for our refutation of other explanations to be valid. At the present time and with cheery candor, we must simply admit that the origin of our sense of right and wrong cannot be identified with unchallengable precision. Neither, for that matter, can we identify the origin of our very consciousness, although we have discovered several of the biological conditions that must be satisfied if there is to be any evidence of consciousness. Note, however, that there can be consciousness in the absence of all evidence of it—except, of course, the private evidence person X has that he is conscious. In the same way, we can identify one of the conditions necessary for the existence of a sense of right and wrong: there must be a personal and, perhaps, forever private awareness on the part of the actor that he has acted on the basis of an intention. We do not refer to accidents or mistakes as right or wrong, but as fortunate, unfortunate, lamentable, etc. We only think we have done something wrong when we know that we intended to do it and were aware of the consequences or likely consequences when we did it. Our sense of right and wrong, therefore, arises out of our ability to weigh what has never happened in the history of the universe— namely, the future. There is, we see, both a logical and a psychological connection between man as an intending being and thought as temporally indeterminative. It is just this aspect of thought that removes it from the context in which both feeling and experience occur. Experience is a function of events occurring in time and space; feeling, of events occurring within the body now. All experience refers to the present, as all feeling refers to the body. Thought, however, can refer to the future, to what is in fact impossible, to what has never occurred and never could occur. Thought is, in this regard, purely propositional. It is not "abstract" in the sense that is evades reality but in the sense that it can propose realities different from that which bathes the senses or excites the viscera. It may be argued, then, that to the extent that morality attaches to intention, and to the extent that intentions are by their nature future-referential and, finally, to the extent that futures can only be proposed—and neither felt nor sensed—all morality entails a rational being. If it were shown that other beings—such as monkeys or ducks—satisfied all these conditions, these other beings would, of course, be numbered among the earth's moral beings, but their inclusion would not vitiate anything said here. The important point is not that man is the only being whom we know to qualify in these respects, but that man does qualify in these respects.

I have set out in this chapter to comment on principles of justice, and I have gone on to discuss what is ordinarily taken to be the character of morals because only a moral being can articulate and comprehend principles of justice. However, what I have called genuinely moral desires are not identical to principles of justice, for the former are held by particular persons and are conceivable in a universe containing only one such person, whereas principles of justice pertain to the transactions taking place between at least two distinguishable beings. That a system of justice emerges from the genuinely moral desires of persons is indisputable, but the system is something different from these desires—something different from even the public expression of these desires. In their purely practical manifestations, the principles of justice make the developed morality of a society's most rational members obligatory by anchoring to it the common moral reasonings of the citizenry. The force of law is identical to the power of enforcement, but the force of justice is the force of logic, that instrument by which rational beings persuade one another to a given course of action. In referring to a society's most rational members, I mean not necessarily the most intelligent persons, but those who have studied and tested various maxims of action and, who have come closer to perfecting moral reasoning than have persons who have devoted less thought to such matters.

It should be noted that at various times there have been strong arguments according to which "justice" is merely the power that society exercises over its members through the combined strength of police, judges, and juries. Early in this century, such arguments were developed by those in the tradition of legal positivism who insisted, as Justice Holmes once did, that by *law* one could only be referring to that which allows one to predict what judge and jury will do in a given circumstance. This, which is scarcely true even of "law," can only be trivially true of justice. Indeed, granting the principles of justice, one surely should be able to predict what judges and juries will do in a given circumstance, but without such principles of justice there could be neither judge nor jury in the first place. Contemporary positivism, as developed by such scholars as Kelson and Hart, retains the traditional skepticism toward law as a "normative" body of universal principles and attempts to locate the essential character of law in what is finally a set of rules. On this account, there is an unbridgable gap dividing the moral and legal spheres such that, in a given cause, the jurist quite properly takes recourse to extra-legal and largely social considerations in his attempt to secure the public welfare. What the positivist specifically rejects is the notion that every jural matter is to be settled by appeals to moral principles; that the jurist "discovers" the law by applying these principles to the facts of the instant case. It is thus part of the positivist's thesis that a law may be morally repugnant and still be a valid law and, accordingly, that the given jurist may well be called upon to hand down a *legal* decision utterly at variance with his own moral sensibilities.

Perhaps the most influential of the recent works in this tradition is H. L. A. Hart's *The Concept of Law* which not only reduces law to a set of rules but specifies the criterion by which a given rule may be classified as a rule of law.* This criterion is *the rule of recognition* which permits one to discern whether or not

* Oxford, 1961. See especially Chapters 5 and 6 on the "rule of recognition."

prescriptions or injunctions derive from the settled laws of the land. Since no *ought*-element figures in the application of this criterion, the classification of rules as *legal* is separated in principle from the classification of laws as *moral*. Take as an example the Constitutional rule according to which Congress shall make no law respecting the establishment of religion. To determine whether the subsequent ruling—that, for example, a Federal tax imposed only on the Lutheran Church—is a valid *legal* ruling, it is only necessary to "recognize" the conceptual (logico-linguistic) connection between the Constitutional provision and the later adjudication. Note that none of this addresses such questions as whether or not Congress *ought* to favor certain religions or whether or not the Lutheran Church *ought* to be taxed selectively. The ruling is legally valid insofar as it makes the necessary connections with the settled law of the nation. The proper business of the courts, then, is that of applying rules in a manner consistent with the established laws of the jurisdiction, not imposing a particular moral point of view. And from this, it is a relatively short step to the claim that the courts are, among other considerations, *social* institutions which must be sensitive to the broad social context within which the laws of the jurisdiction became settled.

Too often the collision between legal positivism and "natural law" theory is staged as a conflict between utilitarians and libertarians. This issue is peripheral to the aims of the present book, but it is worth noting that nothing in the formal character of legal positivism requires a commitment to utilitarianism, and nothing in the formal character of "natural law" theory requires a rejection of utilitarian theses. In his otherwise cogent critique of legal positivism, Ronald Dworkin tends to frame the controversy in these terms.* He finds it appropriate to defend the essentially moral foundations of individual liberty by discovering something illiberal or too consensual in legal positivism. But in significant respects the positivist can only be offering no more than a description of procedures, which by itself conduces to neither a libertarian nor a utilitarian system of justice. Hart's "rule of recognition" as a gambit for deciding whether a ruling from the Bench is "legal" is fine as far as it goes. However, the proponents

Taking Rights Seriously (London: Duckworth, 1977)

of natural law must then chase the positivist's "recognition" back to earlier and earlier "recognitions"; all the way back to such principles as *Congress shall make no law respecting the establishment of religion.* This principle, after all, was not itself grounded in a "rule of recognition," nor did it reflect the very strong sectarian allegiances of the framers themselves. The ultimate grounding, we see, is in a principle, a *moral* principle, which may but also may not express the sentiments of a local majority.

Legal positivism sought to demystify the concept of law, but it succeeded only in reversing the relationship between effects and their causes. We would not even know how to convey to some fellow citizen what we had in mind in asking him to *judge* a matter if we were not able to take for granted that he had a sense of justice. But what this sense of justice yields is different from what is yielded by genuinely moral desires. The difference becomes clearer when we appreciate that one of the genuinely moral desires is *that justice be done,* which is to say that the right action be taken. However, it is in the very universalization of our moral desires that the problem of justice arises, for justice is addressed to transactions between interested parties, each of whom may be purely self-regarding in the given situation. That is, both parties may possess (and on some accounts do possess) identical moral desires, but they will not be motivated to act on these desires in the given circumstance. They may instead be motivated to act on nonmoral desires, which include, of course, immoral ones.

Recall that moral desire or moral wishes cannot be automatically translated into the language of conduct. Smith may desire that good prevail in the world, but he may be guided in his own conduct by more immediate concerns. As it happens, it is just this possibility of a rift between desire and motivation that establishes moral beings as free. They are free not in the sense of being unconstrained in their actions by natural causes or forces, but by being unconstrained in their framing of moral objectives. They are free to wish for what is right, though they may not always be free to do what is right. And in practical matters as opposed to purely abstract considerations, this is where the rule of law enters. It is the very foundation of the concept of legal responsibility that the party in question not only has the capacity to desire that good prevail but that, in the given circumstance, the party had the power to fulfill that desire. The law proceeds from a principle of justice; in this case, that no man can be obliged by the law to do what is not in the power of any man to do, or to do in the circumstance what was not in the power of this man to do. It would be unjust for law to require the impossible, in part because it is irrational and because the principles of justice are the productions of rational beings. In the annals of judicature, this has never been contested. What is debated in courts, both ancient and modern, is whether, in the circumstance, the accused had the capacity to know and desire the right course of action; whether he had the power to act on this knowledge and to give public expression to his desire; whether, in the circumstance, anyone could have acted differently. But all this comes under the heading of evidence, not justice.

I have described justice as something that takes form through the attempt to organize conduct around the judgments of society's most rational members by attaching these judgments to those moral canons that are available to nearly every adult member of the society. It follows from this that systems of justice will vary from state to state, from time to time, and from tribe to tribe—which would be otherwise were moral desires instinctive and at the mercy of the unopposable power that instincts have in regulating the conduct of beasts. But, as we have seen, moral desires are referentially futuristic and are of a propositional nature at their origin. In brief, they must be posited and refined throughout life. They are neither received, as in the case of revelation, nor taught, as in the case of manners. Those who behave in the right way exclusively as a result of training are said to be obedient, not moral. And those who behave according to revelation without consulting their own moral reasonings are also obedient; their actions cannot be assigned a moral value even if lawful. Note that the decisive factor is neither fear nor sincerity nor any other feeling. The decisive factor is reasoning in such a manner as to identify that course of action by which what is right is made to prevail. Few persons in any age will be devoted to such reasonings, and no society can afford the luxury of suspending all actions until every member has so devoted himself. Thus, laws are written, as Socrates said, to serve as the substitute for the Wise Man when he is not with us. These laws are *just* when they oblige us to do what we would genuinely desire to do were we to perform the rational analysis standing behind every genuinely moral wish.

So far I have confined my remarks to what might be called personal justice. Those inclined to read these remarks as abstract fail to distinguish between what is merely private and what is, in fact, abstract. Justice as I have been discussing it is not abstract in the sense that it has no standing in experience, for it does have such standing. What it lacks, or seems to lack, is the ability to elicit public experience—it cannot be "seen" by a group of by-standers. But neither can Smith's toothache, yet we scarcely think of such pain as abstract. Persons who have grown to adulthood have a sense of justice, and this sense is as much a part of their individual experiences as are their toothaches, even though no person can give *his* toothache to another. Of course, there is no experience or sensation or feeling that can be perfectly copied in other persons. This, however, does not diminish the validity of experience. It simply calls on us to develop a language by which nonessential differences are overlooked or cancelled. However, such a language is only possible where there is sufficient common ground occupied by all the individual experiences that make up the linguistic community. The point here is not that there had to be aching teeth before there was a word for toothache—for this is true, but only trivially so—but that toothaches had to be sufficiently similar across cases for the word to lead to social actions coherently related to the individual's meaning of the word.

But justice is, as I have argued, not merely a feeling or a sensation. It is a desire of a certain kind which can only come into being after the operation of reason. The public manifestation of justice is, therefore, one means by which this desire seeks fulfillment. *Practical justice strives to satisfy moral desire by conforming to the logic of moral wishes.* This is the social institution of justice; its instruments are the laws of the state. As history cruelly teaches, however, not every law is just, and on the account I have offered we begin to recognize why this is so. A law may be unjust in either or both of two ways: either by ignoring the genuinely moral wishes of those commanded by it, or by honoring the wishes in a way that does violence to the reasoning on which these wishes are based. A law that forbids the torture of animals on the grounds that such actions are bad for the economy is a law that is obeyed in spite of its reasoning and, therefore, in spite of the fact that it makes no contact with the individual's sense of justice. This is not because there is something unjust or immoral about doing what is good for the economy; less because it forbids us to do what our moral desires would have us do. The citizen does not wish to have animals tortured *and* does wish to have the economy prosper. But a law that forbids torture on economic grounds is, in principle, one that could oblige torture on the same grounds, and this is a possibility we grasp not through our feeling or sentiments but through rational deliberation.

My remarks to this point may occasion smiles in at least two quarters. In one we already found those confirmed in the philosophy of legal positivism; in the other are those who traffic daily in the "real world" of the courts. The positivist will argue, as Justice Holmes did, that the law is nothing but a collection of statements and habits allowing one to predict what a judge and a jury will do in a given cause, and I can add nothing to what I have already said in response to this view. However, there are many who do not subscribe to the ism—many who are not even aware of it—who nonetheless have arrived at a similar position as a result of their battles in the courts. I refer here not to theorists (positivists or others) but to attorneys who are constantly reminded of the vast terrain separating Justice and justice. Without ever committing themselves to an abstract theory of justice, they will oppose the analysis set forth here on the grounds that the courts are essentially social institutions that work, if they work at all, by balancing the interests of parties at odds. Whether it is the written laws of our system of justice—the *lex scripta*—or the *lex non scripta* of the common law tradition, judges are responsible to society, not to pieces of paper, no matter how lofty the words on that paper might be. Every law, this argument continues, is sufficiently amenable to interpretation and sufficiently riddled with loopholes that "justice" in fact becomes little more than what a clever lawyer wins for his client. The exercise of reason may be present in all this, but the phenomenon of genuinely moral desire simply plays no part. Pleas are used as bartering tools for the purpose of reducing the client's possible time in prison. Claims are settled out of court on grounds so removed from genuinely moral desire as to have nothing to do with it. Experts make themselves available for hire and in any given action can be found in sufficient numbers on either side of the

issue. White-collar crime goes unpunished as the courts attempt
to keep pace with the ever-increasing numbers of felonies committed by those least able to protect their rights.

Of course, one need not be an attorney to recognize the truths
contained in this blanket dismissal of the terms I have sought to
establish in this chapter. There can be no doubt that Justice is
often lost in the daily administration of justice. But the same
attorneys who bring such facts to light, if asked to interpret those
very facts, will offer two constructions: first, some of the facts,
properly understood, indeed do honor those very moral desires
that I have set forth as the grounds of justice, and second, our
judicial system is corrupt. In other words, even the most prac-
tical-minded and experienced lawyer will either condemn the very
fact he has adduced in opposition to the thesis of this chapter or
he will take some facts as conforming to the spirit of this thesis.
The positivist fails to acknowledge the ubiquity and the binding
nature of human conscience, and the practical man acknowledges
it as he seeks to dethrone it. The aim of my thesis has not been to
describe what courts do, but to identify the conditions by which
courts, laws, judges, juries, and attorneys come into being and
derive their powers and duties. That once in being they proceed to
neglect or circumvent these same conditions—that their performance in society comes to disregard the very purposes for which
they were instituted and constituted—has no more bearing on the
principles of justice than calculational errors have on the rules of
mathematics. That some persons do not add correctly or do not
know how to add does not suggest a deficiency in the principles of
arithmetic, but a deficiency in the abilities (motives, intentions,
comprehension, trustworthiness, capacities, judgment, character,
etc.) of those who cannot or do not follow the principles. To
insist that the principles of justice are not honored in every court
and at all times is to say no more than that persons are sometimes
mistaken or malicious or unthinking or unqualified. It is surely
not to offer a proof against the principles themselves.

Wedded to the opposition that comes from one sector of the
legal profession is the objection raised by those who think they
have uncovered a fundamental flaw in the sort of analysis I have
given by noting that not everyone has the same "moral desires."
The professional objection is that the courts do not perform in a
manner that is consistent with the analysis. The layman's ob-

jection is that not everyone agrees on what is a genuinely moral desire, for not everyone agrees on what is right and wrong. This objection would amount to nothing if it were based merely on the empirical claim that, in fact, many persons had been asked about right and wrong and disagreements were found. For if the claim were merely empirical, it could only establish that not everyone has genuinely moral desires, not that there are no such desires. And, as a purely empirical claim, it would (perhaps inadvertently) establish that everyone does have a sense of right and wrong, for if they had no such sense they could not even disagree on what is right or wrong. To uncover such differences would be to show only the judgment of certain persons regarding the rightness or the wrongness of certain actions or intentions, not to show that they would not have "right" prevail, and it is the latter that refers to genuinely moral desire. But the ultimate standing of this desire in practice will be determined by the quality of rational deliberation that went into the determination of right and wrong in the given circumstance. Those who defended the institution of slavery in the eighteenth and nineteenth centuries did so for a variety of reasons. Some may have thought that freedom was morally right only for persons and that slaves were not persons. Here we find a defect based partly on factual grounds and partly on analytical grounds. But such a defense would not ipso facto establish that not everyone has the same moral desires. If we take as the moral desire the proposition All X's should be free, then both the abolitionist and the slaveholder could agree on the maxim but disagree as to whether slaves were X's. Others defended slavery on economic grounds, insisting that in the absence of slavery the South could not survive. Let us say that, at least for some, the evil of slavery was counterbalanced by the good it created. Here we have an instance of imperfect reasoning. If it is granted that X's should be free, then the state (any political entity) is brought into being in part to secure the freedom of X's. If it is further granted that slaves are X's, then it it simply inconsistent to argue for the preservation of that which the state was organized to eliminate on the grounds that the state is thereby made stronger. Nothing can be strengthened by enlarging that which it was designed to eliminate. That the given slaveholder might not have carried the reasoning that far is but one of the reasons why we have forgotten him and remembered Lincoln, but in any case it has no bearing on what I have developed in this chapter. There is no more reason to expect rational analysis to occupy the daily life of citizens in the moral arena than to expect it to occupy their lives in nonmoral arenas. Nor is there any evidence that such abilities and capacities are uniformly distributed among the persons of the world. As with any other division of the human imagination, moral reasoning benefits from practice, hard work, diligence, and some degree of native ability. But although every child is not Pythagoras, we can still teach nearly all children his theorem. Similarly, not every citizen should be expected to articulate coherent moral systems; he need only comprehend the logical connections by which such systems are made coherent and compelling to rational beings.

With all this said, exceptions still must be noted. There are and always have been individuals who oppose or ignore or deny or fail to follow the dictates of reason; others who, by whatever means of communication we may employ to reach them, fail to reflect what is ordinarily meant by a sense of "right" and "wrong." If it is this group that the layman has in mind when he argues that "not everyone has the same moral desires," then the layman is presenting cases of disease as an argument against the concept of health. Here it is the empirical part of his claim that works against his own contentions. In recorded history we find only a vanishingly small minority failing to share what has been called "the common moral sense"; that is, failing to desire that right prevail, having asserted that "X is right." The vaunted findings of anthropologists and sociologists are, again, largely beside the point. A society that believes that Pharaoh is a god and that he will need food in the afterlife is not violating the dictates of the moral sense by taking food from the poor and placing it in the crypt. The members of this society may be wrong in their facts, but granting the facts, the actions are proper, for the gods will now smile forever on those who have sacrificed in their name. We may discover communities and tribes lacking not merely moral maxims that match our own but maxims that have that peculiarly moral property. The same communities may also lack algebra, chemistry, and calculus. There is nothing claimed in this chapter, however, that requires as a condition of its truth the actual existence or the universal distribution of genuinely moral desires, only the potentially universal distribution of such desires in any human society in which the refinements of reason have been brought to bear on the native sense of right and wrong. If this has the ring of colonialism to it, I would only urge those still at war with the Victorians to produce one political entity which, having now thrown off the yoke of imperialism, has simultaneously rejected those fundamental principles of justice transported there by the imperialists. Soon after the Visigoths sacked Rome and made sport of any number of Roman traditions, beliefs, customs, and institutions, they issued something called *Lex Romana Visigothorum*. Perhaps they did not have a developed sense of justice when they arrived but they knew one when they saw it!

To recapitulate: Justice as a social institution and a practical matter makes the developed morality of a society's most rational members obligatory by anchoring to this developed morality the common moral reasonings of the citizenry. The law as an instrument of practical justice is just when it obliges us to do what we would genuinely desire to do were we to perform the rational analysis that stands behind every genuinely moral wish. A law that satisfies the desire but defies the terms of analysis is not just, nor is one that honors the canons of reason but opposes the object of moral wishes. The primitive term in all of this is "ought," in that it must be granted a priori in any discussion of justice. As it is not grounded in experience, it cannot be taught.

2. On Science and "Social Science"

There is no question that the developed sciences have an important part in any number of judicial areas in which outcomes depend on facts: Actions brought against corporations for misleading the public on the merits of a product; prosecutions for negligence in designing a building or bridge without paying due regard to the known principles of construction; malpractice litigation where the plaintiff's burden is to establish that the care received fell short of what is standard in medical therapies; ballistics reports germane to the identification of a weapon used in a homicide. These are but a few of the settings in which judges and juries look to experts to provide facts central to the judicial process. We may ask, then, what it is about expertise as it presents itself in these areas that distinguishes it from the claimed expertise of "social scientists."

This book cannot attempt to be a text on the philosophy of science. Instead, it reviews in brief what is now broadly recognized as the nature of science and the qualities a body of knowledge or methods should have to qualify as an essentially scientific enterprise. Let us begin with the recognition that the essence of science is neither measurement nor "objectivity." It is true that measurement is of great importance in all the sciences, and it is also true that genuinely scientific claims are not based on the biases, ideology, opinions, or dreams of the scientific community. But if we were to adopt measurement as the exclusive standard by which to judge the scientific character of an activity, we would find that nearly every activity qualifies some of the time and that no activity qualifies all of the time. Tailors measure the length of the inseam and theoretical physicists posit events that by their nature are immeasurable. Objectivity, too, is an insufficient criterion, if only because it begs rather than answers the very epistemological question that suggests that total "objectivity" is impossible in anything in which the human intelligence plays a part. What science settles for—if only because it must—is what is called *intersubjective agreement*. It insists on the use of procedures and methods of measurement that will yield results on which all trained persons will agree. Nor is the expression "trained persons" one of equivocation, for the degree of "training" in regard to the criterion of intersubjective agreement is generally negligible. It often amounts to no more than reading a meter or a ruler or noting when a light has gone off. Thus, even if we reject the notion of complete "objectivity" on purely epistemological grounds, we will still grant to the developed sciences the greatest degree of intersubjective agreement available to fallible beings.

The distinguishing feature of developed sciences, therefore, is neither observational precision nor the methods by which they explore their subjects. Nonscientists are often careful, methodical, thoughtful, accurate, truthful, and disinterested. The distinguishing feature, as it has been passed on by the history of science, is in the nature of the *explanations* science gives in response to such queries as "Why did X occur?" In the developed sciences, such explanations are couched in terms of universal law such that, if the law is true, the event in question had to occur in precisely the way it did. Newton's law of gravitation is illustrative: *If the attractive force between two bodies is directly proportional to the* product of their masses and inversely proportional to the square of the distance separating them, *then the apple must fall toward the center of the earth.* The historical (not to mention logical) form that genuinely scientific statements have taken is drawn from such universal laws. To put the matter briefly, for an undertaking to be scientific, it must frame its explanations in terms of universal laws, which is to say that it must be in possession of such laws.

Of course, not every enterprise that is headed in the direction of a developed science possesses such laws at the outset. Scientific knowledge increases cumulatively and new facts always appear to challenge older theories and earlier laws. At a given and less developed stage in the evolution of a discipline, there may be little more than a set of reliable generalizations available to workers in the field. The so-called law of supply and demand is an instance of a reliable generalization that is not by any means a universal law. At this stage of development, the aspiring science cannot provide complete scientific explanations but can offer what some philosophers of science have called "explanation-sketches." These are provisional answers to "Why did X occur?," but they are more of a starting point than the goal of science.

It might seem that in this hurried account of the nature of science I have been speaking only of physics and of those specialties within chemistry and biology that are firmly rooted in physics. After all, what "universal law" exists in anatomy or clinical medicine? But here it is important to acknowledge the dependence of science on any number of activities which themselves are not scientific, and to acknowledge further the dependence of many nonscientific activities on science itself. To the extent that anatomy is concerned only with locating and naming parts of the body, it is not science, since a name is not an explanation of anything, nor is it an answer to any question beginning with the word "why." It is simply a descriptive classification of items. That microscopes, scalpels, blotting paper, and animal specimens are used does not qualify the activity as science. The same materials are used by taxidermists, veterinarians, and butterfly collectors. Similarly, the physician who notes the concentration of sugar in the blood, the pulse and blood pressure, the pupils and temperature of his patient, and arrives at the diagnosis "diabetes" is employing scientific explanations that have been developed by others, but is not advancing new explanations of the same kind. He is using science, not doing science. Science is a form of discovery where the object of the search is laws. It is not a form of treatment or play or mere speculation. When it is successful, it is able to tell us that events in class B will, within the limits of measurement, occur whenever events in class A are present, and this *because* "All B's are a function of A's." This constant conjunction of A's and B's and the uniformity with which B's follow A's is precisely what is meant by the scientific claim that A is the *cause* of B. The language of science is the language of causation. The syntax controlling this language is nothing but the laws of science. Thus, science explains a particular event by establishing the universal causal law of which that event is but an instance. Where no such law can be found, science can offer no explanation. It can only note the occurrence and hope for better times. And where an incorrect law is applied, science has also offered no explanation, since the wrong law explains nothing.

With this in mind, let us turn our attention to the "social sciences" in order to respect how different they are from anything referred to so far. At only a superficial level, the first thing that becomes clear is that the "social sciences" cannot provide scientific explanations for the simple reason that they do not possess universal laws. There is simply no statement about human psychology, human society, or human motivation that is known to be true in all cases, for both sexes, at all ages of life, in every culture, and under all specifiable conditions (assuming that all relevant conditions are specifiable). Indeed, except in the most trivial respects, there are not even reliable empirical generalizations that might serve as "explanation-sketches" of significant human actions. There are, to be sure, well-conducted investigations of such aspects of human psychology as perception, trial-and-error learning, memory, reading comprehension, and related basic skills, but these scarcely qualify as the universal laws of a science of human psychology.

But there is a deeper rift between the sorts of things science attempts and what it would take for us to be satisfied that a "social science" had completed its mission. Science attempts to explain events in the material world in terms of universal causal laws. However, significant human actions—as opposed to the behavior of billiard balls or weights hung from the arms of a lever—are generally understood to be based not on "universal causal laws" but on human *reasons*. This is especially so in juridical contexts. When we ask "Why did Jones shoot Smith?", we certainly are not interested in a causal account of the manner in which Jones's brain produced signals which, when delivered to the index finger of the right hand, resulted in contraction of the digital muscles such that the trigger was pulled. The very purpose of the trial is to establish guilt or innocence; a purpose that can only be served by inquiring into Jones's motives or reasons for acting as he did. The same is the case when we attempt to account for historical events. To ask "Why was the French monarchy overthrown?" is to ask something about a set of social conditions, traditions, political realities, human aspirations, governmental policies, and the like. It is not to ask for a causal analysis of events leading up to the beheading of the monarch. Again, it is only trivially the case that the monarchy was overthrown when Louis XVI was executed. It is not to the mere biological fact of his death that we look when we seek to understand the establishment of the French Republic.

There are basic differences between explanations grounded in causes and those grounded in reasons. The two not only carry different meanings and serve as answers to different questions, but they also follow different logics. A causal explanation is utterly neutral with respect to cases. The biological cause of Smith's death would be the same no matter who shot him, as the cause of an apple's falling is the same for all apples. But the reason for an occurrence is unique to each case, for only Jones can have Jones's reasons. It is precisely in this sense that history never repeats itself and that purely natural events nearly always do. The difference in the logic of the two explanations is further revealed by the fact that effects are inextricably tied to their causes, whereas events are not so bound to the reasons behind them. Jones may have every reason to shoot Smith and not do so, but every natural event covered by a natural cause occurs whenever the cause is present.

There is no ready escape here for the "social sciences." Some would argue that, as these disciplines develop, their provisional "reasons" explanations will give way to the causal language of the developed sciences. What this claim boils down to usually is that a developed psychology or psychiatry will be completely grounded in neurophysiology and neurology such that all references to human behavior, perception, motivation, and reason will, in fact, be references to human nervous systems. Of course, anyone has a right to hope for anything, and the generous spirit may even be willing to grant that such hopes may one day be realized. But such a reduction has not yet succeeded. And even if it were to succeed—and there are many compelling arguments leading to the conclusion that the promised reduction is impossible *in principle*—two paradoxical consequences would follow. First, there would no longer be psychology, psychiatry, and sociology, for these would be completely absorbed by the neural sciences. Second, the very phenomena that the social sciences were invented to explain would not now be explained, but would be dissolved! That is, in going on about nerves, muscles, glands, and the like, this new science would be simply unable to explain the end of the monarchy in France since no combination of nerves, muscles, and glands will represent the end of the monarchy in France. The paradox is that the perfected reduction of all psychosocial talk to neural talk would not produce an explanation of history but its elimination. On the assumption that nonspecialists even at the dawn of this promised epoch of scientific omniscience are still speaking, if only by habit, of such events as the Battle of Waterloo, the Boston Tea Party, and the climbing of Mount Everest, these same nonspecialists will continue to treat as droll any explanation of such events in terms of neural discharges and muscular contractions.

What I have attempted to show here is that the "social sciences" are not properly considered as merely the less developed version of what physics and chemistry and biology have already become. They are not, that is, "young" in the sense that time will fill them out, but different in a way that is immune to time. This is not to say that they should be accorded a lower status than physics, for to accord them a lower status is to treat them as inferior members of the same class. Instead, they form a separate class of inquiries, and the separation lingers no matter how many of the methods, concepts, or findings they might borrow from genuinely scientific undertakings. If this separation is not appreciated, its implications will go unnoticed and the data and testimony generated by the "social sciences" will continue to be misused and misunderstood. That they have been so misused and misunderstood remains to be established; it is to this task that I turn in the next several chapters.

3. Morals, Justice, and Opinion

There has never been a time in the history of schooled intelligence in which so large a fraction of the instructed classes displays so confused a sense of the properties of morals, justice, and opinion. The confusion is partly responsible for and partly the result of the increased importance of the psychosocial point of view to questions of value. It is this confusion that produces such odd maxims as "You can't legislate morality." Let us be mindful that if there were no difference between morality and opinion, then the law could punish only those actions that proceed from opinions different from those shared by the legislating majority.

It is common these days, whenever a matter of civic consequence arises, for journalists and political figures to consult public-opinion polls to ascertain how some persons "feel" about the issue. The politician's interest in such findings is understandable. He is eager to retain his office, and he does this in part by supporting the wisdom of his constituency. The press, too, has a valid curiosity here, since popular enthusiasms have always been newsworthy. But all too often, if only insensibly, many persons come to think of the results of such polls as having some bearing on the moral or jural dimensions of the issue. That is, to discover how many citizens would support legal abortions, the death penalty, court-ordered desegregation, busing, the publication of pornographic literature, or the decriminalization of drug use is to discover further the right and wrong of these measures: their morality.

As I hope I have shown, the fundamental quality of all moral discourse is the universalization of "ought" through a rational exercise. It is this quality that renders morals and opinions different in their logic and in their work in the world. Nothing obligatory attaches to any statement of mere fact, and all an opinion can ever be is a statement of mere fact. Once the major premise of a moral argument is asserted, its consequences follow with the binding force of the syllogism. There may be and there sometimes are serious grounds for challenging the validity of the major premise, but there can be no grounds—other than the grounds of irrationality—on which to reject the conclusions of moral arguments if they conform to the formal requirements of reasoning. If it is granted, for example, that No X should ever K any Y, and if it is further granted that T is a Y, then it follows that, No X should ever K a T. Note that the actual reference of these terms is irrelevant to the form of the argument. The X may refer to citizens, trees, sunsets, or postage stamps. The K may stand for killing, falling, rising, or tearing. The Y can stand for persons, forests, planets, and the like. But to the extent that the premise itself is offered as a moral proposition, it must be capable of justification—something that is not required of opinions. If, for example, No X should ever K any Y actually means that "No person should ever torture any animal," it becomes necessary to justify this injunction by adding a "because" clause which, itself, will be a moral premise. Indeed, if the "because" clause cannot be cast in the universalized language of morals, we have come close to establishing that the proposed injunction is nothing more than an opinion. Suppose, for example, it were asserted that no person should ever kill a neighbor because it reduces the tax base. What this "justification" amounts to is not an injunction against murder but an interest in a prospering economy. The beneficiary of the injunction is not any given victim, but the economy itself. Thus, by the logic of the argument, it follows that if we were to contrive a means by which the practice of murdering neighbors produced tax revenues, we might be obliged to murder them. If, however, the "because" clause were simply "because I don't like K," there would be no obligation to K or not to K any Y, since no one is obliged to do merely what pleases or displeases another. In the clause "because I don't like K," we have no universalization of the subject-term, and so we have no moral injunction at all. We have only a declaration of fact which, as only a fact, is neutral with respect to moral considerations. Similarly, were it claimed that "no one likes K," we would only have additional facts. The same is true even if it were proposed that "no one ever has liked K or ever will like K as long as there are human beings in the universe." Note that even a universalized subject-term will not convert the lan-

guage of "likes" to the logic of "oughts," for the basic reason that
obligations never attach to mere facts. It is for this very reason
that the results of opinion polls have no bearing on the moral
aspects of that practice or proposal on which citizens have opinions. The moral aspects become engaged when we learn *why*
Smith favors this or opposes that, not when we discover, as a mere
fact, that he does favor or oppose this or that. One person may
favor on immoral grounds what another chooses on moral
grounds. The polls do not reveal the reasonings of those polled,
only their druthers. I think it will be granted that, had such
surveys been available in America in the 1820s, the majority of
citizens would have favored slavery. But we certainly do not think
that slavery was moral when its proponents were in the majority.
Nor do we think the moral nature of slavery suddenly changed
when the Thirteenth Amendment was brought into being. The
moral argument against slavery is of the form No X should ever
K any Y and the injunction against slavery surfaces once it is
granted that slaves are Y's. It is at this point that matters of fact
become important, for there may indeed be factual grounds on
which to claim or deny that anything is a Y. Some citizens in the
nineteenth century were inclined to treat an Afro-American as,
somehow, three-fifths of a person. But even on this peculiar
theory, it would still be binding that No X should ever K any
$0.60Y$ as long as the three-fifths of a Z that qualify as Y cannot be
removed from the balance of Z. Otherwise, we would countenance
such defenses as, "I didn't kill Smith-the-person, I only killed his
vital organs."

We see, then, that all moral discourse is *formal*, that it is
regulated by the rules of propositional logic. In this formal manifestation it is essentially *subjectless* in that its validity is unaffected by merely factual substitutions for the several terms of the
argument. Opinions share none of these properties and, therefore,
thrive in a different and totally nonoverlapping realm of discourse. That certain opinions seek justification on moral grounds
indicates that, to this extent, they are not opinions at all, but the
first steps in the articulation of a moral argument. It is in their
universalized expression, in the logically valid (or invalid) connection they make with the balance of the argument, and in the
logical implications that emerge from them that we begin to

assess such statements as to their moral worth. All this is the task of analysis, and it is to this task that the purely factual results of surveys are irrelevant.

But, as I have noted, the laws are beholden not only to canons of justice but to certain social "realities." Laws that make no provision for the deeply cherished opinions of the public invite contempt and defiance. This is certainly one respect in which the courts are "social" institutions and not exclusively temples of justice. It is also what permits us to gauge the moral worth of a culture by examining the work it calls upon its laws to do. Over the long run, we generally discover the mutual interdependence of laws, principles of justice, and moral reasoning. To the extent that the laws are firmly rooted in developed principles of justice, they are able to call citizens to a higher moral awareness. This is the sense in which the laws of a good state teach. To the extent that the laws are so obedient to the nonmoral wishes or goals of either the public or the monarch, justice fails to mirror the genuinely moral desires of moral beings and the laws lose the binding power that only "oughts" can give them. In such instances, and again over the long run of things, we find the populace itself serving as teacher. None of this is possible under the reign of opinion, however, or under its near relations: fad, ignorance, whim, and prejudice.

Notes

Specialists will recognize in my brief review of the nature of science a commitment to the Hempelian perspective. Interested readers may consult Carl Hempel's *Aspects of Scientific Explanation* (New York, 1965). The reasons versus causes distinction is an old one fully appreciated by Aristotle and, in modern times, by Descartes and Leibnitz. It is a central feature of Hegelian metaphysics, where it is briefly but cogently found in Hegel's *Reason in History*. The bearing of this distinction on the social sciences is thoughtfully examined by Peter Winch in *The Idea of Social Science* (London, 1958). Most eloquent and detailed of the twentieth-century analyses is R. G. Collingwood's *The Idea of History* (Oxford, 1943). The clearest distinction between the "ought" of moral discourse and exclusively jural prohibitions is made by Joel Feinberg in the first chapter of his *Doing and Deserving* (Princeton, 1970).

In this chapter and throughout the book, students of moral and political philosophy will recognize a general commitment to deontological ethical systems. However, this is not to be construed as a rejection of any and every utilitarian alternative, or even as a denial of the validity of certain utilitarian criticisms of deontology. In couching basic rights in the language of individual desires and suffering, there is an explicit acknowledgement of the utilitarian considerations that enter into assertions of rights. Nonetheless, the controlling perspective in these pages is deontological and, therefore, the inclusion of utilitarian considerations is intended only to illustrate and amplify principles discussed in connection with rights. Specifically rejected in this regard is the claim that the ultimate sanctions of morality are grounded in no more than the net happiness promised by adherence to its maxims. In describing a basic right as, *inter alia*, that which every rational being would choose for himself, would elect to have available at least to his loved-ones, and that whose absence or denial would cause any rational being to suffer (Ch. 3), I mean only to remind the reader of the sorts of sentiments and notions commonly elicited by the concept of a basic right. But if a word in this passage warrants emphasis, the word is "rational," and not the word "choose" or "suffer" or "loved-ones."

The deontologist is not oblivious to the hedonistic factors that often tie actions to principles; nor is the utilitarian aloof to the essentially rational analysis that stands as the foundation for many hedonistic calculations. Indeed, in the given situation, the distance between deontological and utilitarian injunctions may be negligible. The history of moral discourse yields no deontic system utterly aloof to human happiness; no utilitarian system destitute of every element of *duty*. If we compare Benthamist and Kantian arguments, we find any number of compatibilities interspersed with the well known differences between them. I note this not to promote an artificial *pax philosophica*, for the conflicts here are real and heavy with implications. Rather, I would suggest that the jural dimensions of moral philosophy are somewhat less affected by these conflicts than the metaphysical dimensions seem to indicate. Thus, whether the principle on which a system of justice rests is utilitarian or is deontic is a matter that may be and often is irrelevant to the process of adjudication and the setting of penalties.

2 Insanity and Responsibility: Understanding M'Naghten

If there is a single region on the map of justice where the influence of the psychosocial perspective has been greatest, it is that
pertaining to criminal responsibility and, more particularly, to
crimes of violence. In one respect, we should not be surprised by
this influence, since the ordinary citizen is likely to think of a
violent act as the deed of a deranged or "mad" person. Indeed, the
more bizarre the felony, the more perverse the action, the greater
is the tendency to place the actor into one of the categories of
insanity. Needless to say, this is a tendency that has been ex-
ploited more than once. The case of *People* v. *Schmidt* (1915)* is
illustrative, though somewhat ironic. Schmidt had been found
guilty of the murder and dismemberment of a young woman, his
"insanity" defense having failed him. The grounds for appeal
were that new evidence, not available at the initial trial and
bearing directly on its outcome, had since been uncovered. The
"new evidence" was, as it happened, that Schmidt had lied about
his insanity! Actually, the death had resulted from an unsuccessful abortion. Schmidt reasoned that if he were caught he would
certainly serve time in prison for the abortion and its fatal consequences. He thereupon mutilated the body in order to establish
an "insanity" defense should he be apprehended. It was with
some incredulity that Cardozo greeted this appeal and informed

*Citations of cases are given at the end of the book.

counsel for Schmidt that legal protections are not games of chance that allow one to try first this and then that defense until the accused finds one that works. We will return to Cardozo and this case later in the chapter. I introduce *Schmidt* here only to establish a certain connection between society's grounds for excusing a crime and the ability of some felons to commit crimes in a manner that acknowledges and conforms to these very grounds. We have seen this recently in the posttrial remarks of David Berkowitz, the postal clerk found guilty of murdering a number of young women in New York. He admitted later that his tales of demonic possession and commanding "voices" were contrivances designed to give society a means of understanding and, therefore, excusing him. Even more recently, Maryland tried a fifteen-year-old for the fatal shooting of two police officers in their police station. The first homicide was partially excused on the grounds that the perpetrator feared for his own safety. The second was excused completely on the grounds that the first killing had put the killer in a state of "temporary insanity."

What trials of this nature—whether that of Berkowitz or of the teenager cited above—invariably produce is but another reexamination of the *M'Naghten* ruling. Yet, at the risk of offending, I am forced to observe that little of this "reexamination" is any more than a confusion as to the actual nature of the *M'Naghten* ruling or its place in the history of the "insanity" defense. Even American judges who claim to be bound by this ruling are commonly mistaken as to what it was, and many of those who oppose it most vocally treat it incorrectly as a pivotal moment in the evolution of criminal justice. It is not enough to complain about the reasoning in *M'Naghten*. It is necessary to inquire into the grounds of that reasoning and thereby come to grips with just what will survive its abandonment.

1. *From* mens rea *to* M'Naghten

As this is not a text on the history of law, I must gloss over a number of important distinctions that separate English common law, American constitutional law, and European "Roman law." Until the "reception" of the early seventeenth century—when Roman law was "received" into the principalities of Europe, law on the Continent was as much a common law affair as it had been and has remained in England. What the tradition of common law provides is a collection of unwritten understandings that are no less binding because unwritten. The *lex non scripta* of common law is not an invitation to anarchy, just as the *lex scripta* of Europe's Roman law is no guarantee of justice. The distinction usually drawn when the two systems of justice are contrasted is that the judge's role in one is *lex dare*; in the other, *lex dicere*. On this construal, the common law judge *gives* law, whereas his European brother merely *states* what the law is. But in practice, we usually discover that the weight of past precedents and reasonings lies as heavily on the opinions of the common law court as does the written legislation of Europe. There is, to be sure, something of a petrifying as well as a stabilizing effect produced by inscribing rights and duties in stone; something of a capricious and seasonal influence imparted to a system of justice that relies chiefly on the wisdom of any current crop of jurists. But what appear to be the fundamental principles of justice have a way of surviving the nuances of application and technique. A just state will treat its citizens justly even with imperfect adjudicative methods, and a malign state will find some means of expressing its malignant nature even within a perfected system of adjudicature. It should not be surprising, therefore, that the "insanity" defense evolved in essentially the same manner and at very nearly the same pace in Europe, England, and the United States, even though the three were (and are) structurally distinguishable in their systems of justice. This evolution began, if it can be dated reliably at all, with a breaking away from a conception of man and the universe that had held sway for two millennia in the Western world. The evolution began when the nearly ageless Homeric idea of harmony came to be replaced by the Enlightenment idea of progress. It will be useful to review the terms of this very radical transition.

   The earliest sign of a genuinely judicious perspective is found among the earliest *archons* of the ancient Greek world, Draco and his successor, Solon. It was the archons who adjudicated issues growing out of the formation of populous communities and the decline of purely familial patterns of social organization. There were times in the ancient world when, following the death of an archon or the end of his term of office, no replacement was named, and these times were referred to as *an-*

archia, a word that tells us much about what the archon's mission was. Under Draco—whose measures were rarely "Draconian"— the practice of *vendetta* was outlawed. Here, the law formally acknowledged the moral maxim that no one should suffer for crimes he did not commit and could not prevent; that sons are not to suffer for the sins of their fathers. Here, then, we have institutional expression given to that personal awareness of individual responsibility. For a person to be legally guilty, he must in fact have been the one who committed the crime, and he must have had the ability to have done otherwise.

Roman law, which owed much to Greek example, also came to legislate against the *lex talionis,* the law of revenge. It went even further than Hellenic justice in distinguishing among those rights, duties, and moral awarenesses that are natural to all human beings and those that vary from region to region and from culture to culture. Those that are largely confined to certain districts and customs came under the heading of *ius civile.* Those that pertained to the known nations and races of man were part of the *ius gentium.* But it was under the rubric *ius naturale* that the Romans placed those actions, motives, understandings, duties, and obligations that were endemic to any being having the right to be called a *human* being. The *ius naturale* was rooted in the very sense of "right" and "wrong" that established persons as something higher than inanimate or merely animate matter. At the foundation of the Roman sense of *ius naturale* was not so much a religious sentiment as a philosophical or metaphysical perspective: Stoicism, the philosophy of natural law and natural order. Rome was more bookish in its stoicism, but the central element of this ism can be found in nearly every stanza of the Homeric epics. What is celebrated and taught in these works is the lawful connection between actions and deserts, the harmonious establishment that is the universe, the rule of law as the burden and the hope of all that live, the ultimate purpose toward which every existing thing must move. Very little in the following seventeen centuries of the Christian world challenged this antique perspective. Scholastic theology took it for granted and labored to reconcile its pagan terms with the truths of Christianity. Even the triumphant astronomy of Copernicus and the new physics of Galileo are best seen as the culmination of this tradition rather than as challenges to it. Indeed, Newton's physics was seen by its author as the scientific translation of God's ordered scheme for the universe.

Let us now inquire into the view of "insanity" that prospered over these centuries of pagan and Christian Stoicism. The Romans recognized that not every human being was in possession of reason. Some had no power over the workings of their own minds; they suffered from *non compos mentis*—no power of mind, no possession of mind. Synonymous with this description were those of *fanaticus* and *furiosus*, in that all three descriptions referred to a raving, raging beast. The being in question stood as a violation of the law of its intended nature. Let us remember that in the excessive reaches of stoicism, Roman law sometimes stretched the limits of plausibility. There were, for example, provisions made for "thing liability" such that those unjustly assaulted not only won damages but were even awarded the offending instrument. This they could then destroy, since it had been used in a manner for which it had not been intended. (Centuries later a French court at Bâle would hang a cock for laying an egg "in derogation of its proper sex"!) But consistent with all this was the reasoning by which a responsible agent is one who has the capacity to frame actions in his mind, to harbor intentions, and to recognize the connection between his actions and their outcomes. The *furiosus* is not such an agent, for he is not rational; he does not possess mind or the power of mind. Accordingly, he can only be guilty in action, not in mind. He lacks, that is, the essential ingredient in criminal responsibility, *mens rea*, a guilty mind.

It is important to understand that this line of reasoning persisted even during epochs of witch-burning and exorcism. The theory of demonic possession was a theory about causation, not a new theory of the nature of mental or spiritual disturbances. In fact, at the heart of the possession theories was the well-worn rationalistic assertion that the body is the tool of the soul, not its master. On this account, which includes the view that soul (mind) is immaterial and therefore immune to the forces of mere matter, the madness of the sufferer can only be understood as the consequence of the possession of the soul by another spiritual entity. The centuries of doubt about the biological causes of mental derangement are not, therefore, to be understood as episodes of untrammeled mysticism but as residuals of a quasi-Aristotelian and stoical outlook. These same residuals persisted well into the Elizabethan period (and even into colonial America), when more witches were burned in a decade than had been executed throughout the High Middle Ages and the Renaissance combined. On the whole, at least in the matter of theories of human psychology, the later Renaissance and the Elizabethan Age were both given to more voodooism and mystic fluff than any celebrated Scholastic would have considered. Renaissance Florentines were the first in the modern world to revive old superstitions about "the wisdom of the East," and they were hell-bent on exploring anything and everything thought to have been minted in Egypt. An astonishing portion of scholarly energy in fifteenth-century Florence was devoted to the Hermes legends, replete with occultism, magic potions, rites for the liberation of the troubled soul, and concoctions for every malady of body or soul. Elizabeth's famous Dr. Dee is part of this same tradition, whose effects are quite discernible in the works of Francis Bacon, that "patron" of the modern scientific outlook. On the specific issue of insanity, the post-medieval world may be divided into astrological and humoural theories in the mystical tradition and possession theories in the rationalistic tradition. Even in the late eighteenth century, Mesmer would derive a psychological thesis from Newtonian physics, so we see that neither the argot nor the "objectivity" of science is enough to immunize the sincere theorist against mystic excesses. The same is generally true of those who, in the tradition of Galen, would explain insanity on the basis of faulty chemistry. We must remember that much of this speculation was an offshoot of the alchemist's magical stews, and that none of it was grounded in experimental science or reliable clinical findings. Thus, whether the theorist located insanity in the stars or in ourselves, he was, more often than not, taking sides in what was fundamentally a nonscientific dispute. In either case, his sense of "insanity" was the Roman sense of *furiosus, non compos mentis, fanaticus.*

The most direct evidence for this is found in the writings of Sir Edward Coke (1552–1634), who is often described as the greatest common lawyer in the history of English jurisprudence. He became Elizabeth's attorney general in 1594 and chief justice of the Court of Common Pleas in 1606. For two centuries after his death, what Coke had written on any number of issues had the status of

law in England. On the issue of insanity, his position was unequivocal: For a person to be excused of a crime on the grounds of
insanity, it must be proved beyond doubt that he was *non compos
mentis* and *furiosus*. Only the raving lunatic could expect to be
freed from the burden of his actions. In this, Coke spoke for his
age. When he died, John Locke was two years old; the Locke who
would speak in the just emerging language of the Enlightenment
when he insisted that madmen "reason rightly from wrong
premises."

Illustrative of Coke's understanding of the matter is the position taken by Justice Tracy in the trial of Edward Arnold (1723).
Arnold had shot and wounded Lord Onslow. Witnesses were
produced who swore that Arnold's enmity toward Lord Onslow
was based on the belief that Onslow had sent imps and devils to
disturb his sleep. Eleanor Gittings remarked on the accused's fits
of rage. Arnold's own sister recalled the time he attempted to burn
down the family's residence. There is no doubt that his insanity
defense would have succeeded in any contemporary American
court. But in the actual trial, the counsel for the king informed
the jury thus:

> Every man that so departs from reason, every wicked man may
> be said to be a madman; but I hope that shall not skreen all
> that so act, and free and exempt them from punishment.

And then came Justice Tracy's charge to the jury:

> If a man be deprived of his reason, and consequently his
> intention, he cannot be guilty . . . [P]unishment is intended
> for example, and to deter other persons from wicked designs;
> but the punishment of a madman, a person that hath no
> design, can have no example. This is on the one side. On the
> other side, we must be very cautious; it is not every idle hu-
> mour of a man, that will exempt him from justice . . . [I]t
> must be a man that is totally deprived of his understanding
> and memory, and that doth not know what he is doing, no
> more than an infant, than a brute, or a wild beast.

In stating the "wild beast" standard, Tracy was not breaking
new ground but simply giving body to Coke's criterion of *non
compos mentis* and *furiosus*, for the English "wild beast" is very
close in meaning to the Latin *furiosus*. Note, too, the connection
established in the first sentence between reason and intention and
between intention and guilt. On Tracy's account, an Aristotelian

account, intentions are the possession only of rational beings and only rational beings can be legally liable for their actions. It is the guilty mind, the *mens rea,* that stands before the bar of justice. In the circumstance, Arnold's defense became hopeless at the moment he bought the gunpowder. He was sentenced to death, but Lord Onslow interceded and the sentence was reduced to life in prison. Arnold died in jail thirty years later.

It was soon after *Arnold* that the English courts began to make finer distinctions than those fashioned in the patrimony of Coke and Tracy. The first clear sign of this is in Lord Hale's *The History of the Pleas of the Crown* (1736) where there is formal recognition of what would later be called "partial insanity." It is under *Dementia* that Hale exonerates the person who "is absolutely mad for a day." Should such a person kill another while "in that distemper," he "is equally not guilty, as if he were mad without intermission" (Hale, p. 31). However,

> Such persons as have their lucid intervals, (which ordinarily happens between the full and the change of the moon) in such intervals have usually at least a competent use of reason, and crimes committed by them in these intervals are of the same nature, and subject to the same punishment, as if they had no such deficiency. (Ibid.)

Thus, Hale simultaneously recognizes partial insanity and temporary insanity and essentially dismisses both as defenses if it can be shown that

> such a person as labouring under melancholy distempers hath yet as great understanding, as ordinarily a child of fourteen years hath. . . . (p. 30)

Here we have England's most celebrated jurist subscribing to the "lunar" theory of madness, but this is really beside the point. The thesis as developed by Hale was significant because it introduced a seam, if not a crack, in that wall of reasoning that was built in ancient Rome and maintained largely without breach throughout the seventeenth century. Hale did not go so far as to excuse murder on the grounds of temporary or partial insanity, but he did make legal distinctions between those who were *furiosus* and those were, for the moment, in a state of distemper, and he allowed the latter a defense in principle, if not in practice.

The law does not evolve in isolation from the balance of society. Between Hale's *Historia* (1736) and the first successful and celebrated departure from the standards of Coke and Tracy— and I refer not to *M'Naghten* but to *Hadfield* (1800)—it was the troubled life of George III that most affected thinking about insanity. There were, first, the king's notorious psychological eccentricities; his bouts of depression, his nearly pathological need for privacy, his episodes of rage and mania. It was also well known that the king's physician, Dr. Willis, had prepared a therapeutic regimen based on physical abuse and verbal assaults, interspersed with exercise, broths, and a few herbs. But here was the spectacle of a reigning monarch overcome by *periods* of melancholy despair and *episodes* of raving. He was surely not "a wild beast," nor would he qualify for the Roman attribution *furiosus.* These considerations led many to reexamine the abrupt transitions between sound and unsound minds required by Coke and by Tracy.

The life of George III was troubled on still other counts. His colonial policies were the subject of great political divisions within his country, in part because of the tax burdens they imposed. There were several attempts on his life, sometimes involving, as in the case of John Frith, no more than the hurling of a stone at the royal carriage. Some of those who spoke and acted against the king were judged to be "lunatics," but there was great concern that after being acquitted on such grounds they would simply go back into society and make similar attempts. It was this possibility that brought into being the momentous *Insane Offender's Bill* (1800), which made provision for the incarceration of those acquitted of crimes on the grounds of insanity.

It was the king's own "insanity" that gave something of an impetus to the insanity defense. Ordinary citizens still looked upon "lunacy" with horror and shame, and no family was inclined to admit its existence publicly. Now, however, the accused felon could point to none other than George III in attempting to gain forgiveness for his crimes. The most celebrated of these in the last decade of the eighteenth century was the Earl Ferrers, who shot and killed the commoner John Johnson. Ferrers had recently separated from his wife, and Johnson had found occasion to side with her in the dispute. Ferrers pleaded insanity before the House of Lords. Let us listen to the Solicitor General's instructions to the peers in this connection:

[I]f there be only a partial degree of insanity, mixed with a partial degree of reason . . . if there be thought and design; a faculty . . . to discern the difference between moral good and evil; then, upon the fact of the offence proved, the judgment of the law must take place. . . . All cruelty, all brutality, all revenge, all injustice is insanity. There were philosophers, in ancient times, who held this opinion, as a strict maxim of their sect; and, my lords, the opinion is right in philosophy, but dangerous in judicature. It may have a useful and a noble influence, to regulate the conduct of men . . . but not to extenuate crimes, nor to excuse those punishments which the law adjudges to be their due. (*Ferrers*, pp. 948–955)

The earl was found guilty and was executed, the peers having unanimously rejected the plea of insanity.

This brings us to *Hadfield* (1800), perhaps the most significant case in the modern history of the insanity plea. All the ingredients were present at this trial. The crime Hadfield was charged with was high treason; he attempted to kill George III in Drury Lane. The prosecution was headed by Mr. Abbott, who would soon become Lord Chief Justice. Hadfield's counsel, Mr. Erskine, was the most respected trial lawyer in England and would himself become Lord Chancellor. The chief justice was Lord Kenyon, a man of great depth and broad experience. The circumstances attending the act were dramatic. James Hadfield was a nondescript fellow of labile temperament and active imagination. Days before the crime, he was confronted in a field by one Bannister Truelock, who convinced Hadfield that the Savior's second coming was only a short time away. (Truelock would soon be confined in Bethlehem Hospital—the former "Bedlam.") According to Truelock, not only would Jesus be outraged by the state to which the faithful had fallen, but he would find England's sovereign to be an especially repugnant symbol of all that had gone wrong in the world. Accordingly, it was any good Christian's duty to rid the world of said monarch so that a more wholesome climate might greet the Redeemer. On the strength of this revelation, Hadfield headed off to Drury Lane where he fired on but failed to harm the king.

Mr. Abbott undertook a careful exposition of the laws of England since the time of Lord Coke and as understood by Justice Tracy in *Arnold* and by the House of Lords in *Ferrers*. He stressed the grounds on which Ferrers' plea failed, here leaning on Lord Hale's dicta:

[I]t was insisted, that it was not necessary that a person committing a crime should have the full and complete use of his
reason, but, as my lord Hale emphatically expresses himself, A
COMPETENT USE OF IT. . . . (*Hadfield*, p. 1289)

Abbott, we see, is arguing for the "wild beast" test and is rejecting
the claim that any and every form of provable incompetence can
relieve the accused of the burden of his crime. But in rising to the
defense, Erskine for the first time exposes the logic of this test:

If a TOTAL *deprivation of memory* was intended by these
great lawyers to be taken in the literal sense of the words:—if it
was meant, that, to protect a man from punishment, he must
be in such a state of prostrated intellect, as not to know his
name, nor his condition, nor his relation towards others—that
if a husband, he should not know he was married; or, if a
father, could not remember that he had children; nor know the
road to his house, nor his property in it—then no such madness ever existed in the world. (*Hadfield*, p. 1312)

What Erskine seeks to establish is not that the "wild beast"
criterion is wrong in principle, but that it effectively eliminates
any basis in fact for the plea of insanity. The criterion, if it
applies at all, applies only to the person ordinarily referred to as
idiotus, one who has from birth never displayed signs of mind,
will, or reason. The insane, however, do not provide any such
symptoms, according to Erskine. They are known to have lucid
intervals, sometimes standing as the dominant and controlling
fact of their lives. They often conduct their business affairs with
acumen and propriety. They are often good husbands and fathers,
loyal subjects, and honorable persons. Accordingly, the true test
of insanity cannot be the one set down by Coke and embraced by
Hale and Tracy. Rather, says Erskine, the true test is one based on
the phenomenon of *delusion*. The jury must decide whether
Hadfield

when he did the act, was under the uncontrollable dominion of
insanity, and was impelled to it by a *morbid delusion*. . . .
(Ibid., p. 1319)

Going on, Erskine further refines the criterion to include the
operation of "motives irresistible" (p. 1315), and rejects out of
hand the idea that it must be further shown that the actor had no
sense of right and wrong, good and evil:

> [T]here is something too general in this . . . Let me suppose
> that the character of an insane delusion consisted in the belief
> that . . . the man he had destroyed . . . [was] . . . a pot-
> ter's vessel . . . *although to all other intents and purposes he
> was sane* . . . I only put this case . . . (to show) . . . that
> the knowledge of good and evil is too general a description.
> (Ibid., pp. 1317–18)

In basing the defense on Hadfield's delusion, Erskine was
able to avoid the standards applied in *Ferrers*. In that trial, it was
proved that the victim had actually opposed the earl in the divorce action such that Ferrers' hatred of Johnson rested "upon no
illusions, but upon existing facts" (*Hadfield*, p. 1325). What
Erskine prevails upon the jury to weigh is the connection between
the act and the delusion, on the assumption that the contents of
the delusion are true. If, in fact, the Son of God were preparing to
visit England and, further, He specifically commanded that
George III not be there, it would be obligatory for any believer to
take whatever measures were necessary to obey this command.
Not only would such a person know the difference between good
and evil, right and wrong, but would act precisely on the basis of
this knowledge. Was not Abraham prepared to murder his own
son on just such grounds? And had he thus disposed of his
offspring in response to a direct command from God, would any
court sentence him to be executed?

But there is more even than this in *Hadfield*. As Erskine
approached the end of his argument, he noted that James Hadfield had served the king in time of war and had been seriously
injured in this service. He had sustained gunshot wounds to the
head, and expert medical testimony established that such wounds
probably caused irreparable damage to the brain. It was at this
point that Erskine reached over and fingered Hadfield's scars,
drawing the attention of the jury to the pathetic former soldier
now accused of making an attempt on the life of the very sovereign for whom he had nearly died. We see that in the years
between *Arnold* and *Hadfield* the "lunar" theory had all but
been replaced by the "medical model." By 1800, many of the
influential writers on the subject agreed that in nearly every case
of insanity there was disease of the brain, and it is on this claim
that Erskine is capitalizing. Shortly after this, Lord Kenyon called
a halt to the proceedings and, in consultation with Erskine and

Abbott, charged that the prisoner be acquitted and removed to some facility that would guarantee the public safety. This was the same year in which the *Insane Offender's Bill* was passed, but there still were not separate quarters for those like Hadfield.

Hadfield did not rewrite British law overnight. Justices and jurors still had a difficult time extracting the parts of the tradition of Coke, Hale, and Tracy that had to be preserved from the parts of *Hadfield* that had to be honored. Thus, we find Justice Mansfield in *Bellingham* first instructing the jury that the law in such cases is "extremely clear"; that to support the plea of insanity,

> it ought to be proved by the most distinct and unquestionable evidence, that the criminal was incapable of judging between right and wrong. (*Bellingham*, p. 671)

but then qualifying this "extremely clear" standard:

> It must in fact be proved beyond all doubt, that at the time he committed the atrocious act with which he stood charged, he did not consider that murder was a crime against the laws of God and nature. (Ibid.)

Bellingham had murdered Spencer Perceval, the Chancellor of the Exchequer. He had spent time in Russia, had got into trouble, and had been detained in a Russian prison. Once back in London, he petitioned the government to pay him for his "service" in the Russian jail, and finding no satisfaction, he began to pester officials in their own offices. In desperation, he sought to avenge his losses on the life of Mr. Perceval, a popular public official. The insanity plea failed, and Bellingham was executed.

What is unique about this case is the fence-straddling of Chief Justice Mansfield, whose charge to the jury keeps one foot in the courts of Coke and Hale and the other in the court of Kenyon. He instructs the jurors first that the standard is the *capacity* to judge right and wrong and then instructs them that the standard is the accused's *belief* that his act was a crime against God's and nature's law. It was the first standard that put the rope around Bellingham's neck, and the second that resulted in Hadfield's acquittal. The very fact that Bellingham sought revenge proved that he had a sense of right and wrong, for otherwise he could not have judged himself "wronged." That Bellingham was "deluded" in the same sense that Hadfield was there can be no doubt. But there was this difference: Hadfield's delusion compelled him to attempt to kill the king, an act that would be "right" were it commanded directly by God. In *Bellingham,* however, the murder of Mr. Perceval would not have been right *even if Bellingham's delusions were true.* That is, one is not permitted to take a life merely because one has been cheated out of money or not compensated for one's services. And it is this reasoning that finally brings us to *M'Naghten* (1843).

The facts of the case are now widely known in legal and psychological circles. Daniel M'Naghten shot and killed Edward Drummond, secretary to the Prime Minister, Sir Robert Peel. The bullet had been intended for Peel himself, but M'Naghten mistook the secretary for the Prime Minister. It was M'Naghten's belief that Peel was spreading rumors about him and otherwise compromising his good name. In this and related matters, M'Naghten's testimony was disjointed and implausible. Experts were summoned on both sides and testimony was taken from many persons who knew and had dealings with the defendant. The entire nation watched as the insanity plea worked its way through the days of testimony and argument. Then, when the court acquitted M'Naghten, all hell broke loose. Queen Victoria herself made her ire known, and the House of Lords adopted the rare measure of asking the justices to explain the law in this case. I should note that although the last measure was rare, it was scarcely without precedent, for on any number of occasions the peers had sought the opinion of justices. But this had never happened in so notorious a case, and never before was it so clear that, in asking for an explanation of the law, the Lords were really demanding that the court explain its own conduct.

Chief Justice Tindal and Mr. Justice Maule agreed to respond to the five questions put to the court by the peers. The questions are instructive, and I shall paraphrase them here:

1. How is the law to be understood in a case in which a deluded person who knows he is acting contrary to law acts to avenge a grievance?

2. Where "morbid delusion" is the basis of the plea of insanity, how is the jury to be instructed?

3. To what extent is the nature of the criminal's mind at the time of the crime a matter of fact to be determined by the jury?

4. Is it the law that any person who can show that he was deluded at the time he committed a crime is thereby excused of the burden?

5. Is medical testimony *in the abstract* to be taken as evidence when the testifying experts have not examined the prisoner and have not mastered the facts of the instant case?

Let us be clear on what the peers were getting at with each of these questions. The first seeks to establish how far the court in *M'Naghten* departed from the "right-wrong" criterion and how far it moved in the direction of Erskine's "morbid delusion" standard. A man may be utterly deluded but still know the difference between right and wrong. The fact of delusion does not establish Coke's *non compos mentis* or Hale's "wild beast." What, then, is the law in such a case? And this ties in directly with the second question, for it is the judge's responsibility to instruct the jury on matters of law. How will the court so instruct jurors regarding the relevance of "morbid delusion" to the plea of insanity? The third question is a loaded one, and one that remains as vexed today as it was at the time of *M'Naghten*. If the decisive factor is the state of the criminal's mind *at the time of the crime*, how is this to be determined? Is it a matter of evidence or hypothesis or presumption? If it is a matter of evidence, what facts must be adduced in support of the determination? What must the jury know to be able to establish the state of mind of the criminal at the time of the crime? Or is the jury to be *told* what that state of mind was by "experts"? Related to this is the fourth question: Suppose it can be shown that, at the time of the crime, the criminal labored under a delusion. Is that fact enough to justify his acquittal? And with respect to such facts, how much weight is to attach to the testimony of physicians who never examined the prisoner and who are called merely to discuss the nuances of the insane mind?

It is in their answers to that first question that Tindal and Maule gave body to the now famous "M'Naghten Rule." Yet the actual replies were quite matter-of-fact since neither Maule nor Tindal judged the standards employed in *M'Naghten* to be any different from those that had evolved since the time of Lord Coke. Maule answers thus:

> There is no law, that I am aware of, that makes persons in the state described in the question not responsible for their criminal acts. (*M'Naghten*, p. 206)

And Tindal adds only a little more:

> [W]e are of the opinion that, notwithstanding the party
> accused did the act complained of with a view, under the influ-
> ence of insane delusion, of redressing or revenging some sup-
> posed grievance or injury, or of producing some public bene-
> fit, he is nevertheless punishable . . . if he knew at the time
> . . . that he was acting contrary to . . . the law of the land.
> (Ibid., p. 208)

In other words, the simple fact of delusion is not sufficient to
sustain the plea of insanity. But, as it happens, M'Naghten—like
Ferrers and Bellingham—thought of himself as a wronged party
and therefore must have had the conception of right and wrong.
This seems to be what the fourth question is probing, although
Maule was of the opinion that his answer to the first question
settled the fourth one. Indeed, if it did settle it, Maule would have
been obliged by the logic of his argument *not* to permit acquittal.
But Tindal seems to recognize the subtle connection between the
first and fourth questions, and he proceeds to answer the fourth
by qualifying his earlier reply:

> [I]f under the influence of his delusion he supposes another
> man to be in the act of attempting to take away his life, and he
> kills that man, as he supposes, in self-defence, he would be
> exempt from punishment. If his delusion was that the deceased
> had inflicted a serious injury to his character and fortune, and
> he killed him in revenge for such supposed injury, he would be
> liable to punishment. (Ibid., p. 211)

This much had come out of *Hadfield* and *Bellingham,* and Tindal is surely not breaking new ground. The principle in cases of
"delusion" is twofold: the delusion must be functionally related
to the criminal act, and the action taken must be the sort of action
that the law would forgive were the contents of the delusion true.
And it is just this reasoning that permits "experts," including
those who have not examined a prisoner, to provide the jury with
"evidence" about the workings of the deluded mind.

There are several aspects of *M'Naghten* generally neglected
by contemporary writers drawn to this case. To begin, the "rule"
was neither new nor clear. As an approach to the problem of
criminal insanity, it began to take shape as early as Lord Hale's
Historia, when the law first took cognizance of *degrees* of responsibility and thereby began to qualify Lord Coke's (Roman)
standard. Hale still insisted that full responsibility could be as-

signed to anyone whose reasoning was as good as a teenager's, but this was enough to erode the *furiosus* criterion. Nor was *M'Naghten* precedential in terms of "right-wrong" criteria or the requirement that delusions and actions bear some coherent relation to each other. Those who insist that it was *M'Naghten* that cemented the courts to the delphic standards of the felon's knowledge of his actions and knowledge that these actions were wrong fail to recognize that by the time of *M'Naghten* these standards had been common for nearly fifty years on both sides of the Atlantic.

In declining to add anything to the fourth question beyond what he had already said in connection with the first, Maule did make an interesting and ultimately influential observation. Maule thought the question pertained simply to the range of protections provided by "delusion" and remarked, rather in passing, that "this is not a matter of law but of physiology" (ibid., p. 206). The importance of this phrase is twofold: First, it does not make the "delusion" criterion a principle of law, but a question of fact to be decided by the jury. Thus, in the given case, the question becomes, "Now that it is clear that Smith does and did labor under delusions, are these delusions of such a nature as to excuse Smith of the crime with which he is charged?" Second, the phrase virtually removes such considerations from the opinions and reflections of jurors and locates them in the realm of "expert testimony" where questions of physiology must be settled. It is this part of *M'Naghten* that stands as something of an official installation of the "medical model."

Contemporary critics of the "M'Naghten Rule" attack it from both sides. Those who judge it to be too lenient argue that it results in the acquittal of anyone who happens to be wrong-headed about the conduct or motives of his victim; that it frees the felon who can convince a jury that he thought what he had done was right; that it forces the prosecution to prove that the criminal was knowledgable as to the laws of the land at the time of his act. Such criticism is both misdirected and partly groundless. It is misdirected because these putative features of *M'Naghten* came into adjudication much earlier than 1843. It is partly without foundation because the "rule" does not excuse the sufferer of just any delusion, does not address the prisoner's literal knowledge of specific statutes, and does not confer blanket immunity on the person who shows only that he believed he was doing the right thing.

Those who criticize the decision as not being lenient or realistic enough insist that many insane persons do know the difference between right and wrong; do act wrongly by their own admission; are fully aware of the letter and the spirit of laws proscribing such conduct; but are nonetheless not responsible for what they have done. On this account, it is folly to require the insane person to impose logical coherence on his actions such that they are brought into harmony with the terms of the delusion. A man who judges a neighbor to be a potter's vessel, or who judges innocent parties to be demons, or who thinks the king has stolen his sheep cannot then be obliged to do only that which a normal person would do with potter's vessels demons and rustlers.

The problem with this line of criticism is not that it is invalidly directed at *M'Naghten*, but that most courts have not drawn these lessons from *M'Naghten* and so have not been bound by the "M'Naghten Rule." At the very time the British were gasping over the *M'Naghten* decision, Massachusetts was in a dither over the trial of Abner Rogers, convicted of murdering Charles Lincoln, warden of the state prison at Charlestown. The defense sought to prove that Rogers was morbidly fearful that Lincoln would cause him suffering and death. The prosecution proved, through eyewitness accounts, that Rogers proclaimed "I told you I would" at the instant that he stabbed the warden, and that the murder was thus premeditated. The trial took place in 1844 and was not influenced by those *M'Naghten* factors that had yet to surface clearly.

Chief Justice Shaw, in his instructions to the jury, established *Rogers* as one of the authoritative cases in American law. He begins by reminding the jurors that *ignorantia legis nemiminem excusat* even when such ignorance of the law is occasioned by disease. The law makes certain assumptions about "the power of conscience in all persons of ordinary intelligence" (*Rogers*, p. 273), such that mere ignorance of a given statute will not protect one who has ignored "the dictates of his own natural sense of right and wrong" (p. 275). To be justly punished for a criminal act, the accused

> must have sufficient memory, intelligence, reason and will, to enable him to distinguish between right and wrong, in regard to the particular act about to be done, to know and understand

that it will be wrong, and that he will deserve punishment by
committing it. (p. 275)

Echoing the reasoning in *Hadfield,* Shaw then goes on to acknowledge temporary insanity:

> [I]f his reason and mental powers are either so deficient that he
> has no will, no conscience or controlling mental power, or if
> through the overwhelming violence of mental disease his in-
> tellectual power is for the time obliterated, he is not a responsi-
> ble moral agent, and is not punishable for the criminal acts.
> (p. 276)

In such cases, says Shaw, a jury must address three questions: Did
the prisoner suffer from delusions? Were his actions governed by
these delusions? Was the criminal action "an outbreak or paroxysm of disease"? It is this third question that moves the American court away from not only Coke, Hale, and Tracy, but *Hadfield, Bellingham,* and *M'Naghten.* In *Rogers,* it is now not even
necessary to establish a causal connection between the delusion
and the act, as long as it is shown that the act resulted from "an
outbreak . . . of disease." In this same charge to the jury, Shaw
neutralized the linchpin of the prosecution's statement of the law.
Pleading for the Commonwealth, Mr. Parker had stated that, even
in the case of delusion,

> an impulse springing out of such a belief . . . should excuse
> (the prisoner) just as much and *no more* than an impulse in a
> sane man would excuse him. . . . (p. 240)

Parker here is relying on *Hadfield* and *Ferrers,* but Shaw extends
coverage:

> This state of delusion indicates to an experienced person that
> the mind is in a diseased state . . . (and) . . . that the act was
> the result of the disease . . . of uncontrollable impulse. . . .
> (pp. 277–278)

The jury must acquit—even where there is a sense of right and
wrong, even when the delusion and the act have no coherent
relation—when it is shown that the prisoner was of diseased mind
and that the act was the result of disease.* Within two years of

---

*Rogers was acquitted and consigned to a lunatic asylum. He died as a result of
hurling himself through a window. This apparent suicide conferred a form of
sentimental validity on Shaw's interpretation of the law.

Rogers, a number of states introduced new statutes by which no one found to be in a condition of insanity could be punished for an offense. These statutes were the gift of *Rogers*, not *M'Naghten*. And, by 1869, Justice Gregory in *Stevens* v. *Indiana* leaves no doubt about the range of protections introduced by Shaw:

> The will does not join with the act, and there is no guilt, when the act is directed or performed by a defective or vitiated understanding. So far as a person acts under the influence of mental disease he is not accountable. (*Stevens* v. *Indiana*, p. 491)

2. Crime as Disease

Especially in the American courts, a wedge was placed between all the older maxims and what was taken to be the scientific fact of insanity. *Rogers* was that wedge, and the room it created was soon to be filled by a wide variety of liberalizing decisions. *Stevens* v. *Indiana* was decided in 1869. Two years later, speaking for the Supreme Court of New Hampshire, Justice Ladd does not so much build on the past as dismiss it:

> It is entirely obvious that a court of law undertaking to lay down an abstract general proposition, which may be given to the jury in all cases, by which they are to determine whether the prisoner had the capacity to entertain criminal intent, stands in exactly the same position as that occupied by the English judges in attempting to answer the questions propounded to them by the House of Lords . . . and whenever such an attempt is made, I think it must always be attended with failure, because it is an attempt to find what does not exist, namely, a rule of law wherewith to solve a question of fact. (*State* v. *Jones*, p. 393)

In this trial, the attorney general attempted to confine the evidence to that bearing on Jones's ability to distinguish right from wrong, but Ladd simply covered the attempt in a cloud of modernity. To adopt such a standard, he says, would "save the trouble of trying each case" on its merits, but

> No formal rule can be applied in settling questions which have relation to liberty and life, merely because it will lessen the labor of the court or jury. (Ibid., p. 394)

Rather,

in a matter where we must inevitably rely to a great extent
upon the facts of science, we have consented to receive those
facts as developed and ascertained by the researches and observations of our own day, instead of adhering blindly to dogmas
which were accepted as facts of science and erroneously promulgated as principles of law fifty or a hundred years ago.
(Ibid., p. 400)

In 1891 came the famous *Bolling* v. *State* where an earlier
finding of guilt was set aside precisely because the judge in the
lower court had instructed jurors to apply the right-wrong test:

That ruling . . . may have led the jury to believe that if the
defendant was sane generally, he could be held responsible,
although he was absolutely insane upon that subject. (*Bolling*
v. *State*, p. 603)

By 1915, in the case of *New York* v. *Schmidt*, already referred to,
not only has the right-wrong test gone the way of all traditions,
but the very concept of "wrong" as it might be introduced in such
cases can no longer refer to legally proscribed acts. Rather, says
Cardozo,

We hold . . . that there are times and circumstances in which
the word "wrong" as used in the statutory test of responsibility
ought not to be limited to legal wrong (p. 339)

but must include the person's sense of moral wrong and religious
wrong. The test of responsibility, then, must include those tenets
of faith that might bind a person in such a manner as to cause
him to defy human laws.

It should be clear from even so hasty a sketch of the trends in
criminal insanity over the past two centuries that *M'Naghten* was
not *the* landmark, for there has been no such single influence.
There has instead been a continuous erosion, rejection, rein-
terpretation, and revision of the ancient standard of *mens rea*.
The source of these tendencies and practices is no single case and
is no single professional discipline. The tendencies and practices
preceded psychiatry, psychology, and sociology, although these
same disciplines have taken their place in the continuing process
of criminal justice. But they have not only taken their place, they
have been given a place, or at least an invitation.

Here, too, we must not think of the invitation as new. If it
can be dated, we should look to the eighteenth century and the

vaunted rationalism of the Enlightenment. The phenomena of insanity were an abiding challenge to the Enlightenment gospel of progress and human perfectibility. The overarching rhetoric of that age, which was aimed at all forms of authority, sought justification in something called man's "basic nature." It was averred that this was a freedom-loving, fair-minded, and reasonable nature called upon to endure the withering effects of shabby environments and capricious rule. Under favorable political conditions, the argument continued, this "nature" would emerge and prosper, and the accidentally great differences among the several classes would be shown to be no more than man-made.

But how, then, is the "lunatic" to be understood? Is madness too but the creation of a class system or of poverty or religious superstition? Is it always so? The Enlightenment mind, known more for its confidence than the correctness of its theories, had answers to these questions. In many cases, the deranged person was in fact the victim of social, political, and religious forces. But in other cases, the culprit was *disease*! It was to be through education that Rousseau's *Emile* would be spared the consequences of the former and it would be through science that the weight of disease would be removed. But what sort of disease is insanity? In this, the major spokesmen of the Enlightenment were even less halting in their theorizings. They had pretty much arrived at a settled position on what it is that makes us all the psychological entities we are: our brains. Thus, when insanity is a disease, it is a disease of the brain. Gassendi was certain of this in 1640, as were La Mettrie, Diderot, Holbach, and a score of others in the eighteenth century, and nearly every physician in the nineteenth. Gall's system of phrenology, which prospered from 1810 until at least 1850, was grounded in the claim that all the moral and intellectual "faculties" of man were not only based in the brain, but that each faculty was tied to a specific organ of the brain, and that the amount of that faculty was determined by the mass of brain devoted to it. Mesmer's "animal magnetism," which made the rounds in influential circles during the last two decades of the eighteenth century took for granted that purely physical causes stood behind all significant mental events. By the mid-nineteenth century, one of the growth industries in science was the weighing and dissecting of the brains of geniuses, madmen, idiots, and savages. It all fit together very nicely. The Enlightenment preached the idea of progress and the nineteenth century converted it into a religion of progress. Colonial expansion made sense, for the "savage," with his small brain, could only be moved along the continuum of human destiny by the civilizing nurturance of his "betters." The universe is but the machinery of the universe and when a part of it breaks down, it is the mission of science to locate the trouble and fix it. Some of the breakdowns are in the brain, in which case a madman is produced. It isn't right to hold him responsible for what he does, because, like the savage or the child, he simply lacks the necessary equipment to behave himself. By far the best course is to lock him up in the interest of the safety of the community and of himself. To be sure that, in the given case, the brain is truly diseased, experts are to be summoned to give a scientific account. Insanity, correctly understood, is like consumption: the coughing may annoy many and the disease may spread, but the sufferer surely is not morally guilty for the trouble he causes.

The historian's mission is not to hold the past up to scorn but to see it for what it was and to undertand what gave it its essential character. It was not foolish for Ficino, in the Florence of the Quattrocento, to seek the secrets of life in parchments he incorrectly identified as pre-Hellenic, nor was it foolish for the alchemists to attempt to make gold from mixtures of base metals. But it would be foolish for us to do the same. I do not condemn, therefore, the arc of reasoning that covers the two centuries beginning in 1700 and that leads to the quasi-syllogistic certainties I have just reviewed. Instead, like Justice Ladd, I would urge the contemporary citizen not "to adhere blindly to dogmas which were accepted as facts of science and erroneously promulgated as principles of law fifty or a hundred years ago." To avoid blind adherence, we must be prepared to test the merits of each of the terms in that analysis that converts crime into disease.

The test begins with an assessment of the uses to which the term "disease" had been put by the courts as early as the time of Lord Coke. Initially, the term carried a meaning that could be grasped by any juror, for it meant that degree of rational and intellectual impoverishment that converted a person into something akin to "an infant, a brute, or a wild beast." No expert testimony was needed. The bearing of the prisoner established beyond all plausible doubt that the accused was not to be judged as a human being. To prove that the defects were clear from the earliest stages of life was to prove that the prisoner was an idiot. The same signs, occurring at some time during adult life, indicated that something had happened, but etiology was less important than the actual fact of *furiosus*. In all relevant respects, the later criterion of "right-wrong" was included in the Cokean standard; not in terms of whether the accused knew the difference between right and wrong, but in terms of whether he had the *capacity* to know the difference. There is a difference between having knowledge and having the capacity for knowledge. Neither Coke nor any judge since would excuse violent conduct precipitated by insobriety if it were shown that the drunkenness was a state voluntarily established by the prisoner himself. This standard still survives, but let us be clear on what it asserts. It will not extend the protections available to "wild beasts" when the wildness or irrationality has been self-imposed.

As I developed the point in the first chapter, the concept of right and wrong, which is not "learned" in the ordinary sense, is one basis on which beings are judged to be human beings. By virtue of this native capacity, the individual is able to absorb the lessons of social life and to recognize the obligation to absorb these lessons. We do not expect the infant to issue forth from the womb equipped with a knowledge of each of the statutes, ordinances, and regulations defining the proscriptions of his nation, but we also know that, if the sense of right and wrong did not exist, this same being could never be taught just what a proscription is. We can train an animal not to take socks out of the drawer, but we cannot train an animal not to steal. We can train the same animal to give us a bone or a ball, but not to give us a gift. Finally, an animal can be made to kill, but not to murder. Words such as stealing, giving, and murdering do not simply denote specific acts, but connote general relationships. To steal is to take what belongs to another, and there is nothing in the purely physical features of the object that will convey the idea of "belonging to" or "is owned by," let alone the idea of "shouldn't take."

Thus, the moral "ought" must be taken for granted as the very condition for establishing moral conduct. The concept is logically prior to the judgment as it is functionally prior to moral education. It is, then, so basic a feature of all human life that its total absence must be as rare as the kind of insanity that elicited such incredulity from Mr. Erskine in *Hadfield*. What must be the meaning of the question at law, therefore, when it is asked: Did the prisoner at the time of the crime have the *capacity* to distinguish between right and wrong? And how is this question related to one that seeks to establish whether the prisoner, at the time of the crime, actually *knew* the difference?

Let me take Erskine's part, this time addressing moral sensibility rather than insanity. If learned judges have meant, in referring to certain prisoners as not knowing the difference between right and wrong, that we take their words literally, then such prisoners would be indifferent to thefts of their own possessions, unconcerned about the fairness of their own trials, incapable of acting on the basis of having been *wronged*, willing to do anything to reduce their own discomfort or promote their own comfort no matter what the effect of the action might be on any other person or thing, and destitute of the merest ray of moral reasoning. Unlike Erskine, in his estimation of the incidence of "wild beasts," I do not say that such a condition has never existed in the world, but I do say that when it is present, it is the unmistakable sign of a degree of intellectual enfeeblement that qualifies the prisoner as an idiot with the mentality of an infant. Of the ways we could imagine by which to ascertain whether someone has a sense of right and wrong, there will not be two persons in a million who will fail every test once we remove provably moronic or idiotic persons from the pool of examinees. In fact, I would assert that no one capable of planning and executing a capital offense will fail all such tests of moral sensibility.

But then the question is modified to permit a determination of whether this prisoner, though possessing a moral sense when examined, was able to use this capacity at the time of the crime. Was he, instead, overcome by an "irresistible impulse," by a "morbid delusion," by a "temporary insanity"? Cast in these terms, the question is likely to exonerate every person ever found guilty of violating the law, for every violation is occasioned by some condition or consideration or "higher" goal that paralyzes otherwise restraining tendencies. The rapist is overcome by lust; the thief by avarice; the murderer by hatred. And depending on how we choose to define "delusion," all such felons may be said to be burdened by "delusions." The middle-class shoplifter will say with a straight face that he was not really stealing from a person but from a corporation, and that corporate wealth is so unjustly great that reducing it is surely no crime. Can we not all recognize the delusional elements of such an account? And what of the rapist who insists that a person dressed like his victim and having the appearance and bearing of his victim is actually inviting assault? Or the same prisoner who claims that society has so stripped him of his manhood that he must commit such crimes in order to restore it? These, too, are cut from the fabric of delusion, if by that word we mean belief in the existence of an object or a circumstance that neither logic nor the data of sense will confirm. Reasonable beings do not take a woman's grooming as evidence of her desire to be sexually assaulted. Reasonable beings recognize the taking of objects without proper compensation as stealing no matter who the owner is. It is in these respects that every criminal act may be described as irrational or "deluded," but a description is not a justification.

Law is written not only by rational beings but for such beings. It stands as something of a contract between the state and the citizen. The agreement, either written or implicit, is this: *Remain within the boundaries of action set by law and your freedoms are protected by law. Abandon these boundaries and your freedoms are removed.* This is the covenant entered into by civilized persons and it is through this that a state may be said to exist. It thereupon becomes the burden of every citizen to show that his illegal actions should not be punished. This, of course, is the spirit of an older understanding that now seems to have few adherents; the understanding that bears the formal name *retributive punishment.* Even to utter the phrase is, these days, to elicit gasps of horror. Retribution! How barbaric! Let us remain mindful, however, of the difference between revenge and legal retribution. The former refers to actions taken privately against an offender without due process. Retributive punishment is a principle of justice adopted by a society against no one in particular and imposed by a disinterested branch of the recognized government. It is not a means of causing suffering out of anger, but the method by which the state honors its part of the convenant. To fail to punish those who have defied the law is to fail to perform an admitted duty. I speak here not of the practical effects of such misfeasance but of its ethical deficiencies. In crude terms, it is a "breach of contract"; in more elevated terms, a breach of promise.

It is universally agreed that an additional function of law is the regulation of conduct through threats of punishment. This function comes into being precisely because there is no guarantee that all citizens at all times will honor even those laws brought into being by the citizens themselves. To have this regulatory effect, the law must be predictable in its administration. The citizen must know not only what the law requires but also how the law will punish violations—and *that* the law will punish violations. He already knows (or did until recently) that punishment cannot be averted by pleading frustration, depression, anger, despair, moroseness, boredom, or contempt, since, in the absence of such conditions, crimes are not committed, except by "wild beasts," "brutes," or mental "infants." To be guided by the law in his conduct, the citizen must have at least a general awareness of the grounds of forgiveness. One of these, which has never been disputed, is that the law will not and never should punish behavior that the person could not withhold. It does not punish one who has caused injury or damage as a result of being pushed out a window. It does not punish one whose brain tumor caused a convulsion that led to an accident. Briefly stated, it is recognized that the law must not punish those whose conduct is determined by the laws of nature. Human laws appeal to our moral nature and counsel us against actions of a certain type under threat of punishment. Natural laws make no appeal at all, but determine unfailingly the conduct of matter in motion. To the extent that persons are also material entities, they are resistless in the face of natural laws and must not be punished for their compliance since no one can do otherwise.

We see, therefore, that *disease* is and always has been a permissible ground of forgiveness so long as it is not willfully imposed on the actor by himself. And to the extent that this ground of forgiveness is factual in nature, there is no argument in principle against the use of experts for purposes of determining the facts. What is necessary, however, as a precondition of this use is that there be both a disease and a class of specialists whose knowledge qualifies them as experts. This is not to say that all such experts must agree chapter and verse, or that no condition qualifies as a disease until there is unanimity within professional circles. There may be some doubt as to whether Smith was tubercular at the time of the crime, or whether he was suffering from a brain tumor or was weakened by hepatitis. There may even be disagreement as to the causal connection between such disorders and the crime with which Smith stands charged. But in all such cases, there must be agreement on at least this much: *That a palpable aspect of Smith's physiology departs either structurally or functionally from the known norms of his species, and that such departure is significantly great to place his health and well-being in jeopardy.* Only when this is established can a jury of Smith's peers know that there is a disease. It then becomes appropriate to inquire into the known statistical regularity with which conduct of a certain kind follows or attends the disease Smith is alleged to have. This, however, is not the manner in which the "disease" of insanity figures in contemporary criminal justice. Instead, a vicious circle is drawn: the act of the criminal is not shown to be the consequence of disease, but the disease is established by virtue of the act. Smith is said to be a "psychopathic killer," which is then defined as one who commits "repeated homicidal acts without evidence of remorse or conscience." But this is precisely what Smith is charged with, and there is no fact of science or canon of logic that will convert a description of a phenomenon into a causal explanation.

Let us assume for the moment that David Berkowitz did not lie about his mental state, and that in fact he believed he had been visited by demons and "voices" urging him to rid the city of licentiousness. If he felt obliged to obey the demons, he proved at least that he possessed a sense of obligation, which is to say a *moral* sense. And to determine that certain conduct was "licentious," he would have to have a standard of conduct, which is to say a sense of right and wrong. Then, too, by arming himself and driving in search of offenders, he leaves no doubt that his crimes were *intended*. In choosing his modus operandi he provides evidence also of a desire not to be caught, and this is enough to establish that he knew the state would seek to arrest him for what he was doing; that is, that the state classified such acts as wrong. What, then, was his "disease"? Was it mental enfeeblement? A lack of will? A brain tumor? Even on the view that he thought of such voices as divine in origin, we do not have proof of disease, only proof of a God-fearing nature. We may be tempted to rewrite the laws so that no one is ever punished for actions proceeding from religious conviction, but these are not the laws we have, nor are they the laws that faced David Berkowitz on the day of his trial.

A young man in Florida was charged with the murder of an elderly woman who entered her residence at the time her killer was looting it. His defense was grounded in the contention that television violence had so affected his mind as to make murder a "natural" act. Evidence was culled from "experts" to show that depictions of crime give rise to aggressive behavior on the part of those exposed to them. "Social science" again had its day in court. But laws are written precisely *because* the lessons of society are often at variance with the needs of an ordered state. We all know that bad company can have detrimental effects on one's character; that unemployment is frustrating and that frustration often leads to hostile conduct; that abusive parents and incompetent teachers participate in the undoing of the psychological and moral faculties of those in their charge; that intoxication often results in unacceptable behavior; that the glamour of riches tempts some to steal. We surely do not await the results of the next poll or the findings from the university to have confidence in our awareness of all this. Our confidence, if the truth be known, is based largely on the fact that we have all experienced temptations of the same sort. And it is just because of this that we are dumbfounded when such temptations are translated into the language of pathology and "disease." A teenager who sits for hours in front of a television set and witnesses thousands of enacted murders and assaults is, indeed, wasting his time and squandering his talents. He may even be cultivating a certain insensitivity to the lives of others. It is to this boy, and to thousands of others, that the law must speak with unequivocal clarity, and it often must speak through its punishments. If, however, television produces disease, we must know what this disease is, what part of the body is affected, what its incidence is in society, and what connection it bears to the conduct at issue. We must even legislate against those agents who are "carriers" of the disease. We must consult experts who have studied it. But what was the "disease" in Florida, if not the homicide itself? Was it the same "disease" that gripped Berkowitz?

For testimony to be given by experts, there must be a *subject* of expertise. To the extent that the experts are expected to possess degrees in medicine, the subject must be grounded in medicine and physiology. But, for all practical purposes, the only time medicine and physiology figure centrally in the insanity defense is where a disease of the brain is suspected. The experts in this regard, however, are not psychiatrists but neurologists. Psychiatry is a "social science," which is to say it is not a science at all, and the same is true of psychology and sociology. The experts drawn from these disciplines do not bring to the trial a body of durable knowledge, a set of scientific laws, or even an assortment of reliable measures and procedures. At most, they tote a loose collection of question-begging diagnoses that are not beyond dispute even within the small clinical population on which they are based.* The tests and interviews conducted with the prisoner can only provide rough statistical evidence that the prisoner departs from the perceptions and values of the larger community, not that he suffers from a "disease" or even that his departure reliably results in felonies on the part of those whose departure from the norm is as great. But to the extent that the prisoner has already been shown to have committed a grievous offense, we know that his perceptions and values differ from the norm. Nor are we decisively informed on the very rare occasion in which neuropathology is proved—it still becomes necessary to judge whether the disease was the cause of the crime. No one would acquit a murderer merely because he had a case of poison ivy or rickets or gout. Acquittal is based on reasonable proof that the disease was *relevantly* connected to the act, and was not merely coextensive with it. What is required is convincing proof that the overwhelming majority of human beings, were they similarly afflicted, could be plausibly expected to commit the act of which the prisoner stands accused. This is to say that we require proof that the act was governed by nothing less than a law of nature. As Justice Tracy put it, it is not every "idle humour" that will exempt one from justice.

The frequency with which a term is used is no measure of its meaning, only a sign of linguistic convention. Since the nine-

---

*One need only recall here how the American Psychiatric Association recently established the nonpathological status of homosexuality: by a vote of the membership!

teenth century, terms such as "irresistible impulse," "temporary insanity," "partial insanity," "monomania," and "delusion" have filled the criminal courts and have by now numbed judges and jurors into the torpor of monotony. No group of "experts" may agree on just when such ascriptions are in order, but they all use the same terms. How are they to be defined? An "irresistible impulse" is said to be a need or desire or inclination that the power of reason cannot successfully oppose. But is this a measure of the strength of the impulse or the power of reason or the weakness of the will? The life of every person produces any number of such impulses. No one smokes cigarettes in conformity with the dictates of reason. Persons eat things they know to be injurious to health; they drive at unsafe speeds; they risk fortunes at the casino; they surrender their will to an affair of the heart. The issue, then, is not whether there are such impulses, but whether proof of them is a defense against punishment for a criminal offense. The law says, *so far may you go and no further,* and it is speaking here of impulses, for it is not necessary to constrict the domain of rational choice.

How does an "irresistible impulse" differ from "temporary insanity"? It does not differ at all. What then of "delusions"? If we define this word to mean a false impression, a trick of the senses, a belief in what can be shown not to exist, then we recognize that there has never been anyone in the history of our race who has not at one time or another been the victim of "delusions." Anyone who ever set out to "break the bank" at Monte Carlo (including those who did), anyone who judges his children to be better or brighter or kinder than they really are; anyone who thinks of his tastes as superior to those of others; anyone who considers himself to be neglected or misunderstood or not fully appreciated—all are in some sense deluded. The list could be expanded without limit and every entry would include a belief or impression not sustained by the facts and not shared by those able to make objective assessments. Our delusions may lead us to believe we have been wronged. In this case, we clearly have a sense of right and wrong, for if we did not, we could not consider ourselves "wronged." Our delusions may lead us to be suspicious or contemptuous of others or to find them morally repugnant. Here again we are led to evaluative responses that are proof of a certain moral sensibility. At some point, the number and eccentricity of delusions may become so great as to overcome the rational and perceptual capacities by which errors might be detected and corrected . But it is at this point that the "wild beast" standard stands in our defense, and it is also at this point that no "expert" need be summoned. In the throes of such captivating visions of our own creation, we are unable to make contact with the real world, unable to relate rationally and coherently to the facts and persons in our surroundings. We have no more capacity for rational conduct than would "an infant, a brute, or a wild beast." What we do under such conditions is not punishable, for it is not based on a moral choice. We do not act with moral freedom, since we do not have the rational faculty that attends every genuinely moral desire.

At present, given the nature of law as an institution, and given the state of the "social sciences," there can be no meaning attached to the term "expert testimony" as that term is used in connection with the insanity defense. The only experts who might qualify are those in neurology, and they qualify only to the extent that proof of a diseased brain *may* constitute mitigating circumstances. There is no *science* of "mental" disease. All that "expertise" can refer to here is a textbook knowledge of an assortment of hypotheses, a practical knowledge of tests of doubtful validity, and a clinical knowledge of some of the eccentricities of the human mind. By none of the historical standards does crime qua crime qualify as a "disease." By none of the historical scientific standards does psychiatric or psychological testimony qualify as "evidence," since such testimony does not confine itself to publicly verifiable facts. The only exception is in regard to epidemiological findings; e.g., the frequency with which test results of a certain kind correlate with deviant behavior of a certain kind. But all that can be learned from such data is that Smith is not the only one whose perceptions or emotions led to a criminal act. We do not learn that Smith is "diseased" in any legally or morally significant respect. The inclusion of such "experts" places jurors in the position of diagnosticians once they accept the testimony of "experts" as evidence. The real effect is to put justice at the mercy of theory and the courts at the mercy of a professional community in which an anarchy of speculation is the rule and an informed consensus the exception. This part of justice cannot survive the social sciences.

It is an abiding jural principle that equal cases be treated equally and that such differences as might exist be provably relevant if unequal treatment is to be just. All developed arguments that have as their aim exoneration on the grounds of insanity finally can be reduced to the claim that insane persons are relevantly different and that the law is obliged to respect the difference. But again, it is not enough to introduce a label; it is necessary to define the term and to argue convincingly that the category is juridically relevant. In at least one unarguable respect, all persons are "different"—they do not occupy exactly the same space at the same time. There are, to be sure, many other differences whose relevance is subject to dispute and analysis. For purely therapeutic purposes, it may be appropriate to adopt certain clinical labels—neurosis, psychosis, psychopathic personality —and to strive for greater precision and consistency in the employment of such terms. This is a business that might well prosper *apart* from the criminal justice system in much the same manner as the pharmaceutical and automotive industries do. But the institution of justice is too important and too fragile to be rented out to any evolving technology or quasi-science that captures the popular imagination. It is an institution whose survival depends on the disinterested and equable application of principles to causes. For justice to be preserved in any given cause, there must be at least three ingredients: a stated principle of justice; proof beyond reasonable doubt that the accused violated this principle; and further proof that the violation was something the accused had the power to resist. The burden of the second ingredient is the state's, in that the accused is not obliged to prove his innocence. But the third ingredient enters into the process of justice in the form of a legal defense—typically the insanity defense—and this becomes part of the burden of the accused. Under our system of justice, and in keeping with both the Roman and the common law foundations of this system, there are only three bases on which the accused can plausibly plead a want of power. There is, first, proof that the act proceeded according to the irresistible laws of nature such that no person at the time the act occurred would have or could have done otherwise. This is a perfect defense in that it proves that no crime was committed. The second ground, equally perfect but not equally provable, is that of accident or inadvertence. Here it becomes necessary for the accused to prove to the satisfaction of the jury that there was no *malice prepense* and that the action was not intended to have injurious consequences and was not even the product of negligence. Again, the defense is obliged to show that any person in the same situation could in principle have become caught in a web of events not of his own making. Finally, there is the ground of defectiveness, which requires proof that the accused was so lacking in rational or physical capacity as to have been unable to intend *anything* or to realize it as a knowingly causal agent. The defense here is the "wild beast" defense, which, to be sustained, must establish the defendant as mentally indistinguishable from an infant or animal. To expand these grounds may be defensible, but the expansion must be at the cost of what for centuries has been taken to be the very foundation of justice. Let it be admitted that the human race improves in its knowledge and that part of this improvement, perhaps the major part, comes from the facts and methods of science. Society reserves the right, therefore, to reject and replace older understandings in light of new facts. But there must indeed be new *facts*, and not merely the flotsam of narrow specialties. A discipline does not earn rebukes through an admission of ignorance, but through unfulfilled promises. The "social sciences" need not be numbered in the pantheon of the natural sciences in order to warrant our support and respect. The issues addressed by these specialties are the most vexed of any encountered by man, and it is no sign of worthlessness that none of them has been settled. Part of the difficulty is the very size of the problems; another part, the unwillingness to abandon methods already known to be insufficient for the purpose; still another part, the tendency to multiply hypotheses while keeping reliable facts constant. These are some of the reasons for keeping these disciplines alive and active, and they are the same reasons for keeping them out of the courts.

3. Recent Trends

Over the past ten years, the jural dimensions of the insanity defense have gradually been enlarged and at the same time have gradually become less distinct. Perhaps the most fundamental departure from older understandings pertains to the distribution of evidentiary burdens. In all of the United States today, once the defense has successfully raised the possibility of insanity, the state is left with the burden of establishing that the defendant was sane at the time of the alleged criminal act. Any number of appeals have succeeded through a showing that the lower court had failed to recognize this shift of burden from the appellant (defendant) to the state.

In addition to this significant departure, recent trends are also distinctly in the direction of reinterpreting the *M'Naghten* ruling so as to allow moral criteria to substitute for legal criteria in tests of the defendant's capacity and responsibility. Thus, proof that the defendant knew at the time of the alleged crime that what he was doing was legally wrong is now generally insufficient if the defense successfully argues that he judged his actions to be *morally* right. The *United States* v. *McGraw* is illustrative. The defendant-appellant James McGraw had been convicted of bank robbery. The evidence at trial proved that McGraw had passed a note to a bank teller demanding that he be given money. He successfully escaped with the money, only to turn himself over to the authorities two weeks later. Two psychiatrists for the defense testified that McGraw did not appreciate the *wrongfulness* of his actions at the time he committed them, even though he knew such actions to be proscribed by law. The psychiatrist for the prosecution acknowledged that McGraw was mentally ill but that he did have the capacity at the time of the crime to distinguish between *legal* right and wrong. In reversing the ruling of the lower court, the U.S. Court of Appeals for the Ninth Circuit offered the following opinion:

> In *Wade* v. *United States*, 426 F.2d 64 (9th Cir. 1970) (*en banc*), we held that, for purposes of the insanity defense, "wrongfulness" means moral wrongfulness rather than criminal wrongfulness. (at 759)

Both of these trends are fraught with equal shares of peril and ambiguity. The first not only shifts a nearly impossible burden of proof to the state, but in most recent cases goes further and relieves the defense of the additional burden of *weight* of evidence. Thus, the defense is not required to present more evidence in support of insanity than the state can summon in support of sanity; only just as much evidence as is necessary to create the suspicion of insanity. In other words, the statutory presumption of sanity can now be overturned by nearly any evidence, no matter how slight, suggesting the possibility of insanity at the time of the alleged offense. This is not to say that slight evidence, in and of itself, will ultimately result in immunity to prosecution, but that it triggers a shift of the burden to the state; moreover, the burden so shifted is not the same one, but one that is considerably heavier. Put simply, the trend makes it far easier for the defense to raise the question than it then becomes for the prosecution to answer it. The latter now must prove beyond a reasonable doubt that the accused was sane at the time of the crime.

Some will see in this trend a perfect symmetry with the unarguably just principle according to which a person is presumed innocent until proved guilty. Some, that is, will applaud the trend on the grounds that it obliges the state to prove *sanity*, which is taken to be a form of guilt, whereas the defendant must only present a modest sign of *insanity*, which is taken to be a form of innocence. Indeed, this symmetry would be real were the criteria of sanity and insanity symmetrical with the criteria of guilt and innocence. But the latter pertain to public actions and are grounded in data that are in principle accessible to all normal percipients. The former pertain to what are largely the opinions and theories of specialists and are grounded in little more than *ipse dixit*s. The evidence relevant to the question "Was Smith in the store at the time of the shooting?" is of a radically different nature from the evidence relevant to the question "Was Smith sane at the time of the shooting?" The rational part of the human race has arrived at a settled position on what it means to be "in the store." No tutored and responsible person—psychiatrist or layman—can contend that the current position on what it means to be "sane" has this settled status. There is, then, only a superficial symmetry between the state's burdens in matters of fact and these new burdens in the matter of sanity. It is not at all clear that the state can "prove" sanity, as it is not at all clear that modern medicine can "prove" health.

For reasons requiring little amplification, it is always easier to find *something* wrong with someone than it is to establish that *nothing* is wrong. The evidentiary domain of "something" is narrowly bounded; that of "nothing," effectively infinite. To put the state in the position, therefore, of having to establish sanity when there is any intimation of insanity is to require the state to do what is practically impossible. It must find an "expert" willing to testify that there is (or was!) *nothing* wrong with the defendant's mind that could possibly have diminished his ability to conform his behavior to the requirements of law; that the defendant labors under neither delusions nor hallucinations; that the defendant unquestionably knew the nature and consequences of his actions and judged these to be legally and morally, or at least morally, right. Can any of this ever be proved beyond a reasonable doubt? Concurring with the Court in *McGraw*, Circuit Judge Ely seems to recognize this, but does not indicate a comprehension of its implications:

> In the light of the unrebutted expert testimony, the Government could not establish, and, in my opinion, can never establish, beyond a reasonable doubt, that the appellant was legally sane at the time of the robbery. Thus, I would respectfully suggest to the district judge that, upon remand, the indictment should be dismissed. (*U.S.* v. *McGraw*, at 761)

Turning to the other trend, one can only be perplexed by a principle that would exonerate those who judge their illegal actions to be morally sound if the exoneration must proceed from insanity! Those who actively violated Hitler's laws and did so because they judged these to be morally bankrupt—no matter what their legality—surely warrant the admiration of all. We do not think of them as having "insanity" as part of any defense they might bring forth in the face of prosecution. But the felon who takes from others in the belief that it is morally right to do so and who, at the same time, recognizes that his action is condemned by his countrymen and the laws of the state, is, after all, just what we mean by a felon. The entire record of criminality has been written in the main by those who could find some justification for what they were doing—justification based on indignation, envy, wrath, private need, embarrassment, chronic losses in the lottery of life. Surely the terrorist knows that his wanton destruction of innocent lives is against the law, but he will quickly inform the astonished community that his assaults enjoy the protection of higher moral considerations. Sirhan Sirhan was, no doubt, aware of the fact that the laws of the United States did not allow the killing of Robert Kennedy. But would he not insist that he killed for the "morally" justified reason that his countrymen would ultimately benefit from this death?

Gratuitous homicide is rare. In the overwhelming number of cases, the perpetrator is moved by considerations that he judges to have a certain moral quality. What makes his act a criminal act is that it violates the criminal law, and it is this law to which the courts are expected to be beholden. History offers all too many martyrs whose victimization alerts us to the distance that often separates the legal and the moral realms. As discussed in the first chapter, the principal business of a civilized legislature is to measure and reduce this distance. The judiciary is constituted to reflect the point the legislature has reached in this continuing attempt to render morally defensible laws. It does not sit to determine the point the *defendant* has reached in this regard!

It is also once again necessary to recognize how ill suited psychologists and psychiatrists are to determine a defendant's moral sensibilities, even if these are taken to be jurally relevant. When someone explains his actions in terms of his belief that these were "right," he can only be claiming that a rational connection existed between a principle and what he did. The moral standing of the principle itself is not something the social "sciences" are equipped to determine. It is something that grows out of an admixture of logic, culture, history, and analysis. In any society, it is not surprising to discover citizens whose confidence in their own sense of right and wrong is far greater than that elicited by the moral understandings of their neighbors, their government, their clergymen, and their teachers. This confidence is, of course, immune to prosecution as long as it is not manifested in action. But once it surfaces in the form of criminal conduct, the issue at law is not the actor's private system of ethics, but the evidence supporting the judgment that what he did he intended to do. The discovery (or putative discovery) that he thought it was "right" may help to explain why he did it, but it scarcely bears upon the question of his liability. Presumably, there is already sufficient evidence available to establish that the action in question was not accidental. Thus it can be taken for granted that there were reasons. Some might even be interested to learn that, in a given case, the reason was the defendant's belief that he was doing the right thing. But all this can show is that the defendant was able to frame reasons and bring his behavior into coherent relationship with them. What it means is that, indeed, he intentionally did that for which he stands charged.

It is clear that the courts have not yet been able to refine the tests that the state must meet in such cases. The shape of things to come is partly disclosed by decisions such as *United States* v. *Cooper* in which it was held that

> The government cannot carry its burden by attacking the strength of Cooper's case. To meet its burden it must point to affirmative evidence which is adequate to prove sanity without the benefit of a sanity presumption. (at 455)

But the same court, both in *United States* v. *Schackleford* (494 F. 2d 67, 70) and in *United States* v. *Ingman*, (426 F.2d 973, 976), leaves open the question of just what sort of "affirmative" evidence is required. What does seem clear is that the mere cross-examination of psychiatrists and psychologists for the defense is not sufficiently "affirmative." In the circumstance, it is less than surprising to discover a case such as *Alto* v. *Alaska* in which the appellant, convicted of rape, murder, and larceny, has his conviction reversed and remanded because the Supreme Court of Alaska decided that any reasonable man would judge Alto to have been insane, even though the judge in the lower court did not. Alto thus is sent to a hospital, his release contingent upon the medical determination of his mental health. Note that, should the medical staff be of the same opinion as that voiced by the lower court, the release would be immediate!

In all of these recent cases, the decisive element of evidence was the testimony and test results presented by "experts" and comments by witnesses who thought of the defendants as somehow "insane." In these same cases, the state's convictions were reversed because of the state's failure to prove sanity. There are many such cases, of which a few—a representative few—have been cited here. How long it will take for such cases to appear with epidemic frequency would seem to depend on how long it will take defense attorneys to appreciate the possibilities held forth by these recent trends. Given these trends, and on the assumption that nothing succeeds in reversing them, it would be wise for counsel automatically to introduce the defense of insanity in any case in which the defendant (a) displays a convincing belief that his own moral sense of right and wrong is at variance with the sense of right and wrong ensconced in law, or (b) is sufficiently erratic in his emotional life to sustain *suspicions* of mental illness, or (c) is now either volatile or withdrawn or peculiar enough in his manner such that no responsible "expert" would be willing to declare him sane. How many such defenses will actually succeed remains to be seen, but in the process it will be interesting to observe the spectacle of prosecutors attempting to prove sanity. However well they may fare in criminal courts, they will have to anticipate unusual challenges in the Supreme Courts, which are likely to be unimpressed by critiques of psychiatric reasoning and less than moved by even the most careful reconstruction of the actual facts of crimes. They are likely, that is, to come face to face with the sort of reasoning that guided the Arizona Supreme Court in *State* v. *Ortiz*:

> The state did not introduce any psychiatric testimony. The state's evidence dealt with the events which took place at the crime. None of the evidence offered by the state contained any opinion evidence by the nonmedical witnesses on the issue of sanity. (*State* v. *Ortiz*, 114 Ariz. at 286–287, 560 P.2d at 804–805)

If they are able to assemble indisputable proof that the defendant not only committed the crime with which he stands charged, but then proceeded to act purposefully in his attempts to dispose of stolen goods or escape from the police or conceal the weapon used in the crime, the prosecutors may well discover that they now have only half a case, the more important half beginning the moment the insanity defense is raised. All these conditions were met in *Alto* v. *Alaska*, but none was sufficient to defeat the insanity defense. Alto stabbed his victim, raped her, and stole goods from her house—including her husband's boots, which he wore during his escape. He brought the stolen items to the nearby house of friends and there attempted to sell them. He asked to borrow a clean shirt, his own being soiled with the stains of his recent crime. He accounted for his possessions by saying that he intended to move away, and expressed the desire that his friends would buy the stolen stereo. The state established all of these facts and the defense challenged none of them. All the defense did was produce three "experts" and a sister who recalled her brother's nastiness on several occasions when he had been drinking. In addition, a friend of the Alto family told the court that Frank Alto had had an unhappy childhood dominated by quarrelsome parents. On the basis of his examination and "long experience," one of the "experts" concluded that the defendant suffered from "chronic undifferentiated schizophrenia" and that

> it was probably in existence August 6, 1972 as well as 1973. (*Alto* v. *Alaska* at 501)

Of such stuff are reversals now made. It is interesting to compare testimony of this kind with what would be accepted from the nonsocial scientist. Suppose the question at law pertained to whether a defendant was on a train on the night of August 6, 1972, and the conductor were to testify

> He was probably on the train that night as well as a year later.

Would not counsel for the defense press on and require the witness to state whether he was or was not? Would any jury be advised to accept such an offhand remark as conclusive?

To respond to these questions by resurrecting the tired fact that psychiatry is an inexact science is to offer not a justification for the use of such testimony but an additional argument against its use. As has been argued in this and the previous chapter, psychiatry is not an inexact science, but no science at all. In the circumstance, obliging the state to prove sanity when psychiatry thinks there may be insanity is to oblige the state to prove that an opinion is wrong and this, alas, cannot be done. All one can prove is that an assertion of fact is incorrect. But the social "scientist" in the courtroom comes trailing not facts but notions. In the face of these, the state can offer only evidence and hope that on at least some occasions a body of fact will triumph over a psychiatric theory. Again, justice cannot survive this sort of thing.

To close this chapter I must respect at least two criticisms it is likely to inspire. The first is a statistical one. Experienced jurists and defense attorneys will insist that the insanity plea in capital cases is relatively rare, and even rarer in cases of non-violent felonies. The reply here, of course, is that what is at issue is a principle and that we need not wait for epidemic violations of it before coming to its rescue. The willingness of counsel to raise the insanity defense is, all other things being equal, tied to the likelihood that it can be made credible and this likelihood is in turn tied to the influence the psycho-social point of view has had on the minds of jurors. The question, therefore, of how frequently a defense succeeds is separate from the question of whether it is a jurally valid defense. The second concern or criticism will be aroused by the increasing incidence of criminal conduct by "children" and the current habit of judging "youthful offenders" according to psychosocial criteria. The irony here is that the very professions (psychiatry, psychology, and sociology) that eagerly proclaim how "adult" the new child is—how sexually mature, physically enlarged and socially "liberated" he is wher compared with his peers of a century ago—will also plead for special consideration when the "youthful offender" takes the life or possessions of another. Like the Homeric Penelope, the social "scientists" unravel in the criminal court the very fabric they wove to cover children's "rights." Again, for purposes of *justice*, there is no a priori basis upon which age alone establishes exculpation. A person able to take arms against another and plot his demise is accessible to the judgment of the law and vulnerable to its punishments. There is nothing redemptive in the habit of treating youth as a kind of insanity. Society's right to defend itself is meaningful only because its members include those capable of harming others. There is no judicial or moral premise according to which this right is suspended simply because the offending agent is "youthful"—or simply young. Nor is there any moral canon requiring jurists to pardon a fourteen-year-old from a "bad background" while withholding the same consideration from a forty-year-old with just as "bad" a background. Here, as throughout this chapter, the issue is that of guilt and innocence, not that of punishment.

Notes

Significant Contributions to the History of Psychology is a fifty-volume collection divided into six series. Series F is devoted to *Insanity and Jurisprudence* and contains six volumes. Volume V presents the early U.S. cases discussed in this chapter, and Volume VI is devoted to seminal British cases. The pagination given in this chapter is the same as in the original sources. The interested reader will find these volumes a far more accessible source, however, than the bound originals.

I have not subscribed in this chapter to any single theory of justice, although the position implicitly recommended clearly has Hegelian elements. I would not want the reader, however, to think my remarks are

beholden to this or that theory of the "social contract" or as intended for
any conceivable form of political or social organization. "Justice" in this
chapter is taken largely to be that system of laws and justifications on
which Western jurisprudence has rested for the past few centuries. I do not,
of course, accept Bentham's maxim according to which "all punishment
is a mischief," nor would I agree with utilitarians that the only justification for punishment is a plausible belief that greater evils will thereby be
averted. It is W. D. Ross's position in *The Right and the Good* (Oxford,
1930) that felons, by offending the rights of others, have essentially lost
their claim on the state as the guarantor of their rights. This is a mixture of
retributivist and utilitarian thought that does not quite reflect my position
in this chapter. I have not inquired into the nature or number of rights
forfeited by those who have committed crimes, for this is a matter separate
from the state's obligation to honor its own laws. Nor in this chapter have
I even insisted on a free will or nondeterministic theory of social actions.
The issue addressed in the chapter is that of "insanity" as a legal defense.
We do not exonerate all felons on the grounds of scientific determinism.
Thus, the plea of insanity is under the burden of proving that determinism
is relevant in these cases in a way that it is not relevant in other cases; i.e.,
noninsanity cases.

   As a final note, I might mention that the brief characterization of
Lord Kenyon given in this chapter scarcely conveys his pivotal and
sometimes controversial role in the evolution of British jurisprudence. He
was indeed a man of "depth and broad experience," but also a man of some
volatility and crankiness. Some years before *Hadfield*, he and Erskine had
worked as co-counsels in Lord George Gordon's notorious case. Gordon
was acquitted principally through the performance of the junior counsel,
Erskine. Kenyon's performance at trial was as irksome as it was relentless.
In *Hadfield*, however, we find a challenge to the general view of Kenyon as
a jurist who reimposed a severely conservative character on criminal
justice. It is true that his immediate predecessor, Lord Mansfield, had
done much to liberalize jural canons, but it is equally true that *Hadfield*
would have provided grounds for a speedy hanging had it been pled before
a mere ideologue.

3 *Insanity and Responsibility: Testamentary Capacity*

Let us invent a transaction. At nine years of age, Billy donates one of his kidneys to his ailing twin, Dick, who will not be able to live without it. Ten years later, Billy's remaining kidney begins to malfunction, and he demands the return of the one he gave to Dick. Without it Billy will surely die, and the kidney in question he claims was his all along. I must quickly add that I do not pose this dilemma to introduce a problem in "bio-ethics" but to raise a general question about what it means to own something and what it means to have a right to one's property. More particularly, I wish to raise the question: What principles of morals and justice provide the grounds of ownership and on what related or conflicting principles are these grounds justly removed or ignored or violated? Suppose we learned, for example, that Dick had begun to drink excessively at age twelve and that he was now in the process of destroying the donated kidney through chronic drunkenness. Would this be a sufficient justification for returning the organ to his sober brother? That is, were there implicit or stated conditions for the transfer of property at the time of the initial transaction? Suppose, on the other hand, the donor had himself taken to drink and now needed a new kidney because his habits were destroying the one he had. Would our refusal to return the donated kidney be defended on the grounds that he would abuse it were it to be returned? As ethicists usually understand issues of this kind, the original transfer is justified on the grounds that the act will save a life and will not cost a life, whereas the retransfer, although it will save a life, will now cost one too. The principle is that the right to live is a fundamental right, and that the very existence of life requires no justification for its continuation. On the same principle, how a given life began or was sustained has no bearing on its right to continue, and this right takes precedence over any "property" right that may be in conflict with it. Starving parents, for example, do not have the right to eat one of their children solely on the grounds that the child is alive because the parents fed it over the years. Even treated as a kind of property, therefore, life—the ownership of one's life—is thought to be inalienable. But what does it mean to have a right, alienable or not?

1. On Rights

John Locke identified as the basic or "natural" human rights those of life, liberty, and property. Thomas Aquinas, speaking more abstractly if no less convincingly, judged that human beings have only the right to do what is right, since it would be contradictory to claim a right to be felonious or unjust. Over the centuries, and owing to the emergence of popular democracies, the list of putative rights has grown considerably, although the list of defenses has not kept pace. Some would argue that the more recent and numerous rights are derivative, that they are grounded in the few basic rights, and that the same defenses covering basic rights are available to all rights deriving from them. This, of course, does not establish that there are basic rights; only that if there are, others may be conceptually or logically or legally tied to them.

But what, then, is a "basic right"? Among other considerations, it is a potential for action that every moral being would choose to have, would confer on loved ones, and would suffer from the loss of if denied. It is also that which others are judged to be obliged not to oppose or curtail or transgress. To have a right, then, is to be in possession of something for which no justification is required, since any being able to traffic in the language of justifications would not challenge the right in question. A basic right, then, is simultaneously a potential for action, a set of protections, and an entity the possession of which requires no justification. To the extent that every competent being would choose it for himself, would make it available at least to those he loves, and would suffer in its absence, a basic right may also be called a natural right, since it would seem to inhere in the very nature of human nature. This is not to say, however, that all such rights are equally valued or even equally fundamental. One of them—the right to live—is most fundamental in that all other rights are occasioned by it whereas it is not occasioned by any other. And it is to the same extent that basic rights are "natural" that they are spared the burden of justification, since no one is obliged to justify what finally is a law of nature.

It is on these grounds that one may distinguish between rights and privileges, and rights and powers. Privileges are conferred, may be removed, may be denied, and are seldom if ever universally distributed. To claim a privilege is to be called upon to offer a justification precisely because no one has a *right* to a privilege merely by claiming it. Powers, too, by their very nature can be justly opposed, can be redistributed, and can be unjustly expressed. They are, in a sense, in antagonistic relationship with rights in that the latter are thought of as being protected from the former. Power arises from the fact of individual differences as rights emerge from the presumption of equality.

I have referred to moral and competent beings in connection with rights, and such references might lead to confusions regarding the nature of rights. It may be asked, for example, whether infants, animals, or mentally defective persons lose or never have rights because they cannot claim them, cannot be said to suffer in their absence, and cannot wish them for their loved ones—because they are not able to wish for anything. But in citing such factors as the attributes or essences of rights, I did not mean to suggest that these were the only attributes. It is these in conjunction with the obligation to honor rights and the freeing of rights from the burden of justification that fleshes out the skeleton of "rights." And suffusing all these considerations is the idea of *potentiality*, since no right ceases to exist merely because it is not exercised or defended. To the extent that infants, animals, and mentally defective persons have the capacity to suffer, they are thought to have the right not to be caused suffering, whether they "claim" such a right or not. The right is claimed for them by a moral community able to recognize the connection between an agent's obligations and a patient's capacities. Where doubts arise, the benefit extends to the patient in any setting in which a right may be violated on the basis of nothing more than a power or a privilege. Let us assume, for example, that Smith has the power to torture an animal, that the act would please Smith, and that Smith claims the privilege of pleasing himself. To the extent that animals may be plausibly judged as having the capacity to suffer, and since the human right to be protected against torture is grounded in the very capacity for suffering, the right is extended to animals who share the same capacity. In this case, Smith's privilege or alleged privilege is not granted, for it collides with a right. The point here is that the only grounds on which rights may be justly ignored or violated are those occupied by other rights, never those occupied by nothing more than powers or privileges. The right to act freely does not cover homicidal acts, as the right to speak freely does not cover libelous statements. We do not oppose murder or libel because we oppose freedoms of action and speech, but because the rights to act and to speak are not valued as highly as the right to live and to be spared from libelous assaults. In the former instance, the right to live is judged to be more fundamental than the right to act, and in both instances no one has a right to do what is wrong. We would not confer the right to libel on our loved ones; we would not consider proscriptions against libel as causing all moral beings suffering; we cannot imagine all moral beings laboring to secure the right to commit libels; we do not think of the right to be protected against libel to require justification. Thus, the protection satisfies the relevant criteria of "rights," and the act of libel satisfies none of them.

The vast literature on "rights" goes much further than what I have included here, but once we move beyond these fundamental considerations, thoughtful supporters become properly wary and ultimately confused. To say, for example, as many have, that a right is but the promise law makes to an actor is to equate rights with nothing more than any conceivable legislation, including legislation that would offend the moral sensibilities of the overwhelming majority of persons who have ever lived. It is often true, of course, that rights are guaranteed by law and that, to this extent, a right is protected by a kind of promise, but this pertains to the exercise and not to the nature of rights. It has also been proposed to treat rights as but the left side of an equation that equates Smith's *right* with Jones's *duty*. However, I do not think that such an equation defines a right in any but an operational sense, for it only becomes Jones's duty after we have established that Smith has the right in question. Nor is it clear what the allegedly identical duty entails. To say that Smith has the right to live is not the same as saying that Jones, under all conceivable circumstances, has the duty to do everything possible to keep Smith alive. Indeed, in cases of self-defense, it is argued that Jones's duty is to keep himself alive by taking Smith's life. Thus, the part of the "duty" argument that is compelling is just the part that addresses what I have already included among the attributes of rights: their possession requires no justification and, therefore, no one has the right to require a justification. To the extent that this imposes a duty to honor the right in practice, the duty in question is not identical to the right but an obligation brought into being by the very existence of the right. It is in this same sense that there can be said to be a relationship between a right and a claim; not that a right is no more than something actually claimed by those who possess it or seek to have it honored, but that it is something that cannot be reclaimed merely on the grounds of privilege or power. Thus, it is not that the infant has claimed the right to live, but that the right of life, as a basic right, cannot be *reclaimed* from any living entity merely on the basis of power or privilege. Geographically, such rights exist in moral territory in which some beings have shares by nature, others by bequests, others by proxy, and still others by the possession of relevant capacities, such as the capacity to suffer and die. These rights, then, are not something that attaches to bodies or objects but to propositions which, at the root, are moral propositions. We say that "All X's ought not to Y any Z," and Smith or a puppy or an infant is said to be protected against Y-acts by virtue of being Z's or relevantly Z-like. In this case, the right to be protected against Y-acts is not, properly speaking, Smith's or the puppy's or the infant's but a Z-right, meaning it is available to Z's in the sense that space is available to them. They do not "own" it, but it constitutes an indefeasible condition of being a Z. To remove it is to make it impossible for there to be Z's. Thus, for a Z to try to justify its removal is to traffic in contradiction and incoherence. To have a right, then, is neither to *have* a claim nor to *make* a claim, but to be of a nature that is morally immune to claims against it of a certain kind.

With all of this in the background, we can approach the issue of specific rights, in this case the right to property, which Locke accorded the status of a basic right. To avoid an excessively long analysis, let us refer only to property that was not acquired by illegal means and is not being used for illegal purposes. Note, however, that the element of legality is neither a necessary nor a sufficient condition of the moral right to property—if there is such a right. A person might use his property as a sanctuary for those who are the victims of unjust laws, and thus be using the property illegally. But it is not to such instances that I will address myself; only to those in which what Smith claims to be "his" was obtained legally and is used within the provisions and restrictions of the law.

The usual meaning of ownership is *entitlement,* and one is said to have "title" to a thing or property by virtue of having bought it, earned it, or won it. In some instances, the entitlement is granted on the grounds that the thing or property is in one's possession, and no other party has a valid claim on it. That is, no other party can prove to have bought, earned, or won the thing or property in question at the time the present possessor came into possession of it. But "possession is nine-tenths of the law" only when there are no valid competing claims of ownership. Included in the very concept of entitlement is the right to use the possession in any way that will not abridge or violate those rights of others that are of the same or higher standing than the putative rights of ownership. One is not, for example, permitted to mount a high-powered telescope on his property for the purpose of peering into the bedroom windows of neighbors. In such a case, there is no denying that the Peeping Tom has rights of ownership, but these rights do not include the right to violate the privacy of others. Thus the right to own is not synomymous with the right to use. It only establishes the grounds on which legally and morally permissible use requires no justification. This is precisely the sense in which ownership is a form of *right:* its legally and morally acceptable use requires no justification. A man may own a pet, but may not torture it; he may own an automobile, but may not use it to carry contraband; he may own a house, but cannot keep slaves therein; he may own a hypodermic needle, but may not use it to administer illegal drugs to himself or others.

The inextricable connection between life on the one hand and food and shelter on the other has alway given the latter the same sorts of immunities enjoyed by the right to live, but historically such food and shelter had to qualify as "bare essentials" to enjoy the status of rights. That is, to the extent that the right to food and shelter has been taken as part of the right to life, the former has been recognized only as far as survival itself requires. But this has never been the sole grounds on which properties have been said to be covered by rights. Persons have, at least in all civilized epochs, been judged to have rights to things on which survival does not depend, things that pertain to nothing more than pleasure or pride or amusement. No tyranny has ever been so great as to deny all but the barest necessities of merely physical survival. But it is also true historically that, as claimed rights have extended well beyond the perimeter of mere physical survival, contestants have appeared, wars have been fought, and rebellions have been staged. We may say, then, that the purely historical standing of what we now take to be "property rights" has not equalled that of the right to live. Or perhaps more accurately, we may say that historically the right to property has not been covered by the same laws of (universal) distribution as those covering life rights. At various times, there have been monarchs, states, religious institutions, and "landed" families that have assumed proprietary rights over significant parts or even the entirety of the goods, lands, and productions of a nation or polity. These assumed rights were said to be grounded either in birth or the will of God or the weight of tradition or a record of achievement. The first justification pertains to *hereditary* rights; the second, to *God-given* rights; the third to *customary* rights; the fourth to *earned* rights or "deserts."

What is common to three of these alleged rights and what distinguishes them from the basic rights discussed so far is that all of them carry the burden of justification, or at least the burden of proof. To claim that one rightfully owns something as an heir is, among other considerations, to claim that one can prove one is an heir and can prove further that a direct ancestor was the rightful owner of the thing in question. To insist that God has singled out a person or an institution for a special right that is not universally distributed is to make a factual claim, and all factual claims must be settled by evidence. As for customary "rights," if their only standing is that which is conferred by custom, then they can survive only as long as the custom is supported by the community. I submit that, as phrased, none of these property rights is basic. If there is such a thing as a *heredity right*, it does not inhere in the basic rights of the beneficiary, but in the right of the testator to dispose of what he possesses as he sees fit. For a right to be "God-given," its authority must be grounded in certain assumptions about divine gifts and on the assumption that an entity worthy of the title "God" must be all-just, it would be contradictory to contend that such an entity had selected certain persons to enjoy a moral advantage over others. So-called customary rights are equivalently incoherent; rights refer to what *ought* to be honored or respected, and no historical fact can by itself establish a moral obligation.

This brings us to the fourth justification of property rights: that the thing or property in question is earned and that the possession of it comes under the heading of a *just desert*. Where it is won in free and fair competition, it is called a prize. Where it follows from an unusual and unrequired performance, it is called a bonus. In all cases, it is a compensation for the recipient's efforts or stress or concern or risk or achievement. And in all such cases, it would be due to anyone who had expended the same effort or endured the same stress or displayed the same concern or took the same risk or achieved the same goal. In other words, it is a property or thing that is in principle universally available, and it is in precisely this sense that it is right for one who satisfies the conditions to own it. I would argue that this and only this ground of ownership is a basic right: it is one we would labor to extend at least to those we love; one in whose absence we would suffer; one that we grant no other the right to oppose, violate, or ignore; one the possession of which requires no justification; one we cannot imagine any morally competent being to be willing to forfeit or obstruct. If this is accepted, one principle that follows is that no one can be said to have a "right" to luck or good fortune or any bounty that becomes available to a person by accident, inadvertence, or chance. Such proprietorship as that person might come to enjoy can only be a privilege, for he does not have a right to that for which he has had no responsibility. There are, no doubt, many instances where it would be practically impossible to assign or deny responsibility, but I am referring here to a principle of rights and not the actual procedures for determining whether a given entity has qualified.

Let us say, then, that a person possesses a *basic* right to own what his own labor has produced, with the proviso that no one has a right to own any other person even though a parent's labor is necessary for the production of a child. (I distinguish here between the right of ownership and the privilege of custodianship.) Let us say further that such ownership as might be claimed or conferred where the recipient's own labor has played no part can never be a *basic* right, but can only be a privilege or a power and that it always carries a burden of justification. Finally, even the basic right of ownership cannot come into being or be retained as a potentiality if the owner's or prospective owner's right to live is not honored. Thus, the basic right of ownership is occasioned by this more fundamental right and, accordingly, the right of ownership cannot take precedence over the right to live. To the extent that anyone, in exercising the basic right to property, places the lives of others at risk, the right to property may be justly ignored when other remedies have failed, e.g., appeals to the owner's benevolence, offers of compensation, requests for self-restraint. Properly understood, therefore, the so-called right to property is, in fact, the right to compensation, and not the right to unrestricted use. The discoverer of a drug that will save lives does not have the right to withhold his discovery but to be compensated for its use—not because the basic right of ownership is denied, but because it is a right over which life rights take precedence. For the scientist to insist that *no life* is as important to him as his invention is for him to include his own. For him to contend that no compensation is great enough to repay him for his labors is irrelevant, since the rights attaching to labor can never equal that which attaches to life.

There is, however, a conceptual symmetry here between the limitations imposed on property rights and the protections available to those rights. What a man possesses by dint of his labor is his to use as he sees fit provided that this use does not violate a right of higher moral worth. He may use his property and wealth foolishly, profligately, aimlessly, irrationally. He may use it in the interest of no more than his own pleasure or entertainment. He may use it even to anger or disappoint others—for example, by flaunting it—or to teach a lesson or avenge a real or only imagined grievance. He may invest it for the purpose of expanding its worth, divest himself of it for the purpose of enhancing his good name, or give it to those of his choosing. All these and many more similar actions give substance to the basic right to own the fruits of one's labors.

2. On Wills

It is sometimes said that "dead men have rights" and that the power of a will proves it. Dead men, of course, have no rights at all as dead men, though some of the rights of the living exist to protect properties whose disposal was provided for by the owner and made conditional on his death. The justification for wills, which permit the use of properties to be governed by testaments whose author is no longer alive, tends to elude those who have adopted communalistic theories of the good state. Why, they ask, should a corpse stand between properties and those among the living who need and could use them? Even granting that the testator had some "right" to all of this during his lifetime, the right surely does not survive his ability to exercise it!

What questions such as this miss is the fact that a will is a promise and, as such, necessarily refers to future actions. Unlike nontestamentary promises, wills are not specifically dated, but they are, like other promises, conditional. One of the conditions is that the promise is to be kept on the death of the person who makes it. Moreover, although the terms of a will are not executed until the testator dies, the will may and often does have powerful effects long before its terms must be discharged. The testator, for example, may use his will to extract benefits from others; to gain favor in certain circles; to honor persons and institutions and to use the will to publicize his respect for them; to retain the support and cooperation of those who wish to be named in the will. Thus, aside from the satisfaction derived from knowing in one's own lifetime the work that one's estate will continue to do after one has died, there is the additional benefit of being able to enhance one's own life merely by writing a will and making its provisions known.

But a will is also a legal document, not simply a promise. Not every broken promise is actionable. What wills have in common with promises is their future-tense commitments and the right of the promising party to withdraw the promise unilaterally without even apprising the expectant beneficiary. Unlike ordinary promises, however, wills also have a contractual dimension in that they set forth terms that will be respected by courts even though the author or maker of the promise can no longer be consulted as to whether he ever made such a promise and whether he would still have its provisions respected. The testator is now dead; his estate is substantial; a will is produced that requires his estate be transferred to one or more persons according to its terms. But is this will the most recent? Are there others? Were the terms conditional on the performance of some service or action? Was the testator under duress at the time he wrote the will? Was he competent to make such promises? Was undue influence brought to bear, or was a fraud perpetrated? Was the testator the rightful owner of the properties bequeathed? These are but a few of the many technical questions surrounding the laws of testacy, and I offer them only to indicate the many factors that can serve to overturn the terms of a will. But in this regard, one of them is different from all the rest—the factor of *competence*. All other factors are intended either to guarantee that the testator's intentions are implemented or that the properties in question actually and rightfully form his estate. A will can be set aside on the showing of undue influence or fraud because in such circumstances there is every reason to believe that the testator, in the absence of such influence or fraud, would not have made the promises set forth in the will. Where there are several and contradictory testaments, the most recent is the legal one, all other things being equal, on the assumption that the most recent of our wishes came into being in part by relegating other and older ones to a less significant status. However, the issue of competence arises not so much out of a desire to protect and honor the intentions of the testator but as a test to determine the validity of claims brought against the will by interested parties. One interested party, it should be noted, is always the state, not only in its strictly legal mission but also as a possible beneficiary.

Given the nature of wills—and I recognize how varied they are in their provisions, language, clarity, and coherence—and

given the very concept of *ownership,* perhaps the first question
we should raise has to do with the relevance of mental "competence." What does it mean to ask whether Smith is competent
to make a promise? I suggest that, in the circumstance, a question
of this sort can only refer to three attributes of Smith: First, does
the promise fall within the range of actions that Smith has the
power to perform? Second, does the promise fall within legally
permissible boundaries of conduct? Third, is Smith sufficiently
conversant in the language he is using to make his promise so
that we can be certain he knows what he is saying? Only the last
of these questions pertains to Smith's personal psychological
"capacities," the first two being addressed only to the practical
force his will may have. Let me turn, then, to the matter of
psychological "capacity."

3. Competence

I will invent three illustrations of facts that might attend the
authorship of a will, in each case attributing certain motives and
reasonings to the testator even though in practice such attributions are always perilous.

CASE 1. It is White's most deeply held conviction that his
life would have had no meaning to him had it not been for his
short-haired pointer, who remained faithfully at his side for the
last twenty years of White's life. Twin sons survive Mr. White, but
neither had shown any concern for him since marrying ten years
earlier. White's wife died delivering the twins and White never
remarried. A quiet and shy man, and a man of extraordinary
wealth, White spent his last twenty years in nearly total isolation,
going out only to walk with his dog. People made him nervous
and his few dealings with them convinced him that they were
only interested in themselves or in his money. Neighbors would
laugh as they watched White stroll along, talking to his dog,
reading a newspaper to the dog, etc.

The terms of White's will were quite specific. He knew or
had reason to believe that once he died, his dog would not
abandon him willingly. He knew also that no one would give the
dog appropriate attention unless rewarded for it. So in his will he
sets forth the following as the principal provisions:

All of my properties, both real and personal, are to be sold at auction by my trustees within two weeks of my death. Once taxes and fees have been paid, the balance of the proceeds are to be used to acquire a twenty-acre treed plot on which two fully decorated rooms are to be constructed. These rooms are to match as nearly as possible the one that has served as my bedroom and the one occupied by my dog at our last residence. A house is also to be constructed, costing no more than $35,000, to serve as the abode of a keeper to be named by my trustees. The keeper, or his replacement, is to be paid a salary that equals 150 percent of the median income of full-time employees working in the United States. Fringe benefits will provide all retirement and hospitalization coverage available to those at this income level. My dog is to be cared for and is to have access to the grounds and to the new room, which will be my sarcophagus. My trustees will ensure that the care of my dog is of the best sort and will dismiss any caretaker who fails in this regard. I specifically disinherit from my estate my sons, who have been a source of disappointment to me throughtout the past ten years.

Learning of their father's demise, the twins retain counsel and proceed to challenge the will. They produce dozens of witnesses who swear that the deceased talked to his dog, talked to no one else, lived as a recluse, and was otherwise odd in his public behavior on those few occasions when he was seen in public. The sons further insist that it was because of White's eccentricity that they had cut themselves off from him. He was an embarrassment to them and to their families. Nevertheless, they both loved the old man and wished that his behavior had not been such as to drive a wedge between them and him. Surely, they contend, had White known the true feelings of his sons, he never would have cut them out of his will.

CASE 2: Mr. Brown has always loved the quiche served at a local bistro. Furthermore, he has always judged his daughter and wife to be hopeless dunces in the kitchen and not much better in the parlor. He has prevailed on them often to improve themselves and to respect the palates of guests, but neither of them has ever given a hint of changing her ways. Brown writes a will that seeks to correct this. In order for them to share any part of his estate not lawfully theirs to begin with, they must take two hours of cooking lessons each week for ten years, must pass an examination prepared by the owner of the bistro, and must invite all who have dined so disappointingly back for a proper meal once their education is complete. If all of these terms are not honored, the balance of Brown's estate is to pass to the owner of the bistro. (We shall make said owner sufficiently honorable so that the possibility of his failing the women on the required examination for purely selfish reasons is ruled out.)

CASE 3. Mr. Gray has been eccentric in his choice of companions all the days of his adult life. His closest friends include a woman of easy virtue, the spiritual leader of a group of peanut worshippers, and a seven-year-old child who lends Gray his kite on weekends. Gray lived with Mrs. Gray for two years, but they have not lived together for the past forty years. They were never divorced, but as an heiress in her own right, she has never received money or demanded it from Mr. Gray. After he dies, his will is found to require that his estate be divided equally among the prostitute, the peanut-priest, and the child.

What I mean to emphasize in Case 1 is not merely the naming of a pet as beneficiary, but the exclusion of offspring on the grounds of not knowing their true feelings. In Case 2, stress should be placed on an element of vengefulness toward those who would not comply with the testator's wishes during his life. And Case 3 should excite misgivings regarding the worthiness of the beneficiaries as well as sympathy for even two years of wifely comradeship.

Let us approach the case of Mr. White with grave suspicion. Here is a fellow who converses with his dog, but avoids the company of other human beings. He is on record as not trusting most members of his species, so it would not be out of character for him to entertain paranoid feelings toward his own sons. Was such a man competent to write a will? Is it not clear from his conduct and from the very terms of the will that we are here witnessing a mind at odds with reason? Who would expect the children, now married and with children of their own to look after, to continue a relationship with so eccentric and distracting an old man? To exclude them from a will is to punish them for no more than propriety.

The same reasoning will apply to the case of Mr. Brown. For a man to place such importance on cuisine is itself a sign of misplaced values, for he is more concerned with his guests' palates than the welfare of his wife and daughter. What sort of tyrant must it be who would continue to force those around him to comply with his wishes even after his death! What right does he have to compel such ridiculous activities as a condition of inheriting his fortune? And, as for Mr. Gray, any man whose closest friends are a prostitute, a quack, and a child simply lacks the emotional maturity and good taste required of those who would dispose of great estates. The relationship he had with Mrs. Gray, though brief, was at least licit, and certainly ranks higher than any that might have existed between Gray and a prostitute.

There are, to be sure, other objections that could be raised in opposition to the wills written by our three illustrative testators, but I suspect they will be of the same general bearing, i.e., they will either challenge the standing of the beneficiaries, the competence of the testator, or the propriety of the terms as set by custom. But such objections fail to note two significant aspects of each of these cases: first, the properties disposed of were in fact owned by the testator, and second, the motives in each case were cut from the same cloth that covers the common motivations behind nearly every testament. In the overwhelming majority of cases, the testator apportions his holdings according to the esteem or loyalty or sense of obligation he feels toward his beneficiaries. He names them in a will because it pleases him to do so, because they have enriched his life, because he hopes to be remembered by them, because he hopes his fortune will allow them to improve their own lives. White, Brown, and Gray were all returning favors. And who is to say that White's dog, Brown's bistro chef, and Gray's quack had not done favors? Perhaps White did misunderstand the feelings of his sons. But is it not as plausible to argue that many become beneficiaries by virtue of concealing their true feeling from a likely benefactor? Does anyone know the *true* feelings of another?

Now it surely may be argued that in each of these cases, an odd use has been made of money and property. There may even be a unanimous judgment that neither a dog, a cook, nor a quack priest should be allowed to come into possession of fortunes in a needy world simply because of the eccentricities of an old man. But this, too, is common to most wills, for in nearly every case we can find a better use for the fortune, a worthier recipient, a needier recipient, or a nobler cause. But this can amount to no more than an assertion of what we would do were the money ours. The plain fact, however, is that it is not ours, and the added fact is that to force it to do our work is effectively to strip White, Brown, and Gray of one of the central benefits of ownership—the right to dispose of one's property as one sees fit.

It is usually at this point in debates on property rights that one lectures the defenders of absolute ownership on the rights of others. But in the case of White, what in fact are the "rights" of his sons? What of their own labor is mixed with the fortune earned by their father? If none, then there is no right, only a privilege accorded by law to near relations. This privilege has antique Roman roots and, in the absence of a will, is at least arguably sound. But to oppose the express wishes of a testator—to oppose his *right* to what he has earned—on the alleged rights of those who were merely born into his family and who have the means of supporting themselves is to violate a right with a privilege, and this may be legal but it cannot be just.

Let us recognize, however, that the defense of the rights of the testator that I have briefly offered has been honored in law for many centuries, including our own. And it is precisely because of the historically liberal options of testation that challenges to "capacity" have been so prominently represented in the courts. Where great stakes are involved and where the testator has been careful to exclude otherwise predictable beneficiaries, the most common grounds for challenge have been the testator's mental capacity and his victimization by sources of undue influence. It is instructive to review the most important cases pertaining to these challenges to see how the "social sciences" have crept into yet another of the halls of justice.

4. "Capacity" on Trial

We must remember that contracts, deeds, and wills as written instruments have not had an uninterrupted evolution. For two centuries, between A.D. 700 and A.D. 900, the darkness that settled over the European Continent was made even bleaker by illiteracy and by the scarcity of the very instruments of literacy, especially Syrian papyrus. In these years, agreements were established orally before witnesses. It was common to select the latter from the younger segments of the population, since their memories were to serve as the only record of the transaction. Nor was it uncommon for children so selected to be whipped or even scalded at the time of the transaction so that the event would be permanently riveted in their minds.

In these same years, the peoples of Europe were seminomadic, under the constant press of invasion and occupation. The first signs of stability were the gift of Charlemagne in the ninth century, but it was not until the middle of the twelfth century that a return to ordered social and political life was the rule rather than the exception. Moreover, it was in the very nature of feudal organization that so-called *real property* (realty) was confined to a small number of persons and passed on according to hereditary rules developed in ancient Rome. Only with the growth of the Church's power and the corresponding growth of both independent and interdependent monarchies do we find the need for refined laws of property and testation. Indeed, the very concept of an "estate" as land in which parties have an interest and regarding which they have rights of enjoyment for a specified term (e.g., for life or for some number of years) is a concept appearing in the thirteenth century. The term *tenure* refers to the period of time in which the interests are covered or, in common language, the duration of "ownership." In the feudal ages, lords granted their *villeins* possession (*seisen*) and the *villeins* could then apportion the holding in such a way as to become "lords" in their own right, though of course not in name. But in practice, the right to hold property for life and the right to confer the same property on direct descendants in the form of a *fee* allowed many freemen to function as servants of *A* but lords of *B*. Thus, the durability of feudal hierarchies was enhanced by a system of stratification. Feudalism, viewed only in terms of rights of interest, may be said to have died with the *Quia Emptores* (1290), which effectively cut out the middlemen. By the seventeenth century, Lord Coke would treat tenants as absolute owners during the terms of tenure. The power of revocation was vested in "the lord of all" by *Quia Emptores*, and the rights of interest (i.e., the rights of ownership) were held by any tenant unless these were validly revoked by the lord. One effect of this was the elimination of feudal hierarchies and their replacement by an essentially two-class system containing a "landed" aristocracy and a large population of tenant farmers. The most significant feature of this was the increase in the number of legal "owners," for now there were many whose rights of interest were exactly the same as those once held only by the *villeins*. It was the same *Quia Emptores*, however, that permitted the holder of a *fee* to dispose of it without the consent of his lord but only at the forfeiture of his own lordly rights over the new grantee. The holder of property "in fee-simple" passed this property to his lineal descendants, and this devolution followed the historic custom of hereditary succession. With *Quia Emptores*, the custom could be violated, but only at the cost of status. That such costs were willingly incurred was an indication that feudal society was breaking apart. By 1540, the right to "disentail" came into prominence. It was then possible to pass such holdings on to strangers and to exclude lineal descendants in one's will. But there were always courses of action available to heirs, and some of these continue in our own day in the form of regulations against disinheritance.

Let us pick up the thread of this development in 1793, with the well known case of *Cartwright* v. *Cartwright*. Here the direct descendant of the testatrix challenged provisions of the will on the grounds that Mrs. Cartwright was not in her right mind at the time she composed it. Medical opinion had yet to gain a foothold in such cases, and so the court had to rely on nothing more than its own clear-headed understanding of mental "capacity." What it said of the deceased is to the point:

> [B]y herself writing the will . . . [she] . . . hath most plainly shewn she had a full and complete capacity to understand what was the state of her affairs and her relations. . . . She not only formed the plan, but pursued and carried it into execution with propriety and without assistance. (*Cartwright*, p. 933)

The court thus confined itself to three considerations, following the questions I previously proposed: Did Mrs. Cartwright actually have the power to promise the properties stated in her will? Was any law violated by the terms of the will? Does the wording of the will make clear that the language is the language of intention? She knew what was hers, she knew who her relatives were, and she stated how the former was to be treated in regard to (or disregard of) the latter. What we have in *Cartwright* is the extention of "wild beast" criteria from criminal to testamentary cases. I might point out that in *Bellingham*, discussed in the preceding chapter, the prosecutor was careful to remind the jury that if Bellingham had written a will on the day he murdered

Spencer Perceval, its terms would have been honored by any English court. Note, then, that the gambit in *Bellingham* (1812) was to assimilate the question of *criminal responsibility* to the standards of *testamentary capacity*, the latter being far more tolerant of departures from the norms of conduct.

In time, however, the assimilation would work in the opposite direction: as the criminal's burden to establish his insanity became lighter, the testator's *onus probandi* became heavier. Precedential in this respect was *Dew* v. *Clark and Clark* (1826), in which "partial insanity" was sufficient to overturn a will; that is, where the reasoning of Erskine in *Hadfield* now surfaced in a civil action. In *Dew*, the testator's daughter (now Mrs. Dew) alleged that her father had always been morbidly "deluded" regarding her merits. He had contempt for her when she was a child, and this sentiment grew with the passing years. In conveying the bulk of his estate to more distant relations, the Clarks, he was merely acting out the last scene of the groundless hostility he held for his daughter. In their own behalf, the Clarks argued that the plaintiff had earned the low esteem of her father, and, moreover, that the father had a record of great acumen in the balance of his financial and social affairs. The court, however, was not convinced of the former allegation and did not judge the latter to be important:

> People who dwell on the confines of two empires are likely enough to be found in, sometimes the one, and sometimes the other. . . . (*Dew*, p. 446)

> [T]he will propounded in this cause . . . being . . . the direct unqualified offspring of that morbid delusion . . . I, at least, can arrive at no other conclusion than that the deceased was insane at the time of his making the will . . . and consequenty that the will itself is null and void in law. (*Dew*, p. 455)

The court was constrained to note that "partial insanity" would not have nullified any will, and that not any form of such insanity would necessarily nullify any and every will so authored. What mattered were the specific terms of the will and the connection to a demonstrably insane delusion. Again we see a parallel between civil and criminal standards. Ferrers was executed because his enmity toward Johnson was based on fact. Bellingham was executed in part because his deluded sense of the Crown's financial indebtedness to him would not have excused a homicide even if such indebtedness were factual. Hadfield was spared because a diseased mind led him to believe that Jesus wanted George III to die and because the attempted assassination was alleged to be the product of his (alleged) disease. And in *Dew*, the will is found to be the product of "delusion"—evidence of a diseased mind—and is found further to be coherently tied to the specific delusion that the present Mrs. Dew had been insufferable as a child.

In *Waring* v. *Waring* (1848) the trend continued apace. A lower court, the Prerogative Court of Canterbury, had nullified a will on the showing that the testatrix was "partially insane," although no evidence had been presented to prove that this alledged insanity had entered into any part of her will. The appeals court sustained the decision of the lower court and noted in its decision that

> what is called partial insanity has never before been laid down
> in the Superior Court. . . . (Waring, p. 726)

This paved the way for *Smith* v. *Tebbitt* (1866), in which the mere fact that the testatrix had been known to experience religious "visions" was enough to set aside her testament. Justice Wilde tells us why:

> I cannot reconcile the proved hallucinations of the testatrix in
> the matter of religion with the action of a sound and healthy
> mind on the one hand; and on the other, I find them to be just
> such as a diseased mind is known to engender. (*Smith*, p. 436)

It is useful to mark the parallel evolution of Britain's criminal insanity and testamentary capacity standards. In *Arnold* (1723), Coke's *furiosus* is the standard. In *Cartwright* (1793) the woman's mere ability to write a will is evidence enough of her capacity. In *Hadfield*, "partial" insanity provides grounds for acquittal (1800), and in *Dew* the same grounds overturn a will because the part of the mind that is insane is connected to a relevant provision of the testament (1826). And in *M'Naghten* (1843) it is argued that the acts of a diseased mind might exonerate the actor even if the delusion and the act are not entirely of a piece, but that this is "a question of physiology," according to Justice Maule. This, of course, is in the background of both *Waring* (1848) and *Smith* (1866).

In its commendable tendency to backtrack in search of misplaced principles, a developed system of justice must often pay more heed to the past than homage to progress. Thoughtful jurists, reflecting on the immense implications contained in *Waring* and in *Smith,* were ready to call a halt to developments that were clearly at odds with an owner's right to dispose of possessions. We witness this most vividly in the English case of *Banks* v. *Goodfellow* (1870) and the famous American case of *Boardman* v. *Woodward* (1869). In the former, in which a lower ruling was upheld, the court will not permit "partial insanity" to render a testator powerless as long as his alleged disease spares those faculties needed for an informed disposition of his properties. Specifically, the court in *Banks* does not

> think it necessary to consider the position assumed in *Waring* v. *Waring,* that the mind is one and indivisible, or to discuss the subject as a matter of metaphysical or psychological inquiry. It is not given to man to fathom the mystery of the human intelligence, or to ascertain the constitution of our sentient and intellectual being. (*Banks,* p. 560)

Delusion itself will not invalidate a will if

> it presents itself in such a degree and form as not to interfere with the capacity to make a rational disposal of property. . . . (Ibid., pp. 555–556) . . . [T]he standard of capacity in cases of impaired mental power is . . . the capacity on the part of the testator to comprehend the extent of the property to be disposed of, and the nature of the claims of those he is excluding. (Ibid., p. 569)

This scarcely gets us back to the protections advocated in *Cartwright,* but it does reveal a renewed concern for the rights of ownership. In later decisions thought (incorrectly) to be based on *Banks,* the important phrase is "a rational disposal." Clearly, this opens the doors to precisely the sort of mischief introduced by such cases as *Waring* and *Smith.*

Property has always had a nearly sacred standing in American life. Thus in *Boardman* the jury is instructed that a mere proof of insanity is insufficient to invalidate a will if it is further shown that at the time of the signing the testator was aware of the nature of his act and that whatever "delusions" he might suffer played no significant part in the terms of the will. The appeal against a lower ruling argued that the laws of New Hampshire specifically voided agreements entered into by insane parties, and that delusions are unfailing signs of insanity. But the appeals judge (Sargeant) thought otherwise. He was impressed by the widely differing medical opinions on "moral insanity," "delusion," "monomania," and "partial insanity," and reasoned that

> We all have likes and dislikes among our acquaintances and even among our relatives . . . and yet are we all insane because we dislike somebody that some one else likes . . . ? Better make a law that all a man's property should be divided equally among his relatives, without regard to the peculiar views or preferences of the deceased owner, and prohibit the making of wills altogether. (*Boardman*, p. 139)

Yet in this same case, the jury was instructed to treat the question of insanity as a question of fact and even to accept "hypothetical" illustrations from medical experts so long as the hypotheticals were framed in terms of the instant case. The court, we see, may have desired to return to the more innocent protections of *Cartwright*, but it produced no pause in the march of the "experts" toward the witness stand.

5. Capacity and "Expert" Testimony

What are the conditions that ordinarily must be satisfied for us to say that a person has the "capacity" to do something? At the grossest level of understanding, there is one condition and only one that removes all doubt: he does the act in question. That is, the best evidence we can hope to have that someone is able to do something is his doing it. But where a will is concerned, we are interested in more than penmanship and vocalization. The "capacity" in question pertains not to the mere writing of a will or stating of one's wishes, but to the capacity for the free exercise of one's wishes. This is why we are never obliged to honor the terms of an agreement extracted under threats of punishment or death, why we would discount the utterances of a child, and why we would confer no legal or binding force on a document authored by one who had been maliciously misinformed by those consulted on the facts. In these reasons for not honoring a will, we acknowledge our commitment to the genuine and freely expressed intentions of a lawful owner. No one should be held accountable for actions taken as a result of fraudulent representations or those elicited under duress.

The criterion of duress has ancient roots and modern branches. In all of its historical manifestations, the criterion has been asserted as a means of saving parties to a contract from unreasonable and illegal assaults and manipulations by others. But it is only in the metaphorical sense that we speak of a person as defrauding himself or being victimized by his own foolishness. The law must treat equal causes equally, but it cannot make all persons equal in intelligence, maturity, rationality, taste, or a sense of fairness. In every transaction, including all said to proceed from the volitions of the parties involved, there will be the unavoidable participation of caprice, nuances of perception, gradations of intellect, and the command of relevant facts. To insist that all such transactions are void unless it can be shown that some hypothetical rational being would have entered into them is effectively to put an end to nearly all commercial and social institutions, and surely to every form of entertainment and amusement. It would nullify agreements made by passionate lovers, hopeful bettors, fawning parents, and dutiful children. It would raise grave doubts about the validity of gifts designed to secure a higher place in heaven and those intended to perfect the human race. The eighty-year-old man would be proscribed from buying a bond that matures in thirty years. The man who wagers only on long shots would have grounds for recovering his losses. The business of life in all its monetary and possessory dimensions would be engaged in by computers—provided a totally rational being could be found who would program them. Such a being has never existed in the world.

And so we may now inquire into just what an "expert" might tell us about a dead man that will persuade us to disregard his will; further, just what constitutes expertise in matters of this sort. It would serve little purpose to identify contemporary psychologists and psychiatrists who have functioned in this capacity, including those who might properly be described as earning a handsome living in such a role. I prefer instead to present generic cases and testimonies.

There is first, if only in terms of frequency, the case of the "paranoid" whose "delusions" are said to constitute so severe a mental handicap as to make his will little more than an additional symptom of his disturbance. In most cases, the testator is no longer available to be interviewed, and the "social scientist" must rely on what can only be called hearsay evidence even when it is provided by a physician. There are, however, many instances of the testator having been "screened" psychiatrically before his death—a screening often demanded by concerned relatives who have already suspected something odd about the old man's testamentary intentions. Either way, what we are likely to learn from the "experts" is that grandfather had lived somewhat longer than his relevant faculties; that he was, even in his prime, a rather suspicious type; that as he aged he adopted any number of eccentric modes of behavior; that on several occasions he accused his children of plotting his early demise; that neighbors found him rude and reckless in his accusations; that in his final years he even had trouble counting his change and remembering the route to his house. The diagnosis is that of senile dementia or a schizoid personality of the paranoid type. And in light of this diagnosis, "experts" are of the opinion that at the time the will was contrived and signed, the testator lacked the mental capacity to comprehend the nature of the document.

Then there is the habitual drunkard whose alcoholic abuses raise doubts about the integrity of his brain and, therefore, about the validity of his will. Again, the experts provide jurors with an account of brain damage resulting from alcoholism; the psychotic states that follow in the wake of relentless insobriety; the tendency on the part of deeply troubled persons to find solace at the bottom of a bottle; the likelihood that a man of the testator's habits would probably not have sufficient control of his rational powers to be able to understand and weigh all the factors that make up so significant an instrument as a will.

Next we confront expert testimony on the capacity of a testator who spent many years of his life confined in a mental institution. He committed himself voluntarily on the grounds that he could no longer function in the outside world. In this case, the experts are likely to inform the jury that the testator, by his own admission, lacked capacity and that there is no reason to believe his will emerged from any greater psychological reserve than that which failed him throughout his life.

In these and in myriad other cases, terminology is rich and testimony is grave. Judges listen attentively as first one expert and then the next expatiate on problems of adjustment, early childhood traumas, insufficient behavioral control, a lack of cognitive plasticity, diminished judgmental function, vulnerability to episodes of affective outbreaks, paranoid tendencies exacerbated by failing health and advancing years. Perhaps no child is present to suggest the possibility that the emperor is wearing no clothes or perhaps it is merely good manners that constrain jurists from challenging these statements. But the statements themselves fall conveniently into just a few categories: They are either irrelevant, purely theoretical, true of nearly every person some of the time and no person all of the time, or mere redescriptions of what the testator has already stated in his will. He may, for example, have said something like "Since my children would prefer that I die sooner rather than later, I have no intention of giving them a penny." Let us say that it was his *opinion*—rather than his "delusion"—that his offspring wished him dead. Let us go so far as to assert that the opinion was false and groundless. So what? In addition to having the constitutional right to his own opinions—and this covers provably false ones—he also has the right to dispose of his property on the grounds of his opinions. After all, in not conveying his possessions to his children, he is not doing them the sort of harm that limits the exercise of every right. He is not causing them to lose property that is theirs, for the property in question is his. And such mental anguish as they might suffer because of his will is of their own manufacture. No one is obliged to pay money to someone else simply on the grounds that a failure to do so will cause the beggar mental anguish!

The same applies in cases in which alcoholism is thought to invalidate a will. The fact of alcoholism does not establish either extensive brain damage or general mental incapacity. What must be shown is that the habits of a lifetime have rendered the testator so incapacitated that he would be unable to read a will, let alone write one. It is simply frivolous, and vicious in the logical sense, to challenge testamentary capacity on the grounds that the terms of the will are odd or unexpected. As long as a sane man can write a peculiar will, no such document in and of itself can establish that its author was not sane. This is also true of a will executed by a patient in an asylum. It will be clear to anyone who takes the time to visit such a place that very few of the inmates are destitute of reason and intelligence. Even severely disturbed patients will have many periods of lucidity and calm. Should this be the state at the time a will is dictated, there would seem to be no reason for a later challenge. Let us say the patient is only lucid and relaxed ten percent of the time; i.e., that there is one chance in ten the will was written under proper mental circumstances. But the noninstitutionalized citizen also runs the risk of future psychiatric care and hospitalization. How can we ever know whether his will was not written during one of those periods which, when they become dominant, will lead to his institutionalization? We cannot know this, for we cannot know what is in the mind of any person. There is always a chance that we will honor wishes that were the product of fits and fancy, but the alternative is to dishonor those shaped by desire and deep conviction. The question, of course, is where to place the fulcrum. Is it to be closer to doubt or to credulity, and what consequences follow each of these biases? To move in the direction of doubt is to move away from the basic right of property. To move toward credulity is still to respect this right in principle, but to permit it to violate itself in practice. In one case, we abuse the right; in the other, we must permit a person (or his disease) the freedom of self-abuse.

This, however, appeals to a principle of justice, and not to the standing that should be accorded "social scientists" on matters of evidence. As in determinations of criminal responsibility, I can see very little room for such persons in cases of testamentary capacity. The right to dispose of one's possessions is far too fundamental to be challenged on such thin and largely opinionated grounds. A jury, properly instructed and educated by the testimony of those who knew the testator best and longest, should be able to reach a verdict as to the capacities of the testator at the time he wrote his will. They are not obliged to honor the wishes of a raving madman, but no "expert" is needed to identify so helpless and artless a person. All the expert can add is a label and some untried theory of causation. Both are irrelevant, and therefore so is the testimony.

Lest there be any confusion arising from this review of the issues, let me underscore the fact that I do not doubt that there are psychological or medical conditions or states that would strip a testator of his mental capacities, however these are defined. What justice seeks to respect in the matter of testacy are the *intentions* of the benefactor. For this reason, whatever removes or neutralizes or compromises his intentions affects the validity of his testaments to that extent. But there are few certainties in the business of life, and nearly none in the psychology of the individual. Accordingly, there is an inescapable need for the balancing of interests. On the one side, there is the interest of justice in respecting the rights, the *basic* rights, of ownership; on the other side, the related interest in establishing that by his actions and in light of his overall health and intelligence, the rightful owner was able to exercise his rights. If the criteria connected with the latter are made extremely strict, the former becomes the casualty. If they are made recklessly loose, any testament will be taken as valid merely on a showing that the testator signed it. Let us remember, however, that there were wills before there were social scientists, and thoughtful inquiries into such wills before there was "expert" testimony. Such inquiries proceeded from the claim that the testator was unfit to write a will, and it was this claim that carried the heaviest burden of proof. The lighter the burden becomes, the greater the risk that a basic right will be violated.

When the psychologist or psychiatrist is included in the inquiry, the justification is framed in terms of the desire to be certain that the deceased was competent, and the further desire to be certain that assessments of competence are not left to the indefinite and parochial tastes and biases of ordinary citizens or to their ignorance. Where such citizens are jurors, they are thought to be aided by "expert" testimony and are obliged to take such testimony as if it were evidence. But evidence is fact, whereas the overwhelming majority of statements given by the "experts" cannot possibly be factual and known to be factual. Furthermore, whatever it is about a layman that prevents us from trusting his reasoning in such matters must necessarily disqualify him from using such "evidence" for what can only be described as a *diagnosis*. In actual cases, the real evidence has to do with what Smith said in his will, how Smith conducted himself in life, what Smith's neighbors, friends, and relatives are able to say about him. Most of these facts will, of course, be subject to dispute and denial, but here a jury is able to weigh the total mass of attestations on both sides and arrive at a judgment. The only addition an "expert" can make to this mass of attestations is that of a label. He can say, for example, that in his profession those answering to the description that has been offered of the deceased are called "paranoid" or "manic-depressive" or "melancholic." He then might go on to say that these others often do irrational things and occasionally behave in a manner opposed to their real intentions. But this says nothing about Smith and, when examined carefully, it may say no more about the few other persons on whom the "expert" bases his diagnosis. Jurors ordinarily do not traffic in the argot of psychiatry, but they too will describe friends and acquaintances as being morose, vacillating, unpredictable, unreasonable, pleasant, bright, thoughtless, or selfish. Such ascriptions are not to be taken as diagnostic categories unless we are willing to take every display of individuality as a form of disease.

But not every manifestation of individuality qualifies as a disease. Indeed, it is not at all clear that any so qualifies as long as we define "disease" as a pathological conditon occurring in an organ or in organs of the body. This, however, has to do with theory, not with fact. The fact is this: when conduct leaves the boundaries within which ordinary persons function, and when all evidence of a connection between reason and action is lacking, the court of common experience judges the conduct to proceed from a state of madness. Here again we discover the *furiosus* standard, the one that served justice for the better part of two millennia. Every juror can recognize this criterion and can apply it to the instant case. No juror requires a label or the exposition of "experts" to recognize the madman. Is this not, however, all too gross, all too clumsy? Must we not be prepared to make finer discriminations? Well, this all depends upon our understanding of the human mind and our willingness to risk violating the basic rights of another on the basis of this understanding. Were there sound, generally accepted, firmly established, and clearly expressible categories of competence, and were these of a finer grain than *furiosus–non furiosus*, we would have both the right and the reason to adopt them. However, there are no such categories of competence, only categories by which to classify various varieties of individual differences. There is nothing in the fact of difference that establishes incompetence. No two persons are exactly alike in any significant respect, but this scarcely allows us to describe one thereby as being more competent than the other. Each person is at least to some degree eccentric according to the personal standards of another. But the criterion we call competence is, properly speaking, aloof to all such eccentricities except one: rationality. For purposes of testation, we would not even include the criterion of *knowledge*, since one could always insist that the testator would have written a different will had he possessed more knowledge. By competence we mean reason: the ability to anchor conclusions firmly to premises. The testator may be in error as to the premises. For example, he may be wrong in asserting that his sons do not love him, that the quack has enhanced his life, that his neighbor is a communist, that the media are hell-bent on ruining the nation. This, however, is only to establish the fallibility of the human imagination. We surely do not reserve the right to overturn a will merely on the showing that the testator was faulty in his premises, for then there could be no valid will ever written. What we must ask is whether the will expresses the intentions of its author, not whether it qualifies as an authoritative description of the facts of life.

To learn from "experts" that the deceased had this or that "feeling," this or that "morbid delusion," this or that "unreasonable fear," this or that "schizoid inclination" can, at the most, only increase our understanding of the difference between the deceased and other persons, including ourselves. In other words, it can at best only add to our definition of the meaning of "Mr. Smith." In addition to defining him as "the deceased party whose will is being contested," we can now go on to say "the deceased party, given to feelings of frustration and doubt, morbidly at odds with his own sons, and often the victim of his own imagination, whose will is being contested." Note, however, that we cannot tell the difference between Smith's frustration and our own; Smith's "morbid" attitude toward his sons and an enmity that is not "morbid"; Smith as the victim of his imagination and Smith simply as the author of the contents of his imagination. These qualifiers are the gift of the psychosocial point of view, not the gift of science or, alas, of fact. They are expressions of opinion, but the only "expert" opinion here can be that of the deceased. He has the same epistemological authority in the matter of his feelings toward his sons or his assessment of his neighbors as he has in the matter of pains and aches. They are uniquely his, and cannot be denied on the basis of evidence external to him. He may not know that his tooth aches because of a disease not in his tooth but in his maxillary nerve, but he cannot be "wrong" in stating that he has a toothache. Similarly, he cannot be wrong in stating that he believes his neighbors are communists, although they may not be. And the will he writes is based on what he believes to be true. To overturn it on the grounds that what he believes is not true is to subject every will to a fact test and, further, to assert that what counts is not the intentions but the intelligence of the testator. Even in this sorry circumstance, we would surely not be especially interested in the comments of psychiatrists or psychologists, for they are not experts with respect to the facts of the world. Nor are they experts on the nature of mind—and this includes, in particular, Smith's mind. The only possible expert on that subject is now deceased, and what is at issue is not his "mind" but his stated intentions. If property comes under the heading of a basic right, it is these that must be honored, even when foolish, aimless, and grounded in errors of fact.

6. Recent Illustrations

Lest the manufactured illustrations be taken as signs of no more than an active imagination, it is useful to examine actual and recent challenges to testamentary capacity. Let us begin with *Graham* v. *Darnell*, heard before the Texas Court of Civil Appeals in the summer of 1976, with none other than Billy Graham as one of the appellants.

Tom and Sadie Pruett were married in 1930 and had had three children, one of whom would come to be the appellee (Marilyn Pruett Darnell) in *Graham* v. *Darnell*. In 1949, Jimmie Pruett, a son, died, and two years later the Pruetts were divorced. One consequence of the divorce is that Tom Pruett and his surviving children became totally estranged.

In 1965, when the Pruett children were 32 and 31 years of age, Tom Pruett executed a "church will," the first instrument of such a nature ever signed by him. A second will was executed nine years later, naming Billy Graham as beneficiary. Seven months later, Tom Pruett died (29 January 1975). In March of the same year, Marilyn Darnell was joined by her brother in a petition seeking to block the probating of her father's will. In the subsequent non-jury trial, Judge Guy McNeely of the Wichita County Court denied application for probate and granted Mrs. Darnell's application for the continued temporary administration of her father's estate. Billy Graham et al. thereupon filed the appeal.

Of the controlling Texas legislation in such matters, one point is especially illuminating:

> Where contestants at initial stage timely resisted admission of any will to probate, burden of proving testamentary capacity was upon proponents of proffered wills, against whom judgment was rendered, and thus proponents' only available point of error on appeal was that judgment, and underlying findings for contestants, were so contrary to great weight and preponderance of evidence as to be clearly erroneous. (*Graham* v. *Darnell*, at 691)

Thus, once Mrs. Darnell raised a challenge to the testamentary capacity of her father at the time he executed the will, the burden shifted to the proponents (typically, the named beneficiaries) to establish the competence of the testator.

It was Mrs. Darnell's contention that her father harbored an insane enmity toward his children and was "deluded" as regards their true feelings toward him. Here the controlling point of law is:

> "Insane delusion", such as will vitiate last will and testament, is belief of state of supposed facts which do not exist and which no rational person would believe. (*Graham* v. *Darnell* at 691)

On appeal, no party contested Tom Pruett's knowledge of the nature of his estate or his knowledge of his children's existence and the nature of their kinship to him. Nor was there any suggestion that Billy Graham or his church employed any illegal method or in any manner defrauded or improperly influenced Tom Pruett in the matter of either of the wills executed by him. What proved to be decisive in this action was the evidence that the testator entertained "belief of a state of supposed facts that [did] not exist" and was, therefore, suffering from "an insane delusion." (*Graham* v. *Darnell* at 694)

> In brief there seems to be no question but that the deceased had been high tempered, emotional, an exceedingly harsh disciplinarian of his children, and a person disposed to "carry a grudge" against anyone. (Ibid. at 694)

There were many instances in which it was shown that his
actions and reactions to real and to imagined circumstances (in
which there was no foundation in fact) displayed his paranoid
condition earlier than 1949. As applied to many of these there
was medical opinion testimony by which the paranoia was
proved, supported upon delusions as a factor. (Ibid. at 695)

Accordingly, the Court of Appeals upheld the lower court,
convinced that sufficient evidence had been raised regarding Tom
Pruett's "capacity" to shift the burden of proving his sanity to the
proponents of the will. The Tom Pruett who comes out of the
testimony—excluding the delphic pronouncements of the "experts"—is an irascible, cranky, and suspicious fellow who is slow
to accept friendship and quick to dismiss it. It appears that he was
never really happily married and that he concluded, after the
divorce, that his children were sufficiently under the influence of
their mother to be poor candidates for a relationship with him.
There was some evidence—really no more than a claim—that his
son did try to establish contact but that he was rebuffed. What the
weight of evidence seems to support is the conclusion that not
many persons would have found Tom Pruett to be a very likeable
fellow, and that those who succeeded in getting close to him
would soon discover that this was an awkward position. We may
go even further and take the evidence as somehow proving that
Tom Pruett misjudged his children's true feelings and that his
contempt for them was unearned. But against all of this con-
jecture there stands a veritable wall of fact: the estate in question
was Tom Pruett's to dispose of as he saw fit; he intended to leave
his children out of his will; he intended Billy Graham to be the
beneficiary of his will; and he arrived at this position free of fraud
or duress. In addition, those contesting the will had had no
contact with Pruett for the better part of a quarter of a century;
they had given him no service, no kindness, and no comfort.
There is surely no moral sense in which they deserved to obtain
his estate, and there is no legal requirement that a man provide
for persons (including offspring) now in their thirties and totally
self-sufficient. That Tom Pruett's will might have been different
had he not been confused as to Marilyn Darnell's concern for him
is a possibility that has the same standing as any other. Thus, he
might not have named Billy Graham as the beneficiary had he
believed, as some rational persons have insisted, that Christianity

is a false belief. Since no one lived Tom Pruett's life except Tom Pruett, no one can say that his convictions were entirely unfounded or that no rational person would share them. So-called rational persons entertain any number of beliefs that other so-called rational persons judge to be ridiculous, groundless, or utterly impossible. One man's raison d'être is another man's paranoia.

Perhaps the most vulnerable benefactors are those who live long enough for some of their powers to decline. Many states are like Texas in that probate can be blocked by raising the question of "capacity" and thereby requiring proponents of the will to prove sanity. As we have seen in the previous chapter, this is an immense burden under the best circumstances and a virtually unsupportable one where the party at issue is not only dead but lived into his eighties or nineties.

In the *Matter of Kaplan,* just this burden fell to the beneficiary named in Frank Kaplan's will. The deceased had lived and worked for many years after retirement at the Will Rogers Hospital in Saranac, New York. He was essentially a patient who continued to perform odd jobs after his official retirement from the hospital. As Kaplan grew older, he became more emotionally volatile and suspicious, harbored apparently unfounded fears, and suffered from episodes of sullen withdrawal. Nevertheless, he did visit an attorney in the company of his sister, and on that occasion and in the presence of a secretary, the lawyer, and his sister, he made out a will. These witnesses all testified, when the will was subsequently challenged, that Frank Kaplan had comported himself in a reasonable way, had displayed full knowledge of what he was doing, was in full understanding of the nature of his estate and the nature of his relationship to his offspring and other relatives. That is, at the time the instrument was executed, eyewitnesses report that the testator was lucid, comprehending, and self-controlled.

The Essex County Surrogate Court denied probate on the grounds that the will's contestants had successfully raised the question of Frank Kaplan's "capacity." Testimony from hospital staff (particularly one nurse) indicated that the deceased had behaved in a bizarre manner on a number of occasions. A physician, Dr. Blide, testified that Mr. Kaplan's memory was poor for recent events, that he had fits of dizziness, and that he suffered

from "cerebral vascular arteriosclerosis."* Dr. Blide noted that
Mr. Kaplan was also given to "paranoid ideation." Accordingly,
the court decided that sufficient challenges to capacity had been
raised in order to shift the burden to the proponents of the will,
and this decision was upheld on appeal.

Let us recognize, however, the nature of this shifted burden.
Mr. Kaplan asked to see an attorney for the purpose of executing a
will. He made arrangements to be taken to the attorney's office
where he comported himself in a reasonable and proper manner.
He specified the terms of his will in such a way as to create neither
suspicion nor concern in the minds of those in attendance, including the entirely neutral secretary and the lawyer. What more
can the will's proponents adduce in support of their contention
that Mr. Kaplan had the capacity to do what, in fact, he did?
Dissenting from the opinion of the Court of Appeals, Judge
Herlihy noted,

> What the majority does not recognize is that the prima facie
> case establishes a lucid interval in terms of senile dementia and
> the record is devoid of *any* proof that the decedent did not
> enjoy such a lucid interval at the time the will was prepared
> and executed. The medical opinion of the psychiatrist is im-
> material and irrelevant as it is not based upon the *fact* of a
> lucid interval on July 17, 1972. (*Kaplan* at 432)

But of course the opinion of the psychiatrist would have been
equally irrelevant and immaterial had he examined Mr. Kaplan
on the very day the will was signed and found him to be suffering
from "paranoid ideation" if, ten minutes later, a reasonable and
disinterested attorney and his secretary were to find nothing wrong
with Mr. Kaplan. The point is not that a reasonable and disinterested attorney has the same competence as a physician to detect
physical disease, but that "paranoid ideation" is not a known
physical disease and there is no *medical* or *scientific* diagnostic
method available for its detection. If it is to be detected, the
method is just that sort of observation, interview, and interaction
conducted in the attorney's office. As Judge Herlihy went on to
say,

---

*It would be extremely rare to discover a ninety-year-old man who did not have
this condition.

The apparent last wishes of a person should not be set aside upon mere speculation that he was *then* incompetent. (Ibid. at 433)

In such cases, the social sciences again must be largely excluded. If the testator is indistinguishable from "an infant, a brute, or a wild beast," no expert will be required to make the "diagnosis." If, on the other hand, disinterested parties describe him as an outwardly rational and deliberate person who, by all the standards of common sense, seems to know the nature of terms of his will, then, his will be done! The balance to be struck in such matters is that which finds at one end the prospect of denying a person the right to dispose harmlessly of that which is rightfully his and, at the other end, the possibility that his rational wishes are not actually reflected by the terms of the will. Since his preparation of the will is prima facie evidence of the former and since psychiatric opinions cannot claim the same standing, the appropriate course of jural action would seem to be obvious.

Notes

All early cases referred to in this chapter can be found either in Vol. V or Vol. VI of *Series F, Significant Contributions to the History of Psychology,* D. N. Robinson, Ed. (University Publications of America).

A question that will naturally arise in connection with my remarks on inheritance has to do with the "rights" of those named by the benefactor. That is, given that the testator has a *basic* right to dispose of what is his, what is the standing of the ownership resulting from the bequest? Its standing is that of a *derived* right, and this standing remains throughout all successive benefactions. But derived rights are nearly indistinguishable from privileges and other grants. As a practical matter, beneficiaries generally do mix their own labor with their bequests and therefore do earn a *basic* right to that part of the total estate that comes into being as a result of this labor. Typically, the mix is of such a nature that it would be impractical and impracticable to attempt to separate Smith's share from Smith's father's share. Yet there are also cases of Smith's doing *nothing* with a bequest other than drawing against it for his own benefit. There may be sound social reasons for permitting this privilege, but I can think of no basis on which such a practice can enjoy the status of a *basic* right. It is derived, and I doubt it can be "rightfully" passed on by its possessor. Testaments, of course, often refer to, "my children, their children, and their children's children," but this is the language of the potentate, not that of the owner of property. It is the sort of language a pasha uses when he announces what the law will be, "for all time to come." I see no inconsistency in honoring an owner's right to dispose of his possessions and in defining disposal as a complete action which can be taken only once.

What, then, becomes of the estate when the first beneficiary dies? In this case, I believe the issue can only be rightfully settled by examining the use to which the bequest was put. The state should have the right to challenge hereditary claimants on the grounds that the initial beneficiary did not use his derived right of interest in such a way as to convert it to a basic right. I note all this in a merely provisional way to give additional sense to my use of *basic rights, derived rights,* and *privileges;* not to advance a theory of testation.

4 Voluntary and Involuntary Commitments

Over the centuries, and under a wide variety of forms of governance, a number of principles of coercion have been used to justify actions taken against individuals to constrain their freedoms. Before examining these principles, it is important to set forth certain givens by which coercion of any type comes into being. We must take as a given, for example, that social organization itself, as opposed to the life of a hermit, involves persons of differing temperaments, abilities, opinions, tastes, needs, and goals, and that these differences will lead to conflicts and collisions. Under such circumstances, it is also a given that some conflicts or collisions will place in jeopardy the claimed rights of one group as some other person or group exercises the same right or different rights. Accordingly, for there to be peace within any diverse community or state, something more than rational persuasion must be available. Once we adopt methods of persuasion or control beyond that of the power of reason, we are engaged in an activity that is *coercive*. An act is coercive—rather than merely persuasive—when its intended outcome is not simply compliance but the removal of every possibility of defiance or resistance. The goal of persuasion is concurrence; that of coercion, control. The former strives to regulate conduct by altering the judgments on which it is based, whereas the latter regulates conduct independently of the actor's judgments or motives. When the demands of majorities or authorities are implicitly unreasonable, control can be achieved only through coercion, and the same is true when the actor is inaccessible to the power of rational persuasion. Thus, to the extent that any community possesses unreasonable members, and to the extent that any government may be unjust, coercion stands as an abiding fixture of social life. The question, therefore, is not whether coercive measures are just, but when they are. To address this question is to examine the justificatory grounds that have been advanced traditionally in defense of forced compliance. In their largest projections, these grounds may be classified as religious, political, and moral. In practice, there has been much overlap among the three, but in principle each is distinguishable from the other two. Moreover, within each there are subtler subdivisions of justification.

1. Religious Grounds of Coercion

The history of theocracies does not present the spectacle of uninterrupted superstition and irrationalism, as is sometimes averred, but a collection of assertions and practices common to most varieties of social organization. We find laws, magistrates, trials, rules of evidence, measured punishment, and grounds of excuse and forgiveness. What separates theocracies from secular polities is, in large part, the source of *first principles*. In the religious state, the first principles are the gift of revelation. The "truths" and laws are revealed, and their binding nature derives principally from the alleged powers and virtues of the divinity. A law is good and just to the extent that it expresses the will or desire of the gods. The ancient Greek word for justice, *dike*, in its earliest acceptation referred to a bifurcating path, and the "right" way— the *dike*—was the path ordained by the Olympians. It was not for mere man to question the will of the gods, but to conform his conduct to this will. Moreover, it was the obligation of all members of the community to see that this divine will was honored and to do this by forcing compliance on those who, for whatever reason, disobeyed the revealed laws. *Ostracism*, in ancient Greece, was an official ten-year period of exile, a penalty designed to spare the community the wrath of the gods summoned by the crimes and heresies of the ostracized.

Whether revelation takes place through apparitions, signs, omens, or the direct and public intervention of deities, the task that falls to successive generations is that of interpretation. The gods do not reveal themselves to all equally and at all times, and their laws generally do not cover every possible case and context. Thus, the theocracy is governed by priests, prophets, oracles, or magicians—a small group or a single person thought of as having unobstructed access to the gods. It is this class that either announces the law or passes on the validity of those laws written by others. It is this same class that determines what counts as evidence and what establishes guilt and proper punishment. I should note that it was of some benefit to the history of philosophy that the ancient Greek oracles were consistently "delphic" and thereby required ordinary mortals to think for themselves. Still, even at the height of its achievements, the Hellenic world was theocratic enough to execute Socrates for failing to honor the gods.

In the Judaic, Christian, and Islamic worlds—and in the vast majority of all theocracies—the principal divinities are male, and the revealed word is passed on to and through men. Where the deities include goddesses, there will generally be found priestesses, but on the whole, the dominant flavor of theocratic regimes is paternalistic. Within communities thus directed, the chief justification for coercion is *religious paternalism:* the gods have spoken to (or through) the "fathers," and the latter have the right to force members of the community to obey the divine laws. The aim of law is the promotion of reverence, and coercion is just to the extent that it honors the divine commandments.

2. Political Grounds of Coercion

Few states, no matter how secular, are utterly destitute of theocratic elements, and no substantial modern state is destitute of theocratic roots. But there are differences between the genuine polity and the religious congregation, and the most important ones come into being when revealed truth and divine commands are replaced by discovered and disputed truths and secular laws. Where the aim of theocracy is the promotion of reverence, the aim of political law is order. The purpose of order is largely exhausted by the considerations of military defense and material prosperity. Laws are written to control and coordinate the activities of the population. They derive their sanctions from their ability to preserve the state and enhance its powers. Whatever conduces to disunity is a threat to survival and is, therefore, proscribed. The lawgiver, the judge, and the law enforcer may come into being in any number of ways: by force of arms, by hereditary succession, by election, or by valor, but it is not the method of selection that categorizes a state as purely "political." It is purely political to the extent that its ultimate goal is survival and growth. In such a state, coercion is justified on these grounds. What is right or wrong is so only to the degree that the state's ultimate interests are promoted or threatened. As in theocracies, individual freedoms are not necessarily ignored or denied, but are weighed according to the ultimate standard. In a theocracy, one is "free" only to respect the divine will; in a polity, only to serve the state. In both, a high premium may be placed on individual energy, genius, creativity, bravery, and personality. Such talents and traits are not celebrated because they are vested in individuals, however, but because they are useful to the state.

Purely political states are neither invariably ruthless nor invariably injudicious or "fascistic." On Aristotle's account, the good state provides the opportunity for that which all rational beings desire, and one's commitment to the needs and the prosperity of the state is based on this recognition. Whatever rights the individual possesses are inextricably tied to duties, for there can be no right without a corresponding obligation. As the state is the source of all rights, it must be the object of all duties. But Aristotle does not stop with this. He goes on to recognize that the essential mission of a state is to promote virtue it its citizens, and this brings us to the state not as a merely political entity, but as a moral agent.

3. Moral Grounds of Coercion

Where the goal of theocracy is reverence and that of purely political aggregations order, the aim of a moral state is the goodness of the individual. This is not absent in theocracies or in purely political organizations, but it is not present in the same way as it is in the moral state, for in such a state what is "good" is neither revealed nor treated as a means to some higher good. Rather, it is the raison d'être, and it is discovered by the patient application of reason to human desire. On the whole, the moral state turns to coercion only when persuasion has failed. Its legitimacy is not established by power, by divinity, or by prosperity, but by the appeal its laws make to any rational being when he is also a reflective being. These same laws will honor whatever is just in revelation and whatever is virtuous in order, but the force of these laws springs neither from direct contact with deities nor the mere power of enforcement. Such a state may be entirely theocratic in its organization; it may be monarchial, plutocratic, democratic— none of this much matters. But if it is structurally theocratic, the laws will spring from what is finally the rationality of the gods and their commitment to what are the universalized desires of moral beings; if democratic, from the refined expression of the common moral sense; if monarchial, from the sovereign's loyalty to the moral foundations of social life.

4. Libertarianism

Since J. S. Mill's *On Liberty,* there has been something of a principled ground for *privatism,* and a general suspiciousness toward factions, groups, or governments that would exercise coercive means to bring individuals into line. Mill's doctrine limits justifiable coercion to contexts in which the exercise of the individual's liberty violates or is very likely to violate the rights of others. Accordingly, a person is absolutely unconstrained in his thoughts and constrained in his actions only to prevent such violations. Even suicide must be allowed once it has been established that the prospective victim knows what he is about to do and reaffirms his decision to do it.

There are three general categories into which actions of a negative social value fall: *harm, offense,* and *nuisance.* In Milton's *Aereopagitica,* only what conduces to public harm warrants censorship. Mill took the same arguments for a free press and extended them to the entire spectrum of social interactions. Both Milton and Mill offered quasi-utilitarian supports for their libertarianism. In the realm of opinion and knowledge, a society can never be so sure of its understandings as to rule out the possibility of being corrected. The best course for a fallible species is to permit the fullest and freest collision of ideas. What is obviously false is thereby exposed and what is true but hitherto unsuspected now enters the public domain. In addition, citizens in such a climate are made more responsible by having to weigh and act

upon competing ideas and perspectives. The process inescapably
leads to differences of style, outlook, and belief. Minorities accordingly will often be judged as offensive and as dangerous to
the accepted canons of sound judgment. However, the fact that
they offend some persons—even most persons—cannot serve to
justify their suppression. Milton's formulation of the principle
cannot be improved. He speaks of books being

> as lively, and as vigorously productive, as those fabulous
> Dragons teeth; and being sown up and down, may chance to
> spring up armed men. And yet on the other hand unlesse
> warinesse be us'd, as good almost kill a Man as kill a good
> Booke; who kills a man kills a reasonable creature, Gods image;
> but hee who destroyes a good Booke, kills reason it selfe, kills
> the Image of God, as it were in the eye. (*Aereopagitica*, 1644)

Mill was concerned with more than literary pursuits. He was
troubled by the tendency of mediocrity to become dominant and
by the power of conventionality to murder genius in its crib.

> There is one characteristic of the present direction of public
> opinion peculiarly calculated to make it intolerant of any
> marked demonstration of individuality. The general average of
> mankind are not only moderate in intellect, but also moderate
> in inclinations: they have no tastes or wishes strong enough to
> incline them to do anything unusual, and they consequently
> do not understand those who have. . . . Now, in addition to
> this fact which is general, we have only to suppose that a
> strong movement has set in towards the improvement of morals,
> and it is evident what we have to expect. In these days such a
> movement has set in; much has actually been effected in the
> way of increased regularity of conduct and discouragement of
> excesses; and there is a philanthropic spirit abroad, for the
> exercise of which there is no more inviting field than the moral
> and prudential improvement of our fellow-creatures. . . . Its
> idea of character is to be without any marked character; to
> maim by compression, like a Chinese lady's foot, every part of
> human nature which stands out prominently, and tends to
> make the person markedly dissimilar in outline to common-
> place humanity. (*On Liberty*, 1849)

Let us recognize that Mill was not defending *everything* a person
might do that is physically unharmful. There is a difference
between a libertine and libertarian, and Mill was personally and
philosophically the latter, not the former. In this same famous
essay, he acknowledges that

> there are many acts which, being directly injurious only to the
> agents themselves, ought not to be legally interdicted, but
> which, if done publicly, are a violation of good manners, and
> coming thus within the category of offenses against others,
> may rightly be prohibited. (Ibid.)

Thus Mill permits the actor the fullest range of actions—including self-inflicted injuries—short of causing harm or significant offense to others. Private actions are the actor's own business.

What Mill was opposing was paternalism in all its forms. He was not opposed to the public morality but to the imposition of it on those of a different inclination and with uncommon needs. True to the intellectual spirit of his age, he conceived of civilization as an evolving affair, a process of becoming. This was true of nations and of individuals. The growth of knowledge must be at the forfeiture of older opinions; the growth of justice, at the forfeiture of older prejudices. Thus, any threat to personal liberty was not only unjust but lethal to the true interests of society.

Also in keeping with the Victorian belief in human perfectibility was Mill's generous prediction that the unconstrained individual would surely choose the better rather than the worse course and that, on the whole, a tolerant climate would yield goodness by conviction rather than obedience by compulsion. But he did not take goodness itself to be an entirely settled matter. It was to *utilitarianism* that he looked for the best thinking on the matter. Having freed himself of Bentham's troubled version of the ism, Mill calmly insisted that "utility is the ultimate source of moral obligations." He was convinced that, in the last analysis, only that which conduces to pleasure or allows us to escape or avoid pain is *good*; and only that which removes pleasure or the opportunity for it, or causes suffering is evil. There is in all of this a sturdy compatibility between the libertarian political philosophy and the utilitarian social ethics. What has brought more pleasure into the world than liberty? What has caused more suffering than the want of it? How can an action that has pain as its end be defended as "just"? And what added burden of justification attaches to any action that has human happiness as its end?

But this is all only at the grossest and most impersonal level of analysis. Once we cut beneath the surface of libertarianism and utilitarianism, we discover a glut of practical and conceptual problems. For example, suppose we accept the "happiness" principle and commit society to the promotion of the happiness of every member. We soon come to realize, however, that an indissoluble link connects happiness with the capacity for it. How can the pleasures of literature be known to the illiterate citizen? How can the happiness of gainful employment be shared by those devoid of skills of any kind? Thus, in the interest of the individual's future happiness, we compel him to complete an elementary education. Has his liberty now not been abridged? Well, say the defenders of libertarianism, this pertains only to children who, after all, must be educated if they are to have any truly human liberties at all. But what is it that marks a person as a child? Is it merely age, or is there not also the element of intellectual and emotional maturity? And, if the latter, are we not then permitted by the same logic to require the education of childish adults?

One way out of the bind is to remind ourselves that Mill's utilitarianism embraced the happiness of mankind in general, and defined moral obligations in terms of good *on the whole*. This will render the ism compatible with all practices a rational community judges to be essential to civilization, but it will yield one ism at odds with the other, for how can all the terms of libertarianism be honored by a system which, in principle, allows the regulation of individual conduct solely according to what benefits society on the whole? Mill thought of these problems as being drawn largely from the lexicon of the casuist who refused to look to human history for evidence that would put such problems aside. Here again is the hopeful Mill who cannot conceive of significant numbers of persons choosing not to learn, not to evolve, not to prosper in the broadest moral and cultural respects. But even if the historical record defended his optimism, there is no guarantee that the future will. We have every right to demand of a moral system something more than rough agreement with past tendencies. Nevertheless, utilitarianism as framed by Mill possesses unique strengths as a system of ethics, and its flaws are not unique. As with any set of general ethical propositions, it is embarrassed by any number of ad hoc cases. When tied to libertarianism, it does take on the special burden of any "happiness" doctrine that must come face to face with human inertia, weakness, ignorance, malevolence, and confusion. Whether it is the happiness of the individual or that of society that is the goal, the failings of the individual person call for remedial measures which, by their nature, are likely to be constraining or even oppressive. Mill did not find the way out of this, nor has anyone else.

5. American Justice as Eclectic Ethics

America may be said to have borrowed its riches and shared its wealth. Even in the short space of two centuries, it has developed a commendable intellectual history, but the moral and jural foundations of the United States are largely derived from older Anglo-European sources. Our nation has been as much the melting pot for ideas as for ethnic groups and, if anything, the former have been more diverse than the latter. Our laws and our system of justice reveal not only the obvious Lockean and libertarian elements, but, more subtly, transcendental and rationalistic elements as well.

But in referring to "our system of justice," I have in mind a set of procedures designed to create a smaller set of protections. I do not have in mind the actual justice handed down by this system, however, since this has varied considerably over periods in which the procedures have been constant. Perhaps it is too strong to say that "justice" itself has varied; and, if not too strong, it is certainly to risk begging the very question of justice. Let me say instead that considerations of social utility are often in conflict with those of individual liberty and that, over the decades, the conflict has been resolved sometimes in favor of the former, sometimes in favor of the latter. This, however, is not a formal property of the "system," except in the trivial sense that the system was designed by and for the use of social beings.

In its eclectic ethics, American jurisprudence has been tirelessly devoted to the so-called rights of the individual but has not arrived at a settled position regarding the nature of the individual. Throughout the eighteenth century and all but the last decade of the nineteenth, the nation was organized politically as a democracy but was theocratic at its foundations. In those years, the clergy stood as the final authority on matters moral. Although an established national religion was proscribed by the Constitution, the establishment of religion was the gray eminence behind all significant political actions. The last great triumph of the American theocrats was the prohibition amendment, but even at the time of its passage the signs of secular hegemony were apparent.

Under the influence of the theocracy—the government without portfolio—the individual was judged as a child of God, and the law was but one means by which to aid imperfect beings in fulfilling their duty to the Creator. A form of legal moralism prevailed by which free men would fashion a government loyal to the will of God. To be free, however, was to be able to do that which was right. Even Jefferson, whose own metaphysical ruminations led him toward a humanistic agnosticism, was careful to honor religion as the very foundation of the polity. By Jefferson's time, no one could be put to death for the worship of false gods (the penalty articulated in the Colonial Laws of Massachusetts, 1644), but Christianty was so integral a feature of the entire American experience that legislation and politics itself were expressions of it.

At the same time, the existence of an independent United States was won by the rejection of monarchial powers; by the triumph of "common sense" over the pretentions of a sovereign. The case for independence was chiefly one forged in the imagination and daily experience of the common man and tried in the court of ordinary intelligence. American freedoms were not conferred, but won, and the victors were *individuals* driven by personal interests and summoned by a rhetoric beholden to these interests. Central among them was, of course, the right to worship according to one's convictions, but there were utterly secular interests as well. Thus, at the very outset, we discover in the American experience a wedge inserted between practical politics and the ethics of a (veiled) theocracy. By the middle years of the nineteenth century, it was generally apparent that the very grounds on which national independence had been secured provided legal, if not moral, justification for individualism. It was about the same time that Tocqueville alerted the thinking world to the basic tension between liberty and equality; the tension that nearly guaranteed a rigid social and economic hierarchy in any setting in which individual talent and initiative were given untrammeled opportunity for expression.

> The good things that freedom brings are seen only as time passes, and it is always easy to mistake the cause that brought them about. The advantages of equality are felt immediately,

and it is daily apparent where they came from. Political liberty occasionally gives sublime pleasure to a few. Equality daily gives each man in the crowd a host of small enjoyments. (*Democracy in America*, Part II, Ch. 1)

What impressed Tocqueville most and soonest after his arrival in America was "The religious atmosphere. . . . The longer I stayed in the country, the more conscious I became of the important political consequences resulting from this novel situation" (Ibid., Part I, Ch. 9). What he most feared—following Milton, Mill, Jefferson, Madison, and countless students of democracies—was the tyranny of the majority. Together, these two factors, America's essentially religious character and her powerful majoritarianism, had taming effects on each other. The former, with its attachment to universal brotherhood, its emphasis on public responsibility, and its special philanthropy, worked hand in glove with the individual's penchant for liberty, property, and order. When Emerson insisted that "our majesty is work," he was only echoing the Parable of the Talents, which obliged each person to realize the potentialities bestowed on him by the Creator. The nation was united behind two millennia of Christian teachings; teachings that emphasized "just deserts," the "sanctity" of the individual soul, that freedom of the will by which moral beings are ultimately judged. There was already a tyranny of the majority, but it derived its standing not from being a majority but from the nearly universally accepted authority of its moral prescriptions. In the first century of the American republic, we discover a singular rapprochement achieved among the theological, political, and moral justifications for coercion. The spirit of the laws emerged from the first of these; their power from the second; their hold on the public conscience from the third.

With the dawn of the secular state—a state not merely stripped of theological influence but aggressively opposed to such influence—a new source of moral authority had to be found, for in its absence only political power would fill the vacuum. That new source has turned out to be majoritarianism itself, which has installed the social sciences in the office once held by the clergy. Where the majority was once "right" because it subscribed to the tenets of theology, it is now "right" simply because it is the majority. The historical marriage between political democracy and moral theocracy has ended, and the new alliance is one that unites power with popular enthusiasms. The priest has been displaced by the pollster. Under the reign of the psychosocial point of view, the majority no longer condemns individuality as heresy, but as illness. The new justification for coercion is no longer moral, but medical, and the judiciary may be said to labor under what Carlyle called "the noble omnipotence of sympathy."

6. Welfarism

Entire libraries would be required to house all the articles and books addressed to the relationship between the individual and society. This is scarcely the occasion for cooking up another theory or for recounting those that commanded popular assent in the past. Nor is there space to "solve" the free will versus determinism controversy. It is enough to point out that the past century has hosted an increasingly environmentalistic theory of human psychology and that this psychology supports both a "spectator" theory of knowledge and a theory of conduct that emphasizes passivity and reaction rather than action. Today's psychosocial perspective is materialistic and behavioristic. Human activity is judged as being the outcome immediately of biological drives, urges, motives, and states, and more distantly as the result of a "reinforcement" history. Thus, the individual is essentially formed by "society," his behavior being the inevitable consequence of anatomy and conditioning.

The first casualty of this perspective is, of course, the individual himself, who can never rise higher than his past experience and cannot be expected to resist the summons of his physiology. Since he could not choose his family, his teachers, his talents, and his native propensities, he can hardly be judged as being fully responsible for their effects on his conduct and general approach to society. It thereupon becomes the duty of those fortunate enough not to have been victimized to institute remedial measures—not punishment—when one of society's failures departs from the norms of social commerce. Society's proper business is the *welfare* of every citizen. It must see to his education, his health, his diet, his recreation. And when it has failed a person in these regards, it then must own up to its crimes and provide a method by which past denials and neglect are neutralized. There is, after all, an explanation for every infraction: Smith was abandoned by his parents; there were no proper "role models" for him; he was despised by his kindergarten teacher; his peers made fun of his limp; his neighborhood revered violence; television set a bad example. In the circumstance, *anyone* might be expected to turn out as unfortunately as Smith has. Is justice served by consigning such a person to a prison, filled with hardened criminals who will simply continue his education in futility and malice?

The first thing to be noticed in all of this is that it cannot claim to be more than arrant opinion, and that as an opinion it has precious little to support it. The side of it that leans on the "behavioral sciences" is the weakest, chiefly because these "sciences" either fail to support the opinion or provide evidence that is irrevelant to the matter at hand. As I have noted, these are not sciences at all, but a collection of experimental studies addressed to the relationship between the activities of animals and the regimen of rewards and punishments mechanically dispensed in the conditioning chamber. At the height of their modern achievement, these "sciences" recall to us that practice makes perfect and that most living things avoid pain and seek out pleasure, all other factors being equal. None of this is new, of course, except for the need to establish such verities in a laboratory. That they have little bearing on any important part of the debate on "human nature" is obvious. When Thomas Aquinas undertook to prove freedom of the will, one proof he adduced was the efficacy of reward and punishment, for unless we are assumed to be free to choose one and eschew the other, there can be no basis on which either could affect our conduct. In other words, the fact that rewards and punishments influence us is not an argument against, but *for* human freedom, or at least for choice. But more to the point, these studies of rats and pigeons—and occasionally persons—do not proceed under the light of universal laws, are not drawn from the established principles of the developed sciences, and are not able to offer anything beyond modest correlations and immodest generalizations from them. If in fact all human actions are determined, and are determined by something other than the actor's own determination, we do not know what the determinants are. That they include the ordinary seductions and temptations of life there is no doubt, but it was just these that the law and its penalties were designed to control.

It is in the nature of *welfarism* to deny personal responsibility. We only judge ourselves as having the right to step in and manipulate the lives of others when we are satisfied that others have not acted, cannot act, and will not act responsibly in their own affairs. Nor does the welfarist retreat in the face of the beneficiary's protests, for now he simply assumes that the victim is so far gone as not to recognize how desperate his situation is. Having enjoyed few of the bounties of life, he has developed no taste for them.

What separates this from the unblushing imperialism of the old days is, first, the fact that it is imposed on one's own countrymen, not citizens of a foreign state; and second, that it is defended as a therapy rather than as the dictatorial impositions of the mighty. It is not the religious balm of old, since it is not designed to appeal to the moral side of the recipient and is not even drawn from the realm of moral discourse. Instead, it is drawn from the "data"; those morally blind facts that are alleged to tell us what is good, what is sound, and what is desirable. It surely is not political in its aims, for one of the chief objectives of welfarism is to spare those who have misbehaved from the penalties the political community has established. It is not moral; it is not political. What is it, then? It is, I submit, the ultimate triumph of equalitarianism over libertarianism; the sort of enterprise undertaken by implicitly tyrannical majorities when their consciences have been forged in the kilns of utility and democracy. The religious element survives in the form of a mawkish sympathy for "our brothers." The political element surfaces as the actions of a psychologized judiciary. And the moral side—the side that calls itself "secular humanism"—appears as nothing but the "social sciences." The emphasis now shifts from rights and their attendant obligations to needs and their satisfaction. The result in law is the conversion of courts into clinics.

Under the weight of a welfarist theory of society, both the individual and the judicial system come to subscribe to a number of premises, each of which either overlooks, depreciates, or rejects a fundamental principle of justice. This can be seen in both civil and criminal proceedings, and in both voluntary commitment and involuntary commitment to therapeutic centers. A few words on each of these are in order.

7. *Voluntary (Self-) Commitment*

What must be appreciated in the matter of commitment to a psychiatric or "mental" hospital is that the hospital is an institution in which the principles of governance are set by the administrative officers. These principles are different from those that operate in society and are often at odds with any number of Constitutional protections and guarantees. In many states, even at this late date, patients may not be permitted to send or receive uncensored mail. (In most states, this is still the case except for letters to and from counsel and to and from one's personal physician.) Patients are confined to the rooms and grounds of the institution. The right to be visited is governed, as is the choice of visitors and the duration of visits. Codes of dress and conduct are uniformly applied and enforced. Diet is controlled, as are the nature and frequency of medications, treatments, amusements, and assigned tasks. These and many more restrictions are common to all such institutions, and they apply as much to the patient who has committed himself as to those who have been committed involuntarily. Thus for all (libertarian) social and political purposes, these institutions should be recognized as prisons, not as hotels or retreats. They are, like prisons, implicitly coercive environments in that the options made available to the inmates are under the control of others and can be used for the purpose of establishing compliance and control. In principle, such institutions have therapy and not punishment as their objective, and this may be thought of as distinguishing them from prisons. Yet prisons, too, are now spoken of as "rehabilitative" in their mission rather than merely punitive. Moreover, those locked away in prisons are there for a determined period of time set by the nature of their crimes; whereas (it is alleged) those in mental hospitals will be released once cured, and are not actually "guilty" of anything.

Such distinctions, in actual practice, are more argumentative than factual. The specified sentence handed down by the criminal courts is guaranteed by the Eighth and the Fourteenth Amendments and is rooted in that moral principle that requires punishment to be proportioned to the offense. It is just this principle that is violated by indeterminate sentences, and it is just such sentences that are involved when psychiatrists and psychologists are given the power to determine when a given patient is "cured." It is true, of course, that the patient who commits himself can secure his release—usually within two to five days—simply by informing the medical staff or supervisor of his intentions. Still, in practice, the tendency to comply with the judgment of "experts"—to do what the doctor says—is very great indeed. Told that he is still quite ill, that he will be a heavy burden on his family and friends, that he will not be able to function in society, that he needs far greater supervision than the outside world can provide, even the voluntary patient is quite likely to defer to the authorities. And the involuntary patient has no such option.

The voluntary patient finds himself in a mental hospital generally in one of two ways: either he comes to sense that he no longer can "function" adequately in the "real world," or those in his immediate environment reach this conclusion and impress it on him. In most cases, the presenting symptoms are either intense anxiety or severe depression. Not uncommonly there is a history of an unhappy marriage, unsuccessful employment, and unrewarding relationships. There may also be a history of episodic violence, an attempted suicide, a bout with alcoholism or drug addiction, or several confrontations with the law. More often than not, the patient has had some contact with a therapist or counselor. There are also many cases drawn from families at odds with one member; aged relatives who are a burden; eccentric and unemployable relatives who are a burden; intellectually defective persons who, nonetheless, can give their consent to be institutionalized. In brief, we may say that a rich diversity of persons and problems constitute the population of voluntary patients at any large mental institution. All that can be said equally of all of them is that they have *consented* to be hospitalized.

It should be noted, however, that all moral and jural considerations do not evaporate once the element of "consent" has been introduced. We are not entitled to do anything and everything to a person merely because he has consented. We cannot, for example, enslave him, torture him, strip him of his properties, or end his life just because he has consented. This is only to acknowledge that some rights cannot even be given away; put another way, that no one has the right to break the law or to encourage others to break the law even where the lawbreaker or conspirator is himself the victim of the crime. In addition, the very concept of consent entails a degree of competence and knowledge. Suppose, for example, that one were to approach a child of three and were to say in a playfully dramatic way, "Wouldn't it be fun, Tommy, to be dropped from a big building and to fly all the way to the ground?"; then suppose the child were to nod approvingly and ask to be so dropped. We would not count this as a bona fide consent, for the child clearly would not understand the consequences of such an adventure. The point here is that for us to have any confidence in the consent given by the voluntarily committed mental patient, we would have to be reasonably certain at least of the following: (1) that he knew the nature of the setting to which he was committing himself; (2) that he was aware of the constraints on his liberties that would exist within this setting; (3) that he had a knowledge of the sorts of treatments available to him and the prognosis in light of these treatments; (4) that he was correct in his appraisal of the likely consequences of noncommitment; and (5) that he was correct in assuming that necessary therapies and facilities could not be provided as readily, as economically, and as effectively outside the institution.

There is something of a Catch-22 in all of this, however. If a prospective patient were actually apprised of the conditions prevailing in most mental hospitals, if he knew that the prognosis was not significantly different whether he entered or avoided such hospitals, if he knew further that in half or even two-thirds of the cases therapy of any kind would not produce better results than those achieved through the mere passage of time—if he knew all of this and still insisted on being institutionalized, we might be inclined to judge him as mad! But let us take the more relevant case, in which Smith does not walk in off the street and ask to be committed, but in which a judge in a criminal action gives the defendant the "option" of going to prison or committing himself to a mental hospital. Given these alternatives, we can only blush in the face of the word "consent." Prisons are notoriously hostile and shameful places, in which indignity is heaped on indignity. A sensible person will do whatever is necessary to avoid them, and this surely includes "voluntarily" committing himself to a hospital.

It is but one more of the ironies generated by the psychosocial point of view that the jurists we come to think of as humane, enlightened, and progressive are those who look to the "medical model" as an alternative to penal incarceration. In the typical instance, Judge Jones looks down at poor Smith—a (usually) young felon from a broken home; poor Smith who, for the fourth time, has been dragged before the court—twice for dealing in narcotics, once for larceny, and now for breaking and entering. He is (said to be) deeply troubled, at war with authority, adrift in a world that is passing him by. "Experts" note his emotional lability, his diminished social conscience, his longing for a father, his thankless attempts to make friends. They advise the court that Smith would benefit from therapy and surely needs it. The court listens and is moved. Judge Jones informs Smith that he needs help not punishment. If Smith is willing to place himself in the care of those who can provide this help, Judge Jones is willing to drop the charges against him. Smith—who may be disturbed but is surely no fool—jumps at the opportunity and is soon settled within the walls of a mental institution.

Any number of grim illustrations of how all this works in practice could be offered, but one is sufficient to underscore the problem. The case involved a Mr. William Henry Alston, now deceased, whose story was recounted on the first page of the *Washington Post*, 27 August 1979.

Mr. Alston, a now and again taxi driver in the District of Columbia, was arrested for drunkenness on 9 October 1975 and was sent forthwith to the Prince George's County Jail. A routine computer search turned up the name "William Lewis Alston" as a man wanted by the Baltimore police for a number of serious crimes. The description of the much wanted William Lewis Alston was not entirely unlike that of Mr. William Henry Alston. However, when the Baltimore inspectors visited the latter, they apprised the police that he was not the man they were looking for. This fact, however, was not immediately brought to light. Instead, William Henry Alston was presented to a judge as if he were the seasoned felon now withering under the habit of chronic alcoholism.

As reported by the *Post*, the judge mercifully explained to the inarticulate and confused defendant that prison was not the place for him; that he should receive help from doctors:

> I think I am going to send you over to Perkins Hospital . . .
> to see if there is anything we can do to help you. . . . We are
> going to get you out of jail, at least temporarily. We are going
> to make things better. Next case.

It was not long after his "voluntary" commitment that Mr.
Alston began to ask and to write for legal counsel, and to insist
over and over again that he was not responsible for the crimes
attributed to him. The psychiatrists at Perkins wrote an official
report to the judge in which they noted the following:

> In the course of our current re-evaluation Mr. Alston has
> shown definite improvement although he still displays para-
> noid ideation with regard to the current charges. . . . Our
> current diagnosis is: Schizophrenia, Chronic Undifferentiated
> Type with Paranoid Features, in partial remission.

Months later, thanks to letters sent by William Henry Alston
to Howard Campbell in the Public Defender's office, and thanks
to Mr. Campbell's diligence, it was learned not only that the
two Alstons had different middle initials and different dates of
birth, but that William Lewis Alston had been incarcerated in the
District of Columbia during William Henry Alston's period of
hospitalization. Of course, the wrong man was summarily discharged from the Perkins Hospital Center and was awarded modest damages ($20,000). It should be noted, however, that even after
the mistake was uncovered, the state's Attorney General still
insisted that William Henry Alston be detained at Perkins, since
the staff at Perkins had diagnosed his condition as "schizophrenia." Nonetheless, the doctors at Perkins, apprised of the mistaken identity, quickly altered the diagnosis and informed the
court that Alston was a proper candidate for release—as long as
he took some medicine!

It is scarcely necessary to comment on the Catch-22 dimensions of this case. Alston found himself bearing the label of "paranoid" on the grounds that he protested his innocence. Presumably,
anyone else similarly protesting would run a good risk of acquir-
ing the same label. What we have here is a diagnosis based on the
willingness of a patient to accept all the attributions the state
might make in his behalf. Should the state be discovered to be in
error, the psychiatrists are prepared to modify the diagnosis. This
is not science. This is not even medicine. It certainly is not justice.
It is a mixture of pseudoscience and welfarism.

8. Involuntary Commitment

In most states the involuntary or "protesting" patient is guarded by a number of procedural protections, although many of these have come into being so recently that it is not clear how effective they will prove in practice. It is still more the rule than the exception that a person can be involuntarily held for testing and observation at the request of a parent, guardian, or spouse; on the findings of an arresting police officer; at the direction of a judge; or on the urgings of a physician who has examined the person. The trend in most states is to restrict the period of observation and confinement to a few days, seldom more than a week. It is generally also mandatory that, once there has been a determination of need for hospitalization, the committing institution must obtain the approval or orders of a court. Title 21, Chapter 5 of the District of Columbia Code is illustrative:

> An accredited officer or agent of the Department of Public Health of the District of Columbia, or an officer authorized to make arrests in the District of Columbia, or a physician of the person in question, who has reason to believe that a person is mentally ill and, because of the illness, is likely to injure himself or others if he is not immediately detained may, without a warrant, take the person into custody, transport him to a public or private hospital, and make application for his admission thereto for purposes of emergency observation and diagnosis. The application shall reveal the circumstances under which the person was taken into custody and the reasons therefore. (*Subchapter* III)

> A person admitted to a hospital under section 21–522 may not be detained in the hospital for a period in excess of 48 hours from the time of his admission, unless the administrator of the hospital has, within that period, filed a written petition with the court for an order authorizing the continued hospitalization . . . not to exceed 7 days from the time the order is entered. (Ibid.)

> The court shall grant a hearing to a person whose continued hospitalization is ordered under section 21–524, if he requests the hearing. The hearing shall be held within 24 hours after receipt of the request. (Ibid.)

> A patient hospitalized pursuant to this chapter may not, by reason of the hospitalization, be denied the right to dispose of property, execute instruments, make purchases, enter into

> contractual relationships, vote, and hold a driver's license,
> unless the patient has been adjudicated incompetent by a court
> of competent jurisdiction and has not been restored to legal
> capacity. (Ibid.)

On the interpretation of "likely to injure himself or others"
the courts have been particularly tolerant, insisting that such
wording is sufficiently definite to survive constitutional challenges based on vagueness (*In re Alexander*, 1972, 336 F. Supp.
1305). A police force willing to believe what appears in psychiatry
and psychology texts and articles would certainly include all violent persons, all alcoholics, all rapists, all who have used weapons
in the commission of a crime, all disorderly persons as "likely to
injure" themselves or others. The records compiled by many
imprisoned felons make clear that one of the most reliable predic-
tors of injurious conduct is a history of such conduct.

Why, then, do we not have a rash of commitments of those
apprehended in the act of committing violent crimes? The rub, of
course, is that mere conduct does not provide grounds for emer-
gency hospitalization unless it proceeds from something called
"mental illness." The question then arises, What must be added
to such conduct for it to be construed as the product of mental
illness? What we learn when we raise this question is that the
violence must be "gratuitous"; that the crime must be essentially
without motivation or "rational" motivation; that the actor takes
no steps to avoid his pursuers; and that he is unlikely to benefit in
any material way from his deeds. This, however, takes us back to
the insanity defense, on which enough has already been said. The
fundamental legal fact is that persons are innocent until proved
guilty, and guilt attaches not to likelihoods but to actions. Where
injury or death is involved, there is every reason to constrain
perpetrators, the ephemeral deprivation of liberties being of lesser
moral weight than the obligation to save life. However, nothing
in this is confined to allegedly psychiatric cases, for the same
principles are applicable universally—which is what makes them
principles. Note, however, that the steps citizens or authorities
might take where putative insanity is suspected are larger and
more fully protected and encouraged than where simple criminality is not only suspected but established. In the District of Columbia, for example, it is possible to detain a citizen for psychiatric
observation longer than one can detain a felon ("with roots in the

community") waiting to stand trial. In the latter instance, we are dealing not with the possibility of injury, but with the fact of it. This comparison makes evident the tendency of the courts and of society at large, again under the weight of the psychosocial point of view, to turn matters of justice over to a cadre of professionals whose opinions thereby come to have the force of law.

Were such practices limited to instances of grave harm and injury, some might argue that it doesn't make much difference whether the perpetrator is behind the walls of a hospital or the bars of a prison. The fact is, however, that it is far easier to find oneself in the former than in the latter, for one need not commit a crime to be hospitalized. For a variety of reasons, none sound, society has apparently learned to live with crime, but not with eccentricity or with avoidable nuisances. Crime is something we can take steps to protect ourselves against, but society's oddities are unpredictable, usually more public, and in a way far more embarrassing. The psychosocial point of view has trained the modern citizen to accept part of the responsibility for every crime, but has not yet taught him to share the causal burdens of insanity.

The actual horror stories surrounding involuntary commitments have been often recounted. Children have been the most pathetic objects of this sort of welfarism since they carry a double burden. First, their legal incompetence places their interests in the hands of the very custodial parties now seeking to have them hospitalized; and second, there is that peculiarity of court-ordered institutionalization, which strips the proceedings of most of the protections available to those at trial. Think, for example, of *In re Gault*, which involved a teenaged boy charged by a neighbor with making obscene telephone calls. Had appeals failed, the order of the lower court would have had this boy confined to a therapeutic setting for years as a result of allegations which, if true, would not have cost him a night in prison.

When, as a result of revived libertarianism, districts attempt to remedy such problems, the indefensibility of the whole affair becomes clear. Note, for example, the last provision of the D.C. Code cited earlier, which retains for the patient the rights of disposing of property, voting, holding a driver's license, and entering into contracts. The limitation here is that the patient must be judged to be "competent." If so judged he enjoys all the derived liberties of citizenship—but not the basic right of freedom itself. Before commending so humane a provision, we ought first to ask on what grounds a person is kept within an institution when that same person is judged competent to vote, drive a car, make purchases, and form contracts. He has been detained presumably because he is "mentally ill," and, therefore, a risk to himself and to others. Is he not then likely to enter bad bargains and be diverted in his perambulations? Do we really want such a fellow to participate in the election of public servants?

Since I have chosen the District of Columbia in one context, I might stay with it in a more unusual one. I refer here to the infamous "white paper" that is sufficient to detain a citizen in St. Elizabeth's Hospital when any authorized official thinks that person may be a risk to high officials of the government. The sort of person covered by this extrajural device is one who jumps over the White House fence, roams suspiciously around the environs of the White House, or makes threatening statements about its occupants. Any number of harmless citizens have found their way into St. Elizabeth's this way, and once inside, their tenure is determined largely by the findings of examining physicians. When we combine this with the frequent claim made in the professional journals—that perhaps 25 percent of the population is seriously in need of psychological assistance—we see that there is one chance in four that the "white paper" case will have difficulty obtaining a release.

Many who have written on this issue have been excited by the prospects of *political* detention and totalitarianism. I believe this is one reason why general enthusiasm has not gravitated toward the matter. In reality, the overriding motivation in nearly every case is not the urge to control but to "help." Persons are not sent to mental hospitals because of their political convictions. Indeed, as we have seen, most of them still can exercise the franchise. They are sent because they are judged to be needy, and this judgment arises out of a recognition of the differences between "them" and "us." We all become depressed from time to time, but they become too depressed too often. Or they become too anxious too often, or too given to their fantasies too often. We can "function," they cannot. There is in all of this a very definite ideological element, but it is not political ideology. It is a social ideology, one that will unfailingly relegate liberty to a position of secondary importance whenever equality is at issue. Having no means of defining or even recognizing the latter—let alone creating it—society through its courts and legislatures will settle for second best, sameness. The hospitals may not make Smith our equal, but they will make him like the rest of us, or he will not be set loose.

The best protection against the therapeutic state is, of course, numbers. Under welfarism and the psychosocial point of view, there is general agreement that no person is in need of "help" if there is a functional group with which he can be readily identified. Thus, nearly anything done in the name of religion, politics, or art is largely freed from judicial scrutiny, at least where such scrutiny is one of the stages leading to hospitalization. Modern man, as the patron and victim of psychosocial reasoning, no longer defines himself in nonaffiliational terms. Accordingly, he eagerly extends protections to any and every group, knowing that most of them are at least as credible as the one giving meaning to his own being. Thus, he is less able to distinguish between pornography and a free press, obscenity and political expression, trash and art, as long as all of them enjoy roughly equal audiences. His waning power of discrimination is confined to those isolated cases that stand out because they are not part of a parade. So we find the elderly woman who believes all passersby must safeguard their eternal souls to be ripe for psychiatric detention. But the thousand children making the same appeal at national airports, and doing so in the conviction that a Korean industrialist is God, perform their mission under the vigilant solicitude of an army of civil "libertarians." So too with the lonely homosexual whose rootless life is passed in subways and parks rather than in fashionable and populated "gay" bars; so too with the child who physically assaults his playmates but lacks either the whim or the opportunity to join a gang; so too with the vagrant who sleeps wherever a bench can be found, but cannot claim fraternity with those children of privilege who have chosen homeless slovenliness to a directed and ordered life. If we continue to take as a fundamental principle of justice the obligation to treat like cases in like manner, we must recognize in all of this as clear a disregard of justice as a free state is likely to exercise.

9. Confinement, Consent, and "The Right to Treatment"

In *Donaldson* v. *O'Connor*, the Court of Appeals for the Fifth Circuit affirmed that an involuntarily committed mental patient has a constitutional right to treatment under the Fourteenth

Amendment. The decision found support in *Jackson* v. *Indiana*, which involved a mentally defective deaf mute charged with robbery and committed to a hospital until such time as he would be fit to stand trial. In light of his condition, however, it was clear that such a day would never come and that, as a result, his commitment would be for the balance of his life. The court held in *Jackson* that the state can detain a defendant-patient only for a "reasonable period of time"; just so long as is necessary to ascertain how long it will be before the defendant-patient will be able to proceed to trial. Where the evidence indicates that there is little or no likelihood that he will ever be able to do so, *Jackson* requires the state either to release the patient or to take formal steps toward the customary civil commitment. A key passage in *Jackson* is

> Furthermore, even if it is determined that the defendant probably soon will be able to stand trial, his continued commitment must be justified by progress toward that goal.

In other words, the justification for continued commitment is the promise of improvement which, on a certain construction, might suggest a "right" to treatment. This, in any event, was the construction imposed by the appeals court in *Donaldson* v. *O'Connor*, where the court found for Donaldson in his action against O'Connor, the recently retired former superintendent of a Florida mental hospital in which Donaldson had been confined for fifteen years.

In *O'Connor* v. *Donaldson* (422 U.S. 563) the Supreme Court would seem to have taken a decisive step in the direction of protecting the involuntarily committed mental patient. Any number of passages speak to the need for such protection:

> A finding of "mental illness" alone cannot justify a State's locking a person up against his will and keeping him indefinitely in simple custodial confinement. Assuming that that term can be given a reasonably precise content and that the "mentally ill" can be identified with reasonable accuracy, there is still no constitutional basis for confining such persons involuntarily if they are dangerous to no one and can live safely in freedom. . . . [T]he mere presence of mental illness does not disqualify a person from preferring his home to the comforts of an institution. (at 575)

But in his concurring separate opinion, Mr. Chief Justice Burger makes it quite clear that *O'Connor* v. *Donaldson* has not created a right to treatment at all, and that the decision of the court of appeals in *Donaldson* v. *O'Connor* is far from law.

The court of appeals had reasoned thus:

> To deprive any citizen of his or her liberty upon the altruistic theory that the confinement is for humane therapeutic reasons and then to fail to provide adequate treatment violates the very fundamentals of due process. (493 F.2d at 521)

Mr. Burger found at least two defects in this reasoning. First, carried to the end of its jural tether, it would seem to suggest that the state could so deprive citizens of their liberties if it then proceeded to provide them with adequate treatment. Second, the argument suggests that the state loses its power of confinement when, as it happens, there is simply no therapeutic regimen available for the condition that warranted confinement.

> [T]he idea that States may not confine the mentally ill except for the purpose of providing them with treatment is of very recent origin, and there is no historical basis for imposing such a limitation on state power. Analysis of the sources of the civil commitment power likewise lends no support to that notion. (*O'Connor* v. *Donaldson* at 582)

There is

> no basis for equating an involuntarily committed mental patient's unquestioned constitutional right not to be confined without due process of law with a constitutional right to *treatment*. (Ibid. at 588–589)

At present, one cannot safely predict how the rights of the involuntarily committed are likely to evolve. One of the painful ironies in *Donaldson* was the part of O'Connor's defense that sought to establish that, indeed, Donaldson had been treated—he had been given "milieu therapy"! Thus, should one or another form of a "right to treatment" finally appear, it is far from certain that it will ever be possible to prove beyond a reasonable doubt that a patient has been completely denied any and all treatment. Donaldson, as a Christian Scientist, had acutally refused medication, but on the additional grounds that, since there was nothing wrong with him there was no reason for him to accept medication. His refusal in this regard actually weakened his case, a fact that contains the seeds of mischief. Moreover, in light of "milieu therapy," we can surely expect some future defendant-institution to claim "isolation therapy" as a defense. When we look to the data, however, we cannot be comforted by the current enthusiasm for this new "right" to treatment. Studies of those released by mental hospitals suggest that fewer than 10 percent are still on the outside two years later. With the increasing reliance on psychoactive drugs, it may be expected that this figure will improve, but it is not at all clear that such medication can be safely subsumed under the heading "treatment." In any event, the rate of recidivism would ordinarily be sufficient to convince those still accessible to proofs that mental hospitals do not, in fact, have treatments for their patients, so one can only wonder what it is these patients have a "right" to receive. All we can safely assume is that recent decisions will increase the frequency of contact between staff and patients and will probably increase the range and the amount of prescribed medication. However, since such contacts have not had much effect on ambulatory neurotics in the typical psychoanalytic setting, we should not expect them to accomplish much in institutional settings in which symptoms are even more severe. And in the matter of medication, there is no evidence to suggest that any specific drug or combination of drugs will eliminate only that ensemble of feelings and behaviors that resulted in hospitalization in the first place. Practically speaking, *all* psychological therapies are *experimental* when they are not simply exercises in ritual groping. As experiments, however, they are more akin to the things children used to do with their first Gilbert chemistry set than with the activities of serious scientists bent on answering a coherent set of factual questions.

As recently as June 1979 the U.S. Supreme Court has attempted to fashion principles able to protect both the liberties of the citizen and the interests of society. But the decision in *Addington* v. *Texas* so carefully tracks the middle course as to leave matters nearly as equivocal as they were before the ruling. What the decision seems to strike down is that part of the reasoning of the Texas Supreme Court which permitted the confinement of Addington on the grounds of a "preponderance of evidence" conducing to a judgment of mental illness. In *Addington*, the U.S. Supreme Court replaces "preponderance of evidence" with "clear and convincing evidence" that the person whose confinement is sought is a danger to himself or others. Yet, *Addington* specifically rejects the thesis that such confinement-procedures are to be limited in the same manner as criminal proceedings. That is, the court in *Addington* does not embrace the standard of "proof beyond a reasonable doubt" for the nearly droll reason that psychiatry cannot meet this standard! The pivotal phrase "clear and convincing evidence" calls upon us to struggle with a definition of every word except the conjunction.

Professor Szasz has argued in a number of books and articles that one way of understanding the failure of psychological therapies is to recognize that there is actually no disease to be treated. He refers to "the myth of mental illness" as one that supports the immense establishment of psychological therapies, but does so on the strength of nothing more than myth. In a more popular and dramatic way, R. D. Laing makes a similar case, but one that rests perhaps too much on sinister elements. Both of these authors are men of broad experience and lengthy training. I offer their opinions not as a decisive argument against the therapeutic community but only to illustrate the grave doubts that linger in the most informed circles about the value, the validity, and the very conceptual foundations of these therapies. To say, then, that the involuntary patient has a right to treatment may finally be translated to mean that he has the macabre right to be the involuntary subject of an aimless experiment. And this, of course, immediately raises the question of consent, for in conferring a right on a person we do not thereby order its exercise.

When we canvass the range of "therapies" available to the modern patient, we discover measures as benign as hand-holding and others as stark as electroconvulsive shocks and direct stimulation of the brain. All of them are hit-and-miss, for none proceeds under the light of scientific laws; few proceed even under the dimmer light of scientific fact. The so-called mental patient has the added difficulty of his own dreams and distractions. He may be withdrawn, excitable, anxious, inattentive, morose. The more severe his condition, the less value can be assigned to his consent or his protests. The more severe the therapeutic measure, the less predictable its consequences. We must ask, therefore, what the court in *Donaldson* had in mind. Was it lobotomy at any institution whose senior staff might still prefer such treatment? Or direct stimulation of the patient's brain? Or so lacing the patient's physiology with tranquilizing agents as to convert him to a zombie? Are mechanical restraints "treatment"? Are stern rebukes or the denial of cigarettes, candy, and newspapers also "treatment"? And must the recipient know that such measures are intended as treatments? Must he know also what the likely outcomes are, and the effects such measures have had in cases (somehow) like his own? It is one thing to grant the state the right to institutionalize citizens against their will, but quite another to include with this the power to make such citizens the unwitting subjects of practices that can only be described as experimental in the most positive terms.

The reader at this point may be wondering whether a psychiatrist or psychologist can do anything for anybody given the argument developed in this chapter. I will return to this question in the last chapter, but a few observations will not be out of order here. What the psychiatrist or psychologist can do is determined by his abilities and by the developed knowledge of his profession. What he may do is determined in part by law and in part by the standards of the therapeutic community. He surely may not do that which he cannot do, but he also may not—that is, ought not—do some things that are within his power. He must not, for example, employ methods whose consequences are likely to be graver than is the condition being treated. He must not use patients for purposes that are largely experimental. He must not expect to be compensated for efforts that have merely his self-education as their goal. He must not pretend to a degree of expertise at a time when all thoughtful students of the discipline know how little is known. He surely must reserve his ministrations until he is certain that there is a disease that warrants them. Even without the aid of counsel and the courts, he must recognize that his patient is—or at least was and may soon again be—the member of a polity, a citizen, and a person, and that, as such, the patient comes before him with a collection of endemic rights and essentially moral attributes. He must instruct the courts that the adverb "likely" has only a statistical meaning and that in the vast majority of cases, no one can say that anyone is "likely" to harm himself or others unless that person has a history of such attempts. Where there is no history and where no known disease can be found by anyone tutored in making diagnoses, he should withhold treatment, for there is nothing to treat. These steps will often place the entire matter back in the courts and will oblige jurists and attorneys to come to grips with the *justice* of the case, which somehow got lost as everyone played doctor.

10. Remedies Real, Remedies Specious

At the beginning of this chapter, I set forth a short list of givens that come into being the moment a collection of persons can be said to form a political community. There will always be a state of tension between individual persons and the larger assembly as long as individuality is not utterly extinguished. In sketching Mill's version of libertarianism, I attempted to illustrate not only the form of defense traditionally recruited in behalf of individuality but also to underscore the limitations set even by the defenders. Mill was not arguing for a suspension of all the rights of majorities; he was not even defending the individual's "right" to offend others. But in all such regions of social interaction, we are little aided by the axioms of this or that ism. Instead, we must rely on good sense, good judgment, and some measure of analytical agility. There is, alas, no equation or rule or computer program that will relieve us of the burdens of thought and our obligations to fairness.

In recent decades, there has been by all accounts an extraordinary liberalization of the standards of social conduct. Sociologists do not tire of telling us of the breakdown of traditional institutions, the fragility of the modern marriage, the resistance to historic sources of authority, the "relative" nature of all moral and ethical systems, the shifting nature of all codes of deportment and of values. Some of their lessons are clearly descriptive, others patently apologetic and reassuring, still others merely ideological. In any case, the facts need no expert to speak for them, for they speak with stark clarity for themselves. And what they say is that contemporary American life—and contemporary life throughout the Western democracies—is a veritable riot of tastes, standards, eccentricities, inclinations, and transitory commitments, all of which seek the protection of "rights" and all of which have little more than habit as a foundation.

In these same decades, the courts have been nearly sunk by the mass of actions brought by persons against groups, by one group against another, and by some groups against individuals.

The rhetoric of "rights" has not been this prosperous since the eighteenth century, although the new prosperity has not revived either the older eloquence or the older logic. Nonetheless, the effect of the revival has been to create a pervasive reluctance to treat any claim as invalid once it has been presented in the language of rights or under the banner of liberty. The mass of citizens sit, as it were, on the edges of their seats, waiting daily to learn which new right has come into being, which older value has been shown to be mythical, which basic principle has been exposed as nothing more than a matter of taste. With its interminable polls and its candid camera findings, the priests of social science pounce on every *ought* with an *is* and expose the very terms of civilization to the blurring light of statistics. In the inflationary spiral of rights and liberties, none seems any longer to be more basic than others; none more protected than the rest. Having permitted the wisdom of the past, the centuries-old proprieties and manners, to be swept aside, modern man must go to court to discover his relation to the state. Can photographs of his family be published in a national magazine without his permission? Can his telephone be "bugged" by the government? Are his children to be exposed to indecency in public places? Is it really permissible for a person to walk the public byways wearing a shirt emblazoned with four-letter words and obscene slogans? And in each case, the answer comes not merely from the courts, but from the courts as psychosocial agencies keenly loyal to the latest trends and follies unearthed by social science.

Under such circumstances, there is a growing and an essentially compensatory intolerance toward benign eccentricities. The citizens and the courts have effectively joined together, agreeing to overlook each other's forfeiture of principles, and agreeing further to have doubtful cases submitted to the independent judgment of the "experts." That is, neither the citizen nor the judge will arrogate to himself the responsibility of deciding how far a right goes before it offends too many coming within the perimeter of its reach; how much liberty it takes to convert a free state into an anarchy; when comportment crosses the line that divides basic rights from insolent antics. To settle such issues, neither common sense nor jural comprehension is sufficient. Instead, we need data; we need to learn how the nation feels about such things; how many persons do these sorts of things.

It is this perspective that feeds and feeds on the psychosocial point of view and reduces courts of justice into the screening rooms of that enlarged clinic we call modern society. The only alternative—the historical alternative—is the heavy hand of legislation, but, as we are so often reminded, we "cannot legislate morality." Yet let us be mindful of the fact that, if indeed we cannot legislate it, and if some number of persons insist on going beyond its bounds, our *only* remedy is to have them "treated," since we have surrendered the right to have them punished. We refine our sympathies so as not to have to reckon with our fears. We needn't tolerate Smith now that we have agreed to help him. And neither we nor the courts must wrestle with the concept of personal liberty, for in such cases we are dealing with patients, not with citizens.

Notes

For Thomas Szasz's view, consult his "The Myth of Mental Illness" (1961, Harper and Row). R. D. Laing's controversial ideas are set forth in his *The Politics of the Family: And Other Essays* (1972, Vintage). On recidivism, see G. L. Paul's "Chronic Mental Patients: Current Status—Future Direction," *Psychological Bulletin*, 1969, *71*, 81–94. An excellent critical review of the entire problem is provided by Norman Finkel in *Mental Illness and Health* (1976, Macmillan).

5 Education, Testing, and the Judiciary

It was in October 1904 that France's minister of public instruction appointed a commission to consider new methods of assessing intelligence "for insuring the benefits of instruction to defective children." The following year, Alfred Binet and Theodore Simon published their pioneering *New Methods for the Diagnosis of the Intellectual Level of Subnormals* in the influential *L'Année Psychologique.* Eleven years later, the American psychologist Henry Goddard could write:

> It will seem an exaggeration to some to say that the world is talking of the Binet-Simon Scale; but consider that the Vineland Laboratory alone, has without effort or advertisement distributed to date 22,000 copies of the pamphlet describing the tests, and 88,000 record blanks. . . . The Scale is used in Canada, England, Australia, New Zealand, South Africa, Germany, Switzerland, Italy, Russia, China, and has recently been translated into Japanese and Turkish.*

In the same span, any number of countries and several of the American states made the administration of the Binet-Simon tests obligatory for the assignment of children to special schools. And it is one of the ironies of the courtship between law and the social sciences that just two years ago the California judiciary banned

*This passage is taken from Goddard's introduction to the first English translations of Binet's major essays. Consult notes at the end of this chapter for relevant citations.

the use of similar tests as a means of classifying children for special forms of instruction given in various schools. Somehow, between 1915 and 1975, what seemed a fair and objective means of relevant discrimination had become a tool of oppression.

This is not to say, however, that the courts have been uniform in their suspicion of psychological tests. In the landmark decision of *Brown* v. *Board of Education* (1954), for example—the so-called desegregation decision—the justices were soberly interested in the studies conducted by Kenneth Clark, whose tests seemed to indicate that black children in segregated schools had lower "self-images." The actual findings, as it happens, do not support the Supreme Court's interpretation of them (or, for that matter, Professor Clark's own interpretation), but this is less important than is the fact of their inclusion in a landmark case. What we discover, then, is not a general enmity toward or confidence in the results of tests as such, but the selective judicial acceptance of certain kinds of findings and the selective dismissal or even forbidding of other kinds. Where the tests lead to a finding of injury, the courts seem eager to embrace them, but where they may serve as the criterion by which a possible or putative injury comes about, some jurists will not even permit their administration. Our efforts will be repaid if we review the rationale and purposes of psychological tests, and the manner in which their use is alleged to be improper.

Perhaps the most instructive way of beginning this review is through an analysis of Judge Robert Peckham's opinion in *Larry P.* v. *Riles.** The class action suit was aimed at the ten-year-old policy of California's Department of Education which required the administration of standardized tests of intelligence as a means of assigning children to programs for the "educable mentally retarded" (EMR). The same judge, as early as 1977, had ordered a ban on such testing, having discovered that classes for the EMR were racially "unbalanced." His 1979 ruling continues the ban and orders California's school psychologists to develop other methods of assessing black children enrolled in EMR programs. There are approximately 6,000 so classified. The opinion of the court charges the state with the use of "racially and culturally

---

*Filed October 16, 1979, in the U.S. District Court, San Francisco. The opinion runs to 131 pages.

biased placement criteria," tests which would "perpetuate or even exacerbate the very serious overenrollment of minorities in EMR classes."

Eminent psychologists testified on both sides of this cause before Judge Peckham. In the plaintiff's behalf, several psychologists noted that a racist tone accompanied the earliest American efforts in large-scale intelligence testing, and that several of the luminaries in the psychometric movement scarcely concealed their racial prejudices. They insisted also that, such prejudices set aside, the tests themselves were constructed out of a given cultural point of view which took and still takes for granted the validity of white middle-class values and expectations.

The state's experts, in turn, pointed out that the discriminations made by such tests persist even when socioeconomic factors are adjusted and that such "values" as the tests incorporate are similarly incorporated into the state's educational mission. Thus, there was no denying that standardized tests honor a culturally definable position on the very purposes of education, but this in itself does not establish that the tests do no more than rediscover this position.

The several hypotheses revived (again) in *Larry P.* v. *Riles* to account for the results of state-wide testing are now well known to those who have followed this seasonal issue. On one construction, blacks do poorly on such tests with greater frequency than non-blacks because, in fact, there are more intellectually sub-normal persons in the black "race," and all the tests do is recognize what, at base, is a genetically determined difference between the races. Neither of the parties at issue in *Larry P.* v. *Riles* took this approach, but experts for the plaintiff alerted the court to what is at least the implicit hereditarianism adopted by those who defend intelligence-testing. Then, too, environmentalism had its day, here with both sides agreeing that poor performance on such tests reflects the consequences of timeless patterns of discrimination and cultural impoverishment. There was also some speculation on the nutritional correlates of this very impoverishment, and on the possible relationship between this and the developmental "lag" disproportionately displayed by black schoolchildren.

Throughout his opinion, Judge Peckham referred to the EMR classes as "stigmatizing," but it is far from clear that his opinion would have been different had a different label been

involved. No one doubts the stigmatizing effects of being classified as educable but "mentally retarded," but here the stigma is
actually derived from what may be a clinical classification utterly
irrelevant to the issues in *Larry P.* v. *Riles*. I speak here, of course,
of the fact that many mentally retarded persons are *brain-damaged*,
a fact that does not, however, establish that each instance of *mental* retardation is an instance of neuropathology. Still, because of
the habits of the uninstructed, there could be some justification
for requiring the state to find a different label for those who fall
below the criterion-score on I.Q. tests. Note, however, that the
tests are neutral on the question of etiology and that the scores
remain the same whether they are taken to indicate mental retardation, cultural impoverishment, poor nutrition, or a lackluster
pedigree. That a child coming from a class established for the
"educable mentally retarded" is unlikely to excite his next teacher
with his academic promise is doubtless. But even without a stigmatizing label, his inevitable failures in mathematics, reading,
spelling, problem-solving, memory, and general comprehension
will soon call for a readjustment of whatever high hopes his next
teacher may harbor for him. The point, of course—and one that I
shall repeat—is that the scores on such tests survive any theoretical construction we choose to impose on them, and it is these
scores that must be dealt with by a society solicitous of its children's futures.

There are great and fatal flaws in the radical hereditarianism
that has always surrounded I.Q. testing. Several of these are
exposed later in this chapter. But these liabilities do not by themselves give safe passage to just any environmentalistic alternative.
The "cultural bias" argument, for example, must come to grips
with the fact that the tests in question do not yield high rates of
sub-normal performance among American Indians or the children of recent immigrants; further, that the same tests produce
essentially identical distributions of scores world-wide when no
more is done to make them suitable for the non-English speaking
populations than a literal translation of the words. Indeed, the
racial discriminations made in this area become no weaker when
non-verbal measures of I.Q. are employed or when the standard
tests are rewritten in what is called "Black English."* The point

*See, for example, V. A. Hall and R. R. Turner, "The validity of the 'different
language explanation' for poor scholastic performance by black students." *Review of Educational Research*, 1974, *44*, 69–81.

here is not that such findings confirm hereditarianism (they do *not*), but that the traditional arm-waving environmentalistic alternative is put on notice by the facts. It simply will not do, except in purely polemical arenas, to dismiss seventy years of research on the grounds that some of it was conducted by hereditarians or on the equally infirm grounds that it has served only a particular cultural bias. In any event, the courts as such have no part to play and should take no part. His powers of juridical discernment taken for granted, Judge Peckham's difficulties with the facts and theories of modern psychometrics are now permanently recorded in his long opinion in *Larry P.* v. *Riles.* He rejects the "brain damage" hypothesis—one that is vastly more subtle than one would gather from the opinion—on the finding that the incidence of severe retardation is about the same in black and white populations. The embarrassing irony here is that, in order to reject the hypothesis, he must invoke one of its corollaries and must assume at least tacitly that severe mental retardation is the result of brain pathology. What his ruling requires, apparently, is that the psychologists for the State of California develop methods of assessment which eliminate "imbalances" in California's special-education programs. But no such assessment will eliminate the already documented "imbalances" in academic and intellectual proficiency, so the judge's order will only see to it that the normal classroom will now be occupied by a number of children unable to profit from its lessons.

Let us also be mindful that, to the extent that the label "educable mentally retarded" is stigmatizing, the stigma attaches to all who answer to the description. Not every EMR child in California is black. Thus, the question arises, If the EMR designation has no valid physiological correlate, if it expresses only a cultural bias, how do we explain its assignment to non-black children and how are they to be reclassified? That is, on Judge Peckham's reasoning, can there be such a category as EMR? This is an aspect of the judge's reasoning, a consequence of his understanding. But on the side of *fact*, there are indeed mentally retarded children in the world whose retardation is not so severe as to exclude them from education in every form. We can identify these children in a variety of ways, the most efficient being the administration of standardized tests. The tests alert us to the "mental retardation" in that they locate children unable to perform tasks, answer questions, and solve problems which the overwhelming majority of their peers can. They are "retarded," then, in the purely statistical sense of falling behind their peers in the performance of tasks that are "mental." This is not to say that they are retarded in all mental respects; only in those that are involved in the sorts of things schools were designed to teach. The tests are, as such, indifferent to the racial identification of the student *and* to any and every theory of mental development and function. If they are measuring abilities that depend upon certain cultural opportunities, then what they predict also depends upon such opportunities. To order the use of assessments that ignore this factor is only to defer the day of judgment. And, in fairness, it is to order simultaneously that no child be "stigmatized" on the basis of cultural opportunities whose existence is beyond his control. Finally, it must be to order teachers to stop assigning the grade of "F" to those current and prospective EMR students who now pass through the door opened by Judge Peckham's ruling: for short of commanding a suspension of all traditional standards of academic performance, the students who would have been classified "EMR" on the basis of low I.Q.'s will fail in disproportionate numbers. Here we have a judge not easily placed in either the *lex dare* or the *lex dicere* model of jurisprudence, but one who is simply establishing social policy. Now we must wonder whether the social sciences can survive this sort of "justice."

Dilemmas of this sort invariably arise when jural decisions are mired in the quasi-ideological, quasi-scientific bog produced by the psychosocial point of view. Under these conditions, the judge insensibly relinquishes his historical mission and tries to find words with which to sanction what he perceives to be a social goal. The same court that is tempted to accept Smith's "insanity" on the grounds of psychometric data sometimes correlated with brain-damage is next tempted to reject Jones's "mental retardation" as indicated by the very same data, the very same tests. Thus, we have the spectacle, the burlesque, of a jurist attempting to settle questions of fact by appealing to the provisionally settled opinions of a pressure group. In other times and contexts, this has been called political justice, and it is not much more appealing when it seems to confer an advantage than when it clearly removes one. Invariably in such settings ignorance and innocence join with misplaced philanthropy in an unholy alliance against reason. In the present instance, the enemy is the I.Q. test, but the same powers would be brought to bear against any instrument that threatened or even challenged what has become America's official sociology. Let me turn to a few of the modest notions upon which psychological testing rests, not so much out of an optimistic sense that such a review can affect policy, but so that the reader will be aware of what it is this policy explicitly opposes or implicitly rejects.

1. Psychometric Assumptions

The primary assumption behind the vast majority of psychological tests is that human mental characteristics, like physical characteristics, are normally distributed in the human race. Accordingly, one would expect to find relatively few scores at either extreme, and most of the scores hovering around the average. However, unlike physical features such as height and weight, mental abilities cannot be assessed in inches or pounds or any purely physical metric. It becomes necessary, then, to contrive methods and measures that are suited to such nonphysical attributes as intelligence, personality, values, skills, and interests. On the assumption that these attributes are in fact normally distributed, any valid test must, when administered to a large and random sample of the population, yield normally distributed scores. Thus, if 90 percent of those tested performed perfectly, the test would be judged to be insufficiently discriminating and an invalid measure of the true distribution of the talents, capacities, abilities or psychologial makeup of the population.

Now, as with the fundamental assumptions of any discipline, this one cannot be immune to challenge. Let us be aware of the fact that, whereas height and weight are known to be normally distributed in any large and random sample, psychological attributes are only *assumed* to be so distributed. Psychological tests are rejected or refined until they produce results that conform to the assumption and, at least to this extent, may be said to impose the normal distribution rather than discover it. This is a nontrivial difference between psychological and physical measurement, but it is not one that matters in the present circumstance. It is obvious that persons differ in their psychological features and that systematic observations will reveal the differences. Therefore, whether the differences are normally distributed or not, they do exist and can, therefore, serve as the basis for discrimination.

A second assumption—though scarcely unique to psychological testing—is that a valid estimation of a given attribute is possible through a limited sampling of the attribute. To learn, for example, whether someone is able to multiply numbers, it is not necessary to have him solve twenty thousand multiplication problems, or for that matter, even twenty. With only one such problem we can ascertain his possession of the rules of multiplication. The same is true of very nearly all basic skills: spelling, vocabulary, memory span, geography, rules of grammar, etc. The first step in constructing such tests is to determine what members of the population of interest should be expected to know; for example, what schoolchildren in the fifth grade should know about arithmetic. A provisional test is designed and is administered to a representative sample of this population. Alterations, readministrations, and revisions follow until a standardized test results. This test may now be expected to be passed with average scores by about two-thirds of all fifth grade students; passed with slightly above and slightly below average scores by another 27 percent. About 5 percent of the entire population of students will be divided into those who fail completely and those who succeed preeminently. The test will be judged as *valid* if it meets these conditions, if its items are judged to be valid on their face (i.e., if it has so-called "face validity"), and if scores on the test are correlated significantly with such other measures of arithmetic ability as grades earned in mathematics courses.

A third assumption in psychometrics is that genuinely basic abilities and attributes are relatively permanent once they have been acquired or have appeared following the necessary stages of maturation. In isolated cases, scores might undergo sudden and extreme change as a result of disease or injury, but on the average they are expected to remain relatively constant, at least over periods of weeks or months or (even) years, depending on the attribute under consideration. Tests proceeding from this assumption are required to yield highly similar results on repeated administrations. When they do, they are said to be reliable; that is, to have a high *coefficient of reliability*. Since we do not think of arithmetic skills as varying greatly from month to month in an adult population, a test that displayed great variability when repeatedly administered to an adult population would be dismissed as unreliable.

To this abbreviated list of psychometric assumptions, I will add only that of *predictive efficiency*, which is part of the test's practical validity. It is assumed that if a psychological test is valid, the results will, *on the average*, permit nonchance levels of predictive accuracy. If, for example, most of those who failed the test of arithmetic ability went on to distinguish themselves as engineers and accountants, the test would be judged to have been invalid because of its low predictive efficiency. One measure of this efficiency is the correlation between scores earned on the test and estimates of success or performance on the job.

2. Validity

I have cited "face validity" as one index of the overall acceptability of a psychological test, but it should be noted that this is not always a necessary attribute of psychological tests. It finally depends on the use to which the test is to be put and the conclusions that are to be based on the results. Suppose, for instance, that Company A has had a very high turnover rate in personnel, and that most of the employees hired were soon discovered to be unable to do their assigned tasks. Let us assume further that, for economic reasons, Company A is not able to launch elaborate training programs but must, instead, hire only those who will reach the desired level of performance in less than one week on the job. Specialists in testing are retained and begin to study the characteristics of those who succeeded and the characteristics of those who failed in the past year. To everyone's surprise, they discover that the one factor that predicts on-the-job performance, with 90 percent accuracy, is the length of the employee's nose! They pass this fact on to the company, and on the strength of it, all future applicants are screened for nose length. As an added dimension, let us assume that Company A employs 70,000 workers, must screen thousands each year, and must therefore have a rapid, reliable, and valid measure of likely performance.

I offer this odd situation and solution to underscore the difference between *face validity* and *predictive efficiency*. In many settings, the former will be forfeited in favor of the latter, even though the measurement in question seems to have absolutely no connection to the demands of the job. Recent rulings by a number of courts fail to comprehend the difference and seem tempted to conclude that the plaintiff has won his case once he has shown that the test items do not obviously relate to the requirements of the job at issue. The courts in such matters have arrogated to themselves the right to mandate the adoption of one technical standard at the expense of another, when in fact the courts generally do not understand either. And lest the reader think that predictive efficiency will generally work to the disadvantage of those who earn low grades, I should mention that many occupations are poorly suited to those who obtain very high scores on, for example, tests of intelligence. It is well known that high I.Q. groups will, on the whole, become quickly bored with routine operations, will relax their vigilance, and will soon perform at substandard levels. Accordingly, an employer might screen applicants in such a manner as to eliminate those whose I.Q. scores fall *above* a certain cutoff.

3. Discrimination and Injury

Because of the charged climate surrounding the issue of racial discrimination or discrimination based on sex, it is all too easy to be misunderstood, particularly if one chooses only to be disinterested. I should begin this section, therefore, by repeating that fundamental canon of justice according to which *equal cases are to be treated equally, and unequal cases unequally only to the extent that the inequality is relevant.* This being a principle rather than a slogan, a few words must be devoted to it.

It is a settled axiom of moral reasoning that "just deserts" attach to individuals, and that the justice of any desert is determined by the connection it makes with the intentions and the actions of the individual. Persons are to be neither praised nor blamed for anything beyond their power to control, prevent, or bring into being. Among other protections, this entails that we will not be punished merely because we share certain characteristics in common with another or with several others whose actions have been judged as worthy of punishment. That every felon is a human being does not mean that every human being is a felon. At the same time, there is nothing in the fundamental principle of justice or in the settled axiom of moral reasoning that stands as a bar to any and every form of discrimination. The principle of justice includes the concept of "relevant inequality," and that of morals the concept of "desert." In plain talk, the former is not violated by the fact that most professional basketball players are more than six feet tall, and the latter is not neglected when the winning team earns more than the losers. In the realm of prizes, for example, losing is *relevant* to unequal compensation. Nevertheless, all this pertains to the arenas of open and free competition. A different problem arises when steps are taken to determine who is to be admitted to these very arenas, and it is this problem that stalks psychological testing. In the whimsical illustration offered above, have we not told all those whose noses were too short or too long that they would not even have a chance to show their worth? Is not the effect of such testing to eliminate large numbers from those very competitive arenas in which "just deserts" are won?

Let us move from whimsical illustration to actual issues. It has been argued that, on the average, black workers take more time off for illness and other reasons than do their white co-workers, and that newly married women resign from their positions more frequently than men, much older women, and never-married women. Suppose, in light of such findings, that neither black nor female applicants were even considered among the pool of candidates for employment. That is, on the basis of their each having one characteristic in common with a group known to be "high-risk," the black applicant and the female applicant were told that they would not even be considered; or, if considered, their applications would be negatively weighted to reflect the on-the-job records compiled by blacks and by women in the same company over a period of years. Is this any different from the nose-length criterion? Is it any different from adjusting the cost of automobile insurance to the age and sex of the driver, based on the incidence of accidents among given age groups and between the sexes? Is it different from the requirement of the Rhodes scholarship that no applicant be older than 23, or the statutory requirement that all voters be 18 or older?

As we attempt to weigh these questions, we must also remain cognizant of another side of that settled moral axiom; the side which frees persons of blame *for any action that they could not avoid.* That is, we must be mindful that in honoring justice in principle, we may not always be able to honor it in practice; we may simply lack the means, the opportunity, the resources, or the knowledge necessary for our actions to conform undeviatingly to the letter of the principle. That there is room for mischief in this is further evidence that earthly life is the art of the possible. But beyond the boundaries of practicality we enter those of genuine morality, where the first and last question is one of *intention*. It is an unavoidable feature of statistical groupings and an unavoidable consequence of the quest for predictive efficiency that individual cases will be ignored. But it is precisely because these are inescapable and unavoidable that they carry no moral burden in and of themselves. Where such factors are introduced *so that* certain groups will be injured, we have clear evidence of immorality, but this is not the case merely as a result of the factors themselves. There may have been a seventy-year-old man in 1942 who, even with one eye missing and with one wooden leg would have performed admirably in the service of his country; who, had he been given the opportunity, would have been decorated for valor. However, with the need to process millions of citizens, and with the defensible decision to enlist only those having a high probability of completing basic training, was it "immoral" to remove from the pool of potential draftees those in their seventies or those missing limbs and eyes?

In one sense, the answer must be *yes*. Old men were treated differently, as were the handicapped, even though both included in their ranks some individuals who could have performed as well at some of the tasks that fell to young and healthy inductees. Thus, "like cases" were not treated in like manner. Moreover, individuals were put at a disadvantage merely because they shared certain characteristics with a group. But other aspects of justice and morality were also involved in these cases—aspects associated with the government's obligation to preserve the nation and defeat the enemy.

Setting aside considerations of warfare and looking at only commercial life, the urgencies seem to evaporate. Yet corporations have duties to their investors, to their other employees, to their customers, and to the overall prosperity of the society. Corporations are not laboratories for the conduct of experiments in social theory, nor are they temples of justice. To the extent that their policies and practices in the areas of hiring and promotion lead to the glaring under-representation of identifiable groups of persons, and to the extent that this outcome cannot be explained by provable and judiciously obtained facts, the charge of discrimination may be warranted, and appropriate action should be taken. Indeed, where all the criteria of employment are lacking in face validity—that is, where all the tests and standards are of the "nose length" variety—there is cause for inquiry. *However, the cardinal test of justice in such settings is not the proportional representation of all discernible groups in the final pool of employees, but the adoption of measures that are blind to all factors other than likely performance on the job.* Proportional representation can be achieved only by discriminating against applicants whose group is now fully represented. From a moral point of view, there is no difference between a sign announcing that "Blacks need not apply" and one announcing that "Blacks need no longer apply."

When we turn from commerce to education, the issues become even less complex, at least from the moral point of view, although they are more complex from the psychosocial point of view. It is the latter that dictates sameness and that will abandon liberty on the first showing of the equalitarian alternative. Twenty years ago, this would have been hyperbole; now it is a commonplace. The irony, of course, is that the equalitarian defense is often wed to something called a "pluralistic society"—an oxymoron in its own right. But it is surely not diversity that is celebrated by this defense; it is mediocrity. At the root of the issue, of course, is the question of just what sort of society America should be. At the root is exactly the tension recognized by Tocqueville and other observers a century ago. The traditional vision, and if I may say, the Constitutional vision, encompassed a nation in which ideas and talents were nurtured so that the best in every person might survive and prosper, and so that excellence would be the standard. To be sure, we will seldom want to give more than two cheers for meritocracies, but do we want to give as many as two for anything else?

Psychological testing comes face to face with this sudden skepticism toward excellence because it has accumulated a commendable record in the matter of predicting it. Now, this is not to be interpreted as a myopic ignorance of the problems endemic to standardized tests. They do not predict "geniuses," and they may

even be hostile to them. They are not foolproof, for many a fool
has done well on them. Nor do they tell us whom to vote for, or
the qualities of humanity, or the road to virtue. Typically, they
tell us the most efficient and prudent course to follow in making
various educational and vocational facilities available to very
large numbers of youngsters. They are unquestionably essential
to any system of education designed to instruct the millions if that
system is not to neglect the needs of both the most and the least
able in the enrollment. Moreover, they are the only safeguard
against those very tendencies toward prejudice and favoritism
that commonly dominate the ordinary classroom. That such tests
are less than perfect is an argument not for their abandonment
but for their improvement. Nonetheless, of all the specialties
within psychiatry and psychology—of all branches of the "social
sciences"—the field of psychological testing has made more numerous, more effective, and more reliable contributions to the
national life than any other. It charts for us annually the drift of
the national intelligence; it points to deficiencies and strengths in
our diverse approaches to education; it helps us recognize talent
in its crib; it keeps a finger on the pulse of our literary and
technical standards; it informs each student of his standing on
any number of dimensions in relation to those of the same age
and years of education; it permits distinctions among motivational, cultural, and intellectual sources of failure. I find it more
than interesting that many who claim to have the welfare of
minorities at heart are opposed to the one gift of psychology that
might give direction to programs of remediation as well as quan-
tification to allegations of past injuries. It is one thing to accuse
the majority of injustice on the basis of the performance of
minorities on tests, but quite another to forbid the administration
of tests on the grounds that they are discriminatory. Of course
they are discriminatory—they were designed to discriminate! But
is it unjust discrimination?

The answer here is a resounding *no*, for the simple reason
that justice does not enter into the tests at all. Justice enters, if it
ever does, when some benefit or penalty is made contingent on the
results of the tests. There is nothing unjust about measuring the
height of citizens, though it is surely unjust to pay tall ones twice
as much as short ones for doing the same work. Height, like a
scholastic aptitude score, is a *number*. It is neutral with respect to

theories of politics, governance, social organization, and justice. The Hispano-American and Afro-American children of California whose low scores led to proscriptions against testing retain all their deficiencies once the courts have adjourned. They will either improve in their basic academic skills—in mathematics, grammar, vocabulary, spelling, and reading comprehension—or they will be unfit for higher education and for those professional and commercial opportunities reserved to those who have such skills. In the absence of the tests, the deficiencies remain either unnoticed or ignored or unknown at a sufficiently precise level. With the tests, the children and their families and teachers know what must be done. If the courts wish to serve the interests of individuals and society, they might begin by making such tests mandatory.

On the face of it, the decision to bar or restrict psychological tests is, of course, frivolous, but it is not difficult to grasp some of the considerations influencing it. Every war takes innocent lives, and the war against racism is no exception. To the extent that some, like the Nobelist William Shockley, would defend discriminatory practices on the basis of psychometric data, it was inevitable that the tests would bear the brunt of the reaction. Although Dr. Shockley has never had more than polemical enthusiasm to support his peculiar and offensive proposals, competent psychologists such as Arthur Jensen unwittingly aggravated matters in the early 1970s by permitting complex aspects of heredity and psychometrics to surface in the popular media. The net effect was to reduce the entire issue to no more than ideology, with Shockley's views standing at one end of the know-nothing continuum and CBS's "The I.Q. Myth" at the other end. The attacks on Shockley soon extended to Jensen, and the matter seemed to be settled once and for all when a British journalist and Leon Kamin of Princeton University discovered that Sir Cyril Burt may have misrepresented the facts in his authoritative publications on the heritability of I.Q. Thus, by the mid-1970s, the psychosocial point of view enjoyed another of its triumphs, and the specialty of psychological testing was put on official notice.

If these developments are to be seen in the proper light, it is necessary to unravel the technical, political, and emotional threads that have become so knotted in the past decade. Perhaps the first shot was fired by Jensen when he published "How Much

Can We Boost I.Q. and Scholastic Achievement?" in the *Harvard Educational Review* (1969). It was in this article that the infamous "Jensen thesis" was given a quasi-public airing. The thesis itself is a very old one and can be found in many psychological journals from the 1920s and thereafter. In its earliest incarnations, it was addressed to the "immigrant problem," and the first victims of the thesis were the Irish and Italians. The most recent victims are blacks, but the terms of the thesis have remained relatively constant even as the particular racial or ethnic targets have changed. Let us be mindful, however, that an essentially "racist" thesis can be advanced by one who is not himself a prejudiced person, and this would seem to be the case with Professor Jensen. In the form given by him, the thesis is as follows:

1. I.Q. is known to be highly heritable.
2. On the average, blacks display less of it than whites.
3. I.Q. is highly correlated with scholastic achievement.
4. Given (1), (2), and (3), programs of enrichment such as "Head Start" are doomed to fail.

The first term of the thesis requires some analysis, since the concept of heritability is a subtle one. To say that any characteristic displays high heritability is to say that most of the variation in the expression of the characteristic is attributable to genetic diversity. We may take height as illustrative. If we plot the fraction of a large sample whose height falls in each of several ranges of height—for example, 4.6 to 5.0 feet, 5.1 to 5.6 feet, etc.— the heights will approximate a normal distribution. The most frequently occurring height will be the average of the sample, and the further from this average the other heights fall, the less frequent are they. All of the measured heights will fall somewhere under the normal (bell-shaped) curve depicting the distribution of heights. That is, all of the variation around the average value will be found under the curve. The technical way of stating this is that the total variance of the distribution is, in fact, the area under the normal distribution curve. Now, as it happens, height is highly heritable, usually producing a coefficient of heritability (h^2) in excess of 0.90, where the maximum value is 1.0. What this means is that genetic influences are responsible for approximately 90 percent of the total variance displayed by height in the sampled population. *It does not mean that 90 percent of a person's height is genetically determined!*

When it is alleged that I.Q. is highly heritable, the claim is based on the variance of I.Q. scores earned by large groups classified according to the degree of genetic relatedness. What many studies have shown—and Sir Cyril Burt's data constitute only a modest fraction of the total—is that the variance of I.Q. scores is significantly *unaffected* for samples consisting of pairs of identical twins even when different nurturing environments are involved. In other words, environmental variation does not contribute significantly to I.Q. variation.

There are, to be sure, immense difficulties in practice connected with research of this kind, and we have every right to be reserved in confronting estimates of the heritability of I.Q. We do not know, for example, which aspects of the environment are most important for the development of those abilities tested by I.Q. tests. Accordingly, we do not know whether "different environments" are different in relevant respects. Identical twins, as look-alikes, may be treated in highly comparable fashion in *any* environment. Adoption agencies tend to assign adoptees to families bearing certain physical similarities to the child and, to this extent, separated identical twins may find themselves in more similar and comfortable settings than do nonidentical twins. Moreover, estimates of heritability are known to be inflated in any setting in which relevant aspects of the environment are selected on the basis of the genetic composition of the specimen—plant or animal—and, although we cannot measure such gene-environment covariations where human subjects are involved, we have reason to believe that they do occur. (For many years, for example, being black in the South would result in assignment to the rear of the bus as part of one's environment—this being a clear case of the "environment" being selected on the basis of one genetic factor.) Accordingly, any estimate of the heritability of something like I.Q. will be burdened by a variety of infecting variables practically beyond control. Nonetheless, it would be surprising if there were not a significant genetic influence in the final development of *any* human characteristic. Let us, then, give Jensen the benefit of the doubt and accept that I.Q. scores can be taken as reflecting high heritability or, perhaps, moderate heritability. As we shall see, conciliation on this point will not spare the thesis.

Jensen's second proposition is based on numerous studies in which "black" children, on the average, obtain lower I.Q. scores than "white" children. We must always think of these adjectives as residing within quotation marks since they surely do not constitute any precise genetic designation. We do not have "pure strains" of human beings, only tribes and races whose recent history has been marked by relatively little out-breeding. Let us also recognize that black-white average differences generally hover around ten points, and that these differences display some sensitivity to geography, to the monies a community devotes to education, and to the racial features of the examiner. Let us also be mindful of the fact that the vast majority of "blacks" and "whites"—and everyone else ever tested—can be safely categorized as delightfully *average*, so that ten points either way will be cause for neither alarm nor celebration. But, again in the spirit of conciliation, let us simply take the data as they have been reported and accept that, on the average, the "nonwhite" I.Q. distribution falls a bit to the left of the "white" one. Less equivocal is the correlation between I.Q. and measures of scholastic achievement, whether the latter are based on other standardized tests or grades earned in school or evaluations by teachers.

What is interesting about Jensen's thesis is that it fails in its conclusion even if all its premises are accepted without challenge. Heritability, as it happens, has nothing to do with the *average* value of a characteristic, but with the *variance* displayed by that characteristic in a population. Thus, to know that the heritability is high—even 1.0—is not to learn that the environment will not have an effect on its average value, but that environmental manipulations will not affect its variance. The heritability of eye color in one strain of fruit flies is 1.0, but the *average* eye color of the sample of fruit flies depends on the altitude at which they develop. What does not change with altitude is the *variance* of eye color. In other words, even if it were the case that I.Q. had a heritability of 1.0, and even if it were the case that "blacks" had "fewer I.Q. genes" than "whites," it would still not follow that environmental enrichment would fail to increase the *average* I.Q. (and scholastic achievement) of the "black" population.

But this is surely not all that is wrong (and wrong-headed) with theses of this sort. In any comparison of groups of human beings segregated according to one or only a few criteria, there will always be great regions of overlap. The dominant blood types found among Eskimos differ from those found among Bantu, but some Bantu have Eskimo types, and some Eskimos have Bantu types. This is not to say that the concept of a race is meaningless, for it is not, but only that the assignment of any given *individual* to a race will require an element of arbitrariness. If we catalogue as many physical features as we can find among Eskimos, and if we count the frequency with which these appear, we will find one population that can validly be called "Eskimo." But now a stranger appears, and our task is to determine if he is an Eskimo. Whatever we say, we will either be entirely correct or entirely wrong. That is, the assignment of any *single* person is fraught with dangers. What we can say, however, is this: If we employ the measured frequencies of traits observed in the Eskimo population to assign large numbers of persons either to the Eskimo or the non-Eskimo category, we will be correct in X percent of the cases; and the fewer the physical characteristics we employ, the further we depart from the maximum of X percent. Suppose, however, that the only datum we had was the average I.Q. of Eskimos. Now a stranger appears and we administer the I.Q. test. Let us say that the Eskimo average is 100 and our stranger earns a score of 96. Is he an Eskimo? The point, of course, is that we would be as well off flipping a coin as using such a score for the purpose of locating an individual in a group. *To know the average performance of a group on any test does not allow us to predict the performance of any individual within that group.* To know, then, that "blacks" as a group obtain higher or lower scores tells us nothing about what the next black person will do on the same test. To find out, we must give the test *to him*.

We are now in a position to remove the term "racist" from the lexicon of insult and place it in that of analysis. A racist is one who assigns values to individuals exclusively on the basis of the *average* value attained by some racial group with which those individuals are (arbitrarily) identified. For purposes of justice and fairness, there are not "blacks" and "whites," but *persons*, who must be judged one at a time, and whose deserts are earned one at a time. If we were to use only I.Q. scores for the purpose of racial assignments, we would misclassify nearly half of those now classified as "black" and "white" on the basis of color and other physical attributes. Thus, as stereotypes go, I.Q. is especially poor in what is never more than a bad lot.

It should be clear from the foregoing that the problem is not with psychological tests, but with the sort of nonsense made of the results even by those who should know better. A child enters the testing room, sits down, is instructed as to procedure, and completes a standardized test of English, mathematics, and general science. The examiner scores his responses and discovers that the child is seriously deficient in all three. On this basis, he advises the family and the school officials that the child should be given a remedial program. The next child comes in, and the same results are forthcoming. So too with the next, and the next, and the next. When the week is out, it is discovered that 58 percent of the children in the school require remedial education, and that 84 percent of this 58 percent happen to be black or Hispanic. What conclusions are warranted? Some will see in the results clear evidence of past discrimination. Others may think of the findings as genetically suggestive. Still others will insist that such facts will only diminish each child's self-image. I would urge that only one conclusion is warranted, and that is that 58 percent of the children tested require remedial education. All the rest is potentially hazardous speculation. If we are to address it at all, it is only to expose it. Suppose past discrimination is, in fact, the cause. There is still the problem of academic deficiency, and if it is not solved we can expect a fair and proper amount of future "discrimination" unless illiteracy becomes a national goal. And as for the hereditarian theory, we may treat it as an empirical prediction and see what happens to successive generations of well-educated, highly motivated, and generally accomplished members of the various minority groups. So too with respect to the child's putative "self-image." We have every reason to expect it to prosper as the child comes up to par in those abilities that are coextensive with modern and civilized life.

The great mistake of the Court in *Brown* v. *Board of Education* was not simply that it misunderstood the studies conducted by Kenneth Clark and others but that it consulted them in the first place. Chief Justice Warren went to great lengths in reflecting on the "injuries" of segregation in the matter of the "self-esteem" and "dignity" of the children and in their overall scholastic standing. But suppose there had been no evidence of this sort, or even contradictory evidence (as there was)? Would it follow, then, that the schools could and should remain segregated? The principle of justice to which the Court should have confined itself is the historic one: that equal cases be treated equally. No child should be denied access to any school merely on the grounds that he happens to have some feature in common with the members of some group unless the feature in question is provably relevant to the expressed mission of the school. Put another way, denying a child entrance to a school because the child is black is morally repugnant on its face no matter how the child feels about it and no matter what the effect may be on his subsequent scholastic achievement. The issue is not one of real or alleged "injury" to the child, but one of *injustice*. Segregation of the sort under examination is unjust in part because it is irrational and in part because it violates our genuinely moral desires. The plain fact is that segregation was not and could not be shown to result in "injury" in every case. Nor would such a showing be sufficient to establish the practice as unjust. Every tyro who fails to make the major leagues is injured, his self-image tarnished. Every rejected suitor sustains similar injuries. In most situations, the practice of discrimination will be a source of disappointment and injury to all who fail to be included, but every such discrimination is not *ipso facto* injudicious. The justice of it all depends on the *grounds* of discrimination, not on the mere fact of it. More than 60 percent of the players in the National Basketball Association are nonwhite. We do not take this as evidence of injustice but as a sign of the distribution of talents and opportunities for the development of these talents. Justice is preserved by the openness of competition and by the uniform application of relevant standards. It could be that white children are not as encouraged to perfect the skills of the game; that surburban environments are not well suited to early education in the rudiments of the game; that, on the average, the black population contains a relatively higher fraction of those physically suited to the game; that the relative absence of non-athletic opportunities for high earnings encourages blacks to pursue athletics. As in most significant human endeavors, the causal elements are numerous and somewhat different in each case. On the psychosocial vision of humanity, these elements must be uncovered and homogenized for the dogma of sameness to be vindicated. Psychological tests unfailingly expose this vision as perverse and therefore are the subject of relentless attack. Were justice to stand as the properly disinterested witness there would be no problem, for the facts will always speak out against the levelers. The problem comes into being with a judiciary that shares the vision and that has the temporary power to impose it.

164

4. Recent Cases

A number of perplexing cases followed in the wake of the civil rights legislation of the 1960s and it became grimly clear in *Bakke* that the courts—including the Supreme Court—had been hoisted by their own psychosocial petards. Predictably, the problems began in the very legislative language with which the courts have had to contend.

In 1972, Congress brought into being something called The Equal Employment Opportunity Coordinating Council which later issued a now famous *Affirmative Action Policy Statement* (1976). Let us sample passages germane to the question of psychological tests:

> When an employer has reason to believe that its selection procedures have the exclusionary effect . . . it should initiate affirmative steps to remedy the situation. Such steps, which in design and execution may be race, color, sex, or ethnic "conscious", include, but are not limited to, the following. . . . Revamping selection instruments or procedures which have not yet been validated in order to reduce or eliminate exclusionary effects on particular groups. . . . The initiation of measures designed to assure that members of the affected group who are qualified to perform the job are included within the pool of persons from which the selecting official makes the selection. . . . The goal of any affirmative action plan should be achievement of genuine equal employment opportunity for all qualified persons. Selection under such plans should be based upon the ability of the applicant(s) to do the work. Such plans should not require the selection of the unqualified, or the unneeded, nor should they require the selection of persons on the basis of race, color, sex, religion or natural origin.

This statement does not require hiring on the basis of race, religion, or gender, but it does permit "remedial" steps to acknowledge these factors by being "race, color, sex, or ethnic 'conscious.'" But for such measures to constitute a "remedy," there must be a preexisting *injury* or *injustice*. Now, the bald fact that certain racial groups are under-represented in one or another sector of the workaday world is not sufficient to establish that they have been injured or unjustly treated. The overwhelming majority of employees in Chinese restaurants are oriental, although few of the patrons actually speak Chinese and many of the employees (waiters, for example) have not perfected English. For purposes of communicating with the chef, let us note, the non-Chinese waiter is under no greater handicap than is the English-speaking patron who must communicate with the Chinese waiter. Of course, such establishments are known to be ethnic by their very nature, and their commercial success depends on this. Still, such establishments are regularly found in regions having negligible numbers of Chinese-American residents and having significant numbers of unemployed and qualified non–Chinese-Americans whose ethnic status effectively excludes them from consideration. Some of them may be Afro-American or Hispano-American; others Italian, Anglo-, or German-American.

In situations of this sort—and they could be multiplied into the hundreds—the employer surely "has reason to believe that its selection procedures have the exclusionary effect . . ." and must, on the wording of the policy statement, "initiate affirmative steps to remedy the situation." But is a remedy called for in such cases? Most, I suspect, will say no, in part because the exclusionary factor does not single out a particular group and does not arouse general suspicion toward those so excluded. It is true that being Chinese is a nearly necessary condition of employment, but only because the establishment is recognized as a *Chinese* establishment that strives to bring part of the Orient into American culture. Without pausing to analyze the situation, most observers would say something like "All things considered, it makes good sense for a Chinese restaurant to hire only Chinese waiters and staff, and no one would conclude from this that any other ethnic group is thereby stamped as inferior or denied anything that might be called a basic right." But now let us take the case of a group of Italians opening a Chinese restaurant, and hiring only Italian waiters, chefs, and staff.* Let us add the condition that the establishment is located in a region in which there are many unemployed Chinese-Americans. We now approach the proprietor, armed with the 1976 affirmative action policy statement, and demand a justification. Embarrassed and somewhat testy, Mr. Rinaldi defends himself thus: "The whole idea, you see, is—how do you say? —a gimmick. People think it's funny to come to a Chinese restaurant operated by Italians. They have a good time."

*Those who have visited "Mr. Chow's" in London know that this illustration is not far-fetched.

But, say we, don't you know that many qualified Chinese-Americans in this very neighborhood are out of work and that most of your waiters travel many miles to get here? Why are you discriminating against Chinese people? Nonplussed, Rinaldi exclaims, "But I do not discriminate *only* against Chinese. I discriminate against everybody who is not Italian. In fact, I discriminate against every Italian who is not a Florentine!" Will most observers now agree that it makes equally good sense for a Chinese restaurant to hire only Italians?

On a purely practical level, these illustrations will appear to be far off the mark since the numbers involved are trivially small and since under the weight of psychosocial reasoning, only the numbers matter. For courts and legislatures to become interested, Rinaldi would have to open a chain of such establishments, use the revenues to acquire trucking firms, airlines, and department stores, and use these profits to take possession of three medical schools staffed exclusively by Florentines in oriental dress. That is, once the very principle of justice is corrupted into the delphic language of "groups," it becomes impossible to consider *injury* in individual terms. As long as Rinaldi owns only one restaurant and discriminates against all who are not Florentine, there is no problem. However, he cannot discriminate against any single group even when he owns one restaurant, nor can he favor a single group once his possessions become great. What is the principle here? Alas, there is none. There is a policy, but not a principle, and because of this the courts can only hand down decisions as incomprehensible as *Bakke*. The policy statement insists that plans for affirmative action "should not require the selection of the unqualified . . ." nor should selection be obligatory on the grounds of race, religion, or gender. But all this can mean is, in principle, that all are free to compete for available places and that the result of the competition will be determinative. However, one consequence of this *principled* position seems to be the preservation of nonrepresentative groupings in various sectors of the labor market, and especially in the professional sectors. When we look for the proximate cause of this consequence, we discover more often than not the scores obtained on standardized tests of aptitude and ability.

The courts, however, are not given to quailing in the face of principle where a policy is at stake. Thus, in *Griggs* v. *Duke*

Power Co. (401 U.S. 424), the court found for the plaintiff simply on the showing that selection tests had substantially "racially disparate" effects. In such instances, the burden falls to the employer to prove that the tests are unequivocally related to the actual demands of the job. In *Albemarle Paper Co.* v. *Moody* (422 U.S. 405, 425), there is this additional burden:

> [I]t remains open to the complaining party to show that other tests or selection devices, without a similarly undesirable racial effect, would also serve the employer's legitimate interest in "efficient and trustworthy workmanship."

Discussing the latter case in its *amicus* brief in *Bakke,* the United States argued that

> in *Albemarle Paper,* in dealing with a test that appeared to screen out black applicants . . . the Court concluded that, in validating such a test as job related, employers could be required to counteract its racially disparate effects by resorting to racial criteria. They could, in other words, be required in appropriate circumstances to "differentially validate" their employment tests—to use one passing score for blacks and another for whites, so that the test would predict success on the job equally well for both racial groups. The conscious use of race in making such employment decisions can help prevent subtle discrimination and help the employer to achieve a result that ultimately will not be racially biased. (*Amicus* Brief, pp. 32–33)

What Griffin Bell and the Justice Department did not make clear in this brief, however, is precisely how using "one passing score for blacks and another for whites" would "ultimately . . . not be racially biased." Let us suppose, for example, that a given company uses the cut-off score of 80 on a particular test and will not even interview those falling below this criterion. Those finally hired all do very well on the job. Let us assume further that, in the original pool of applicants, there were 25 whites and 25 blacks who failed to reach the cut-off. Through further testing, it is found that many applicants with scores of 60, including many black applicants, also 'o well on the job. If we rely on the principle of fairness, this means that the employer now should lower the criterion score to 60 for all applicants, but this is not what the Justice Department wants, and it is not what was mandated in *Griggs* and in *Albemarle.* The fundamental conflict here is between the sound *principle* that opposes unjust discrimination and the ragged *policy* that requires proportionate racial or ethnic or religious or sexual integration.

The court in *Bakke* attempted to reconcile these opposing forces, but the reconciliation by its very nature had to be at the cost of the principle. It finally makes little difference whether race is to be one factor in the admission of students to medical school or whether it is to be the decisive factor or even the only factor. In all cases, its inclusion involves the sacrificing of one person's opportunities in favor of what the court sees as a faceless group. Wed to such a policy, even agile minds are found to wither. Here, for example, is Archibald Cox during the oral argument in *Bakke*, as counsel discusses the medical school's policy of reserving 16 of 100 places for minorities:

> *Mr. Cox:* I want to emphasize that the designation of sixteen places was not a quota, at least as I would use that word. Certainly it was not a quota in the older sense of an arbitrary limit put on the number of members of a non-popular group who would be admitted to an institution which was looking down its nose at them.
>
> *The Court:* It did put a limit on the number of white people, didn't it?
>
> *Mr. Cox:* I think that it limited the number of non-minority, and therefore essentially white, yes. But there are two things to be said about that: One is that this was not pointing the finger at a group which had been marked as inferior in any sense; and it was undifferentiated, it operated against a wide variety of people. So I think it was not stigmatizing in the sense of the old quota against Jews was stigmatizing, in any way.
>
> *The Court:* But it did put a limit on their number in each class?
>
> *Mr. Cox:* I'm sorry?
>
> *The Court:* It did put a limit on the number of non-minority people in each class?
>
> *Mr. Cox:* It did put a limit, no question about that, and I don't mean to infer that. And I will direct myself to it a little later, if I may.
>
> *The Court:* Do you agree, then, that there was a quota of eighty-four?

Mr. Cox: Well, I would deny that it was a quota. We agree that there were sixteen places set aside for qualified disadvantaged minority students. Now, if that number—if setting aside a number, if the amount of resources—

The Court: No, the question is not whether the sixteen is a quota; the question is whether the eighty-four is a quota. And what is your answer to that?

Mr. Cox: I would say that neither is properly defined as a quota.

The Court: And then, why not?

Mr. Cox: Because, in the first place—because of my understanding of the meaning of "quota." And I think the decisive things are the facts, and the operative facts are: This is not something imposed from the outside, as the quotas are in employment, or the targets are in employment sometimes today.

It was not a limit on the number of minority students. Other minority students were in fact accepted through the regular admissions program. It was not a guarantee of a minimum number of minority students, because all of them had to be, and the testimony is that all of them were, fully qualified.

All right. It did say that if there are sixteen minority students, and they were also disadvantaged, then sixteen places shall be filled by them and only eighty-four places will be available to the others.

The Court: Mr. Cox, the facts are not in dispute. Does it really matter what we call the program?

Note in these exchanges the unwillingness of counsel to accept the sixteen places as evidence of a quota; to accept the 84 percent limit on nonminority admissions as a quota; to weigh the implications of the very concept of "fully qualified." He takes for granted that when racial discrimination is "undifferentiated," it is not unjust, and believes, or at least argues, that a quota must be "stigmatizing" for it to be indefensible on moral grounds. Finally, he can only conceive of an inequitable system of quotas where the numerical differences work against "disadvantaged minorities." Can this be the voice of justice?

Most of the facts in *Bakke*, like the alleged facts in *Brown*, are largely irrelevant to the fundamental issues. There are more than

24 million Americans of African and Hispanic ancestry, and this immense population is only scantily represented in law, medicine, and scholarship. On the face of it, the disinterested observer would certainly find this suspect. As he inquired further into the matter, he would learn that professional attainments—even the modest one of certification—come at the end of many years of motivated study, helpful tuition, familial encouragement, and financial support. He would learn also that a very large fraction of black and Hispanic families are weighed down by uneducated adults, meager or modest economic means, and limited opportunities for employment. Where these families are concentrated, the elementary and secondary schools often are unable to attract the better teachers or to insulate students from the negative lessons taught by the immediate surrounds. Our disinterested observer would predict that most children reared under these conditions will be less fit for advanced study than those nurtured by educated and affluent parents. He will conclude from all this that the only genuine solution, at least for future generations, is the creation of intensive and high-quality educational programs in the elementary grades, marked by the constant imposition of rigorous standards of achievement. In time, the products of such programs will compete successfully for places in the better colleges and in professional schools thereafter. *There is no just alternative to this,* and it is only the blinded ideologue who argues otherwise. The double crime of such an argument is the disregard of truth and justice and the inescapable continuation of those very conditions that are responsible for the facts in the first place. What is the inducement to improve education when the traditional rewards of the instructed mind are *legislated* into being for those who are uninstructed? What is the motivation for self-development and what can be the pride of industry when opportunities are mandated solely on the basis of race? And what becomes of the individual, and the concept of the individual, when the courts, the laws, and the politicians can be summoned only in defense of groups, factions, and subcultures? What becomes of the *person*?

5. Culture-Free, Culture-Fair . . . Culture Gone?

That psychological tests have been abused in practice is a fact accepted by all capable of forming a judgment on the matter. Any measurement can be put to odd and venal purposes. Nonetheless, the field of psychological testing, at least as it pertains to the testing of basic intellectual abilities, must rank as the most developed specialty within the social sciences, and the one that has already made the greatest contribution to the practical affairs of society. It is through such tests that we can come to learn both of the effects of past discrimination and also of the success of our remedial attempts. The tests, to be sure, must not dictate educational policies nor be used in such a way as to have us ignore every aspect of the developing citizen except his intellect. Furthermore, the mere fact that mental abilities figure in nearly all human activities does not mean that every opportunity is to be doled out on the basis of such abilities. I think it is safe to say that 90 percent of existing occupations can be mastered by men and women of average intelligence and that at least 50 percent demand even less than average intelligence. On the whole, then, the part such tests are likely to play in the selection of employees will be a limited one, although one that increases as the intellectual requirements of the position become stricter. What part tests should play is, finally, an empirical question, not a legal or moral one. Where tests are used as an integral part of hiring or admission to special programs, those responsible for selection may be summoned to prove that the results of the tests correlate significantly with performance, but this is all they must prove. Neither the school nor the business should have to account for disproportionately lower scores among this or that group or to devise some other method by which the differences can be (artificially) concealed. In all of this, we finally do find a place for the social sciences; ironically, this is the one arena from which they are increasingly barred. The psychometrician arrives with a message: All persons are not equal in all relevant respects. But the message does not conform to the policy. Shall we kill the messenger?

The perennial complaint against standardized tests, and especially those that attempt to assess intellectual abilities, is that they are biased in favor of the dominant culture and therefore place members of other cultures at a disadvantage. This complaint has been taken very seriously by those who specialize in the construction of I.Q. tests, since the goal is to develop instruments by which to assess those intellectual capacities thought to be essentially independent of educational or cultural nuances. There are, for example, so-called performance tests that yield I.Q. scores on the basis of completely nonverbal tasks. But even these are possibly contaminated by such factors as the child's exposure to toys and games, his opportunities for exercise, his diet, and the broad environmental conditions that might conduce to attentive and motivated performance or to desultoriness and early surrender. The issues here are technical and formidable, but they are not directly germane to the argument of this chapter. Only rarely are standardized I.Q. tests the decisive instruments by which decisions are made to admit persons to schools or to hire them in the business world. More frequently, a battery of tests is employed in which different abilities and aptitudes are separately assessed. These too are standardized tests with norms established on the basis of scores earned by a large and representative sample.

It should be clear that the very process of standardization not only fails to be "culture-free" and "culture-fair," but quite properly fails even to attempt to be. Modern American society, "pluralism" to the contrary notwithstanding, has the choice of remaining a society or fractionating itself into distinct tribal communities, each with its own language, values, customs, super-stitions, and laws. In light of its Western foundations and its historical evolution, American society has distinguishing cultural features, not the least of which are those very constitutional safeguards utterly unknown in noncivilized or uncivilized or less than civilized reaches of the world. American culture places a premium on personal initiative, literacy, computational agility, linguistic fluency, originality, and perseverance. In noting that a premium is placed on these attributes, I do not suggest that all Americans continue to revere them, but only take cognizance of the fact that a citizen's economic and social standing is determined more by these attributes than by any others. The exceptions are to be found in the fields of entertainment, but even the extraordinary wealth and celebrity of performers generally will not confer on them the special status accorded to leaders of thought, of science, and of industry. By and large, a person's future in the United States continues to be determined disproportionately by a combination of motivational and intellectual attributes essential to success in settings that are at least quasi-academic. Technology has placed a high price on its gifts. Today's farmer must understand complex machinery, subtle tax laws, soil chemistry, world markets. Even the file clerk and typist must go home every night and tend to personal financial matters, matters of health, and matters of social life all bloated with complexities unheard of just a few decades ago. Today's American citizen is expected to wrestle with ecological issues, energy crises, the rights of tenants, the maintenance of appliances and automobiles— with an awesome assortment of challenges all converging on his mind. If America is "greening," the color comes more from our envy of a simpler age than any tendency to recapture it. There is, no doubt, a good deal more jogging done and much more yogurt consumed, but these and related diversions remain at the extreme periphery of life's daily obligations.

The question that emerges from these indisputable facts is how we are to prepare succeeding generations for the America that is to be bequeathed to them. And let us not be lulled by the promises of imminent revolutions in "life styles" or by what are finally pathetic attempts to revive romantic innocence. Even the future generation that decides to return to Walden Pond will require great strength and focus of mind just to dismantle what we have already created. Each year, the American world becomes a more demanding one, and the greatest demands are of an essentially intellectual nature. It is not that *better* minds are required, but that the mind is more regularly engaged than ever before. Accordingly, the role of the schools is now more significant than at any other time in American history. Whereas education was once a desirable adjunct to an essentially agricultural life, it is now a necessity. Indeed, the poorer the schools become and the less developed are the student's basic skills, the greater will be the disparity between the (shrinking) class of those who have mastered these skills and those who have not. Nowhere will the law of supply and demand operate more ruthlessly.

In the circumstance, the demand for tests that are "culture-free" would be ludicrous were it not so pregnant with tragedy. The courts and the Congress can play roulette with the *lex scripta*, but in the real world, life is anything but a game. Thanks to the courts and the Congress, we have nearly perfected the means of getting children on and off buses, but in the process we have not accomplished much by way of educating them between stops. Meanwhile, the specialists in testing continue to record diminished national abilities in such basic realms of mind as reading,

writing, computing, and reasoning. There are, of course, cultures
in which such abilities are irrelevant, even counterproductive.
But ours is not one of them, and it is not likely to become one.
Even if we set out to transform American society into something
closer to Samoa, our friends and enemies around the world cannot
be expected to follow our example.

Alas, even if we kill the messenger, the contents of the message cannot be evaded. America is richer and stronger for its
ethnic diversity. It is exemplary to the extent that it cherishes this
heritage and seeks to preserve a climate in which every individual
can retain or abandon the customs of his ancestors. How drab a
nation it would be without the spectacle of aesthetic differences
and the parade of older traditions. With these gone, only the
machinery of progress and production would remain. But for all
its noise and rubbish, the machinery is here to stay. It is this
machinery that every mind must reckon with, either as master or
slave. The business of the schools is the preparation of the mind,
not conformity to the will of a subculture. To prepare the mind,
the school must be apprised of its strengths and deficiencies, and
in this regard our very best instruments are standardized tests
constructed out of the facts of modern American life. The alternative to this is not a different culture, but no culture at all. The
alternative is anarchy—a mass without a standard.

The most recent report of the Educational Testing Service at
this writing, "National College Bound Seniors, 1979," tells us
that national scores have again declined in English, mathematics,
and the achievement tests in various specialties. The "verbal"
score is now at 427, an all-time low, and the "quantitative" has
dropped to 467, another record. What is particularly troubling
about the numbers is that they reflect the performance of a group
more given to special tutoring for these tests than were earlier
groups. Ironically, one of the charges heaped on such tests is that
students can be "prepped" for them, putting less affluent students
at a decided disadvantage. However, by most demographic and
economic standards, the "affluent" constitute some 70 percent of
the testing sample. If larger and larger numbers of these students
are availing themselves of special tutoring every year, the national
average should be climbing, not sinking. Indeed, it is a fair
assumption that there is now far more special training for these
tests than ever before and that, in fact, the scores would be even

lower were the current crops to enter the testing room as innocently as did students in the 1950s or early 1960s.

When these facts are illuminated by the occupational trends in American society, they become even more alarming. Whether one adopts liberal or strict criteria, the current rate of illiteracy in the United States is shocking. A recent study for the Ford Foundation* indicates that between 18 and 64 million American adults are either completely or "functionally" illiterate; that 23 million have severe reading problems; that another 23 million are so deficient as to be unable to function competently in contemporary society. In nine states, more than half the adults have not finished high school. The deficiencies that today qualify a citizen as "functionally illiterate" would have placed him under no special burden at a time when American social and economic life was passed in unpopulous, unhurried, agricultural climates. Today, however, the illiterate cannot find the right bus to take home; cannot read the lease he signs; cannot learn the contents of the food he is eating; and cannot determine the provisions of his own insurance, let alone his legal protections and obligations. As a voter, he is at the mercy of clowns. As a consumer, he is the constant potential victim of fraud. His life proceeds in a world he but darkly comprehends and cannot help to manage. Presumably, the state will invent (should invent?) a special sign language for him so that his handicap will not work to his disadvantage. Note, then, that it is in the very spirit of welfarism not only to aid the handicapped but to increase their numbers. Note, too, however, that the laws of daily life pay little heed to the machinations of social theorists. What current trends guarantee is a two-tiered society: one occupied by an ever-dwindling number of literate, motivated, capable persons—in white collars and with a full grasp of how the world actually works—and an ever-enlarging pool of drones. Such trends are always difficult to discern on a day-by-day basis. As of now, we have only the imperfect device of the achievement test to aid us. As we do no good for the sick by shattering thermometers, we do no good for the deficient by proscribing the use of those instruments that measure the extent and the distribution of the deficiencies.

*"Adult Illiteracy in the United States," by C. St. John Hunter.

Notes

The issues addressed in this chapter have guided many discussions I have had with my former colleague, Prof. Hadley Arkes, and I have benefited greatly from them. Some of the material in the chapter comes from parts of a manuscript we wrote but did not publish. I would urge all interested in the part played by psychological research in *Brown v. Board of Education* to read Professor Arkes's "*The Problem of Kenneth Clark*" (*Commentary*, 1974).

For the briefs and oral arguments in *Bakke,* consult Vols. 99 and 100 of *Landmark Briefs and Arguments of the Supreme Court of the United States,* Kurland and Casper, eds. University Publications of America, Washington, D.C.

Goddard's remarks and the translation of major works by Binet and Simon are given in Series B. Vol. IV of *Significant Contributions to the History of Psychology,* D. N. Robinson, ed. University Publications of America, Washington, D.C., 1977–78.

6 Persons: Their Nature and Their Rights

Without using the terms, many have perceived in the combination of welfarism and the psychosocial point of view that diminished regard for ordinary individuals that inevitably constitutes a threat to extraordinary ones, particularly those unable to protect their rights. The trend is most visible in the rhetoric associated with "death with dignity," in jural opinions of the sort handed down in the case of Karen Quinlan, in the powers courts have given to those treating "mental" patients, and in the Supreme Court's reasoning in the landmark *Roe* v. *Wade* and *Doe* v. *Bolton*. Behind each of these trends is a theory of *personhood* and one that is irredeemably either wrong or incoherent. In such areas, the courts increasingly look to technology and to the social sciences for guidance in what are finally issues of principle rather than matters of fact. The net effect is not that the resulting decisions are clearly wrong, but that they fail to settle the issues of justice bound up with these cases. The decisions, then, are neither right nor wrong, for they are not *jural* in the received meaning of the term. Every jurist grants that persons have rights, but there is now a reigning confusion as to the meaning of "person." This confusion is intensified by the habit of looking to technicians—psychologists, psychiatrists, sociologists—for answers to what have always been and will necessarily continue to be philosophical questions. I should quickly add that I use this adjective in the

narrow and academic sense, not in the way laymen rely on it
when they seek to depreciate the importance of something. By a
philosophical question I mean one that must be addressed in
terms of an analysis of the form and content of the propositions
that create the question. Answers that are forthcoming will depend on the meanings assigned to the major terms of the proposition and the implications logically flowing from it.

When issues such as those of abortion, euthanasia, and psychosurgery arise, their legal and moral dimensions can always be
recast as a relatively neutral expression, which helps us comprehend the nature of the problem. What is involved in all these
issues is the performance of a certain action (A) on a certain entity
(X). The issue arises when there is reason to believe that A is
wrong, in and of itself, or is wrong only because the X in question
is judged to possess protections against A-type treatments. In the
latter case, X is said to have a right (R) not to endure A. The
question at law thus becomes: Does the law allow the performance
of A on X? and the moral question becomes: Should A be performed on X? The legal and the moral sides of the issue come
closest to each other on the related question of how the relevant
R is distributed. To use a trivial illustration, let us say that the A
in question is forcibly preventing an X from pulling down the
lever in a voting booth. We then discover that X is a chimpanzee.
Now, since the right to vote (R) is reserved to citizens of the United
States, and since the chimpanzee fails to qualify as a citizen, the
performance of A is not illegal. But is it immoral? This is a far
more difficult question. The chimpanzee, for example, will be
personally affected by legislation pertaining to the treatment of
animals and by economic conditions as these influence attendance at zoos or funds for veterinary care. We can show that the
animal is able to distinguish the several candidates for office and
that, in terms of his gross behavior, is able to demonstrate a keen
preference for one of them. There are, moreover, many adult
human beings who, by virtue of congenital, genetic, or traumatic
factors, are less able to learn, remember, and perceive than is the
chimpanzee. On what grounds, therefore, would we argue that it
is *morally* right to perform A on this particular X? Put another
way, on what moral ground may we insist that this X does not
possess that R which would protect it against A-type treatment?

The most obvious answers to such questions invariably carry

undesirable implications. We might say, for example, that the chimpanzee lacks the intellectual and rational faculties needed to participate fully in a life of citizenship. But to say this is to say that the relevant R is contingent on the possession of specific intellectual and rational attributes such that every X must be tested before claiming the relevant R. Or we might reply that the chimpanzee is not a citizen, does not support the nation, and exercises none of the obligations of citizenship. However, it may well be that this particular chimpanzee has had salutary effects on the local economy and has contributed far more to society than he has taken from it. Moreover, he was brought here against his will, has lived in captivity within the continental United States for five years, and has been as much involved (or as little involved) in the affairs of the nation as any number of vagrants, drug addicts, and alcoholics, who now have the relevant R whether they exercise it or not. Moreover, to deny this R to the chimpanzee on such grounds is logically symmetrical with requiring such participation and industry of anyone who claims R. In desperation, we might then simply insist that the chimpanzee is not eighteen years old, but this is a purely statutory classification whose *moral* standing is precisely what is at issue.

The most obvious answers having failed, we find ourselves compelled by the very nature of the case to become philosophical. Having analyzed the concept of "voting," having come to grips with the moral foundation of participatory democracy, we begin to recognize that the relevant R can only attach to that class of X's properly described as *moral beings*. This is not to say that every member of the class is such a being, but that only members of this class are such beings. We are saying, therefore, that the R in question is available only to that subset of X known as *persons*, the subset we designate as P. Thus, when it comes to voting, we merely have to answer the question, Is this X a P? in order to settle the *moral* side of the issue and thereby complete the essential part of settling the legal side. But, then, what is a P? And is every imaginable R attached *only* to Ps? What is the standing of a given R when a once-P becomes a non-P? What is the standing of a given R when a non-P is very likely to become a P? These are the questions that suffuse such issues as that of abortion. It is instructive to observe how they have been dealt with by the courts, and how they might have been dealt with.

1. *Roe* v. *Wade*

It may seem somewhat out of place to include this celebrated case in a book devoted to the interaction of law and the social sciences, but there seems to be every reason to believe that the psychosocial point of view operated as the Invisible Hand here as much as it has operated more openly in the areas considered in the preceding chapters. In the last analysis, the decisions in *Roe* v. *Wade* and *Doe* v. *Bolton* hinged on implicit assumptions about the legal standing of the fetus given the psychological standing of the same fetus. In these cases, "expert" testimony was not sought from the psychological specialties, although a number of psychological claims were made regarding the perceptual, cognitive, and affective attributes of prenatal beings.

Of all the odd reasonings embodied in the court's decision, perhaps the most peculiar was that leading to the conclusion that medicine and theology have not been able to determine when life commences after two thousand years of speculation. Students of the modern Court had already discovered its difficulties with ordinary propositional logic long before *Roe*, but in this decision what had only been remarkable now took on legendary proportions. A representative sample of the most telling parts of the opinion is offered:

> The appellee and certain amici argue that the fetus is a "person" within the language and meaning of the Fourteenth Amendment. . . . If this suggestion of personhood is established, the appellant's case, of course, collapses, for the fetus' right to life is then guaranteed specifically by the Amendment. . . . The Constitution does not define "person". . . . But in nearly all . . . instances, the use of the word is such that it has application only postnatally. None indicates with any assurance that it has any pre-natal application.
>
> All this, together with our observation, supra, that throughout the major portion of the 19th century prevailing legal abortion practices were far freer than they are today, persuades us that the word "person", as used in the Fourteenth Amendment, does not include the unborn. . . . We need not resolve the difficult question of when life begins. When those trained in the respective disciplines of medicine, philosophy, and theology are unable to arrive at any consensus, the judiciary, at this point in the development of man's knowledge, is not in a position to speculate as to the answer. (*Roe* v. *Wade*, 410 U.S. 113, 93 S. Ct. 705)

And, joining the majority in the related case of *Doe* v. *Bolton,* Mr. Justice Douglas offers these opinions:

> Elaborate argument is hardly necessary to demonstrate that childbirth may deprive a woman of her preferred life style and force upon her a radically different and undesired future. . . . When life is present is a question we do not try to resolve. While basically a question for medical experts, . . . it is, of course, caught up in matters of religion and morality. (*Doe* v. *Bolton,* 410 U.S. 179, 93 S. Ct. 739)

How the nineteenth century used the word "person" would seem to be no more relevant to the issue at hand than how that same century used the word "lunatic" if, as the Court reasons, the question falls in the domains of "medicine, philosophy, and theology." All three of these specialties, and particularly the first two, have undergone dramatic alterations of perspective in the past century, and since the Court has shown a decided inclination to rely on narrow technical expertise in all sorts of cases, there would seem to be no reason to abandon them here in favor of century-old dictionary definitions. The same applies in regard to the failure of the Constitution to define "person." Years after the Constitution was written, many were prepared to count the freed slave as three-fifths of a "person" for voting purposes, and many others who doubted he was a "person" at all. But these ancestral ignorances surely are not to serve as guiding lights for the modern world! Similarly, it is entirely unclear that the permissiveness of the last century in the matter of abortion has any bearing on the issue at all. Slavery was also permitted "throughout the major portion of the nineteenth century." It may well be that the authors of the Fourteenth Amendment did not consider the fetus as worthy of its protection. They also did not consider women worthy of the franchise. The fundamental judicial question is not what they considered in light of what they knew, but how our expanded knowledge and understanding allow us to honor the intention of the law without saddling us with conceptual or technical errors that prevailed at the time the specific words were chosen. The Constitution does not define "press" either, but we surely honor the intentions of the First Amendment by extending its protections to television and radio, although neither of these could have been predicted at the close of the eighteenth century.

Thus, this part of the reasoning in *Roe* is simply fatuous. What the last century knew or didn't know about the biology and psychology of the fetus is a matter to be explored by historians of science. A contemporary court is obliged to acquaint itself with what *we* know.

This brings us to the second leg of the logic in *Roe*, the putative fact that "medicine, philosophy, and theology are unable to arrive at any consensus" on the question of "when life begins." As a statement of fact, this is simply wrong, for there is absolutely no difference of opinion as to whether the fertilized egg—or, for that matter, the sperm or the unfertilized egg—is alive. The metabolic physiology of such cells has been studied often and carefully and is known to display all the features of any entity said to possess life. But giving the Court the benefit of the doubt, let us say that what was meant was that medicine, philosophy, and theology had not reached a settled position on when *human* life begins. This is a more reasonable claim, although it too is false, at least if we are willing to accept the basis on which the modern biological sciences classify any form of life. Such classification proceeds from modern genetics and permits us to name a given living specimen according to its genetic composition. A cell, therefore, may be said to be a human cell when its genetic structure is drawn from the gene pool of *Homo sapiens*. Thus there are human eggs, human sperms, and human fertilized eggs or zygotes. I don't know that philosophers or theologians traffic much in these designations, but there is no room here for differences of opinion, since what is involved is a fact, not a point of view. Note, then, that even before conception, we are dealing with human life. However, before conception, are we dealing with a *human being*?

At this point, matters become more tangled but not entirely arbitrary. In the trivial sense, every existing thing is "in being" and, to this extent, may be said to be "a being." But it is ordinarily accepted that a *being* is differentiable—that it possesses one or more than one attribute by which it may be distinguished from other beings. Genetically, each egg is indistinguishable from other cells taken from the same body, and the same is true of each sperm. With fertilization, however, a new genetic combination is achieved that differs from the genetic makeup of either parent. This fertilized egg may split to form two genetically indistinguishable zygotes. In this case, differentiation can no longer be based on genetic uniqueness but on spatial or geographic uniqueness. The point here is that no violence is done to the concept of *human being* by applying it to fertilized human eggs, but that some violence is done by applying it to sperms cells or unfertilized eggs—or cells of the liver or spleen.

Still, in treating the zygote—or, later, the embryo or fetus—as a human being, we do not establish that the entity is a human *person*, since personhood implies something different from biological uniqueness. It implies, among other considerations, an ensemble of perceptual, motivational, intellectual, and moral attributes found widely and historically in human communities.

The Constitution did not, of course, define "person," if only because no exhaustive definition is possible. This should scarcely trouble the Court, however, since the same document leaves undefined such crucial terms as "rights," "powers," "freedoms," "states," and "war." The Constitution is not a lexicon but a body of principles written by intelligent men who assumed that the common experiences of mankind would permit their meanings to be known. If we attempt to define "person," we are likely to insist that at least two classes of attributes are essential: one class containing some number of purely physical features, and a second class containing some number of psychological or mental features. On this construal, we would call a corpse a human being but not a person. But the room for disagreement becomes great indeed once we attempt to list either the necessary or the sufficient physical or mental attributes. Must one be awake to be a person? Must one have thoughts, feelings, plans, sensations, pains, or language? Must one have arms, legs, kidneys, a brain, intestines, or a heart? These are not medical questions at all, for they have to do not with biological facts but with what philosophers call the extensional (denotative) and intensional (connotative) properties of words. This is not to say that philosophy can settle the matter, however. What philosophical or, in this case, linguistic analysis will yield is an account of the work such a word as "person" does in our language, and what the logical implications and entailments are once we settle on a specific set of definitional criteria.

In the simple notation I used at the beginning of the chapter, the Fourteenth Amendment may be said to protect every X from all actions of type- A, by virtue of conferring rights of type- R on every X. What the *Roe* Court construed was that the fetus did not qualify as an X whereas the appellant did, and this on the assumption that X must be a *person*. If the fetus were a person, "the appellant's case, of course, collapses." It must be noted, however, that there are some Rs available to non-Ps, so it does not follow that the fetus is stripped of every R once it is assumed that the fetus is not a P. The law, for example, forbids the torture of animals who may, therefore, be said to have a *right* not to be tortured. Thus, if the fetus is granted the status of "animal," and if it can be shown that abortions cause suffering as well as death, we then must weigh the pregnant woman's alleged right to privacy* against the fetus's right to be spared unnecessary suffering.

This, however, is a separate (though related) matter. Let us remain with the Court's understanding. We learn that the inability of doctors, philosophers, and theologians to settle the matter of "personhood" is, somehow, a justification for the Court's refusal to take a position. Let us recognize *in passing* how preposterous a line of argument this is for any institution bearing the name of Supreme Court. It is, after all, only when irreconcilable differences of interpretation occur that disputants must approach a *supreme* court for a ruling. Yet there is more than irony in the Court's uncommon diffidence. If, in fact, the status of the prenatal human being is in doubt—if, that is, there is room for the argument that the fetus is a person—and if the relief sought by the appellant entails the death of the fetus, then doubt alone is sufficient to refuse the relief unless the appellant's life hangs in the balance. It is perhaps true that "Elaborate argument is hardly necessary to demonstrate that childbirth may deprive a woman of her preferred life style," but it is unequivocally true that abortion deprives the fetus of life itself. The remedy for a childbirth that deprives a mother of her preferred life style is adoption. We do not think of her as having the right to kill her child under the protection of the Fourteenth Amendment. What, then, is the difference between the prenatal human being and the postnatal one? Physically (if this matters at all), there is only the difference between intrauterine and extrauterine sources of nourishment and oxygen. Psychologically, there is no measurable difference at all, since the progress of mental abilities is too gradual to admit of daily discriminations. The famous criterion of "viability" is a

*Also not mentioned either in the Constitution or the Fourteenth Amendment.

shifting one that depends on advances in science, bioengineering, and medicine. In invoking this criterion, the Court guaranteed periodic challenges to its own decision, but this was a small island of tactical awkwardness in a vast sea of conceptual error. No infant is "viable" in the sense of being able to survive on its own. The difference between the fetus and the infant is that the former can live only as a result of maternal nurturance whereas the latter can be kept alive by anyone caring to do so. However, there is no moral argument known to me that confers the right to live in amounts inversely proportional to the potential victim's degree of dependency. Rather, the right is judged to be particularly designed to protect those least able to fend for themselves.

In joining the majority in *Doe*, Mr. Justice Douglas was constrained to add other phrases of note:

> [R]ejected applicants under the Georgia statute are required to endure the discomforts of pregnancy; to incur the pain, higher mortality rate, and aftereffects of childbirth; to abandon educational plans; to sustain loss of income; to forgo the satisfactions of careers; to tax further mental and physical health in providing child-care; and, in some cases, to bear the life-long stigma of unwed motherhood. . . . The protection of the fetus when it has acquired life is a legitimate concern of the State. Georgia's law makes no rational, discernable decision on that score. For under the Act the developmental stage of the fetus is irrelevant when pregnancy is the result of rape or when the fetus will very likely be born with a permanent defect or when a continuation of the pregnancy will endanger the life of the mother or permanently injure her health. (op. cit.)

In the first part of this passage, the concerns expressed by the Justice remain unaffected by substituting "motherhood" for pregnancy and childbirth. The second part is a jumble of paradox and contradiction. The fetus has life, it does not "acquire" it. Moreover, if the Court is distressed by the Georgia statute because it fails to protect fetuses resulting from rape or those that may be defective, the remedy is surely not the decision in *Roe* or in *Doe*! What is most salient in the passage, however, is the psychosocial list of burdens imposed on the child-bearing women. Hospitals, doctors, nurses, aides, laboratory technicians, and business officers must now preside over a million abortions annually so that some pregnant women can continue their studies, increase their incomes and not "forgo the satisfaction of careers." Is all of this covered by the Fourteenth Amendment? Is any of it?

Somewhere in this storm of premises and welfarism the fetus got lost. The Court was not prepared to confer personhood and was not moved by the fact that this status is nearly invariably the consequence of undisturbed pregnancies. Through Mr. Justice Douglas, it acknowledged a wide range of future possibilities in the life of the appellant, but it was not carried by this same logic to notice the foreclosed possibilities of the fetus. In refusing even to review the question of personhood, the Court may also have presented future appellants with attributes they do not have. Both *Roe* and *Doe* were given unchallenged status as persons. Suppose, however, one of them was feeble-minded. Suppose one was sadistic and took pleasure in the pain and death caused by abortions. Suppose one had been eleven years old. The point here is that whatever one's definition of personhood may be, the mere fact of pregnancy cannot plausibly be taken as a sufficient condition for the attribution. A comatose patient could conceivably be artificially impregnated and the pregnancy could be maintained through the marvels of modern technology. This same patient would display fewer psychological attributes than those already found in prenatal human beings. I mention this only to underscore the point that the condition of pregnancy does not automatically establish personhood. Nor does the right of "privacy" automatically protect anything that might be done in private. A surgical abortion is not a private act, but one that involves at least three beings: the surgeon, the mother, and the fetus. To permit the first two of these to do to the third something that would not be allowed were the third a child must be based on not merely manifest differences but unarguably relevant differences between the fetus and the one-hour postnatal infant. To the extent that personhood is assigned largely on psychological grounds, there is no unarguably relevant difference. And to the extent that there can always be found an adult whose psychological equipment has been ravaged by disease, injury, or calamity, any decision that allows killing in cases of doubtful "personhood" cannot rationally be limited to fetuses. In summary we discover two propositions of consequence:

1. To the extent that personhood is assigned on exclusively biological grounds, there is only one criterion satisfied by all who

have ever been called persons, and that is the genetic criterion. On this head, every human fetus is a person.

2. To the extent that personhood is assigned exclusively on psychological grounds, the criteria of consciousness, moral awareness, intellect, memory, and emotion are traditional. On this head, no fetus is a person, nor are any number of defective human beings of all ages.

The effect of adopting the first proposition is to deny the right to an abortion in every case except those involving self-defense. The effect of the adopting the second proposition *might* permit abortions in all cases *and* also permit the killing of all human beings who are as burdensome as fetuses and who fail to qualify as persons in the same way that fetuses do. I say it only might permit abortions because the fetus is not entirely like the defective adult. The latter in many cases can be classified as irremediably defective; i.e., as one who will never qualify as a person. The fetus, however, has a better than 95 percent likelihood of so qualifying; even though the relevant test is failed now, the life is preserved on a promise. The closest the courts have come to embracing the second proposition is the case of Karen Quinlan. In this instance, the psychosocial point of view was not the Invisible Hand, but the visible one.

2. Karen Quinlan

The facts in *Quinlan* have been the subject of books and articles, as well as one television motion picture. I will review them only briefly.

On 15 April 1975 Karen Quinlan was discovered by friends to be unconscious and labored in her breathing. Subsequent tests led to the conclusion that her condition had been precipitated by the combined ingestion of alcoholic beverages and barbiturate medication. Early in the course of her hospitalization she displayed some awareness (it was reported that she blinked on command), but her abiding condition has been that of a vegetative state. Her life was sustained by intravenous feeding, feeding through a gastric tube, and artificial respiration through a tracheal tube. Physicians described her case as hopelessly irreversible. Sometime in late July or early August of the same year, Karen Quinlan's parents, in consultation with physicians and a priest from their parish, concluded that the mechanical supports of respiration should be discontinued. After initially agreeing to follow the wishes of the family, the attending physician, Dr. Morse, refused to disconnect the respirator because he could find no relevant precedent in the annals of medicine. On the advise of hospital administrators, Miss Quinlan's father, Mr. Joseph Quinlan, sought the legal sanctions of custodianship in the Superior Court, Chancery Division, Morris County, New Jersey (12 September 1975). The decision of the Court, as rendered by Judge Muir, was that none of the appellant's arguments succeeded, and that a neutral party be named as custodian (10 November 1975). Notice of appeal was filed one week later, but on the same day the New Jersey Supreme Court issued an order by which it came to review the appeal.

In opposing the Quinlan family, the State of New Jersey argued that it had a compelling interest in the life of every citizen, and that it would seek criminal sanctions against any party or parties acting in such a manner as to end the life of Karen Quinlan. But during the oral argument, the Justices pressed the state's prosecutor, Mr. Collister, on the reach of such criminal sanctions. Would the state prosecute physicians who failed to perform the tracheotomy in the first place? Would it prosecute the physician who, after learning that the respirator had ceased to function, decided to take no corrective action? Suppose the doctors had met with the Quinlans and had informed them that their daughter was irremediably comatose and had recommended that she simply be allowed to die. What then? In response, the state labored to make a distinction between the duties that attach to physicians once therapy has begun and the absence of those same duties before it has begun. The hypotheticals presented by the Justices were very demanding, and the state was not able to find a cogent principle for any of them. Thus, its argument boiled down to a pair of contentions: Karen Ann Quinlan is alive, and the state is obliged by *parens patriae* to protect her life.

The court, as we now know, ruled for the Quinlans in this action. The decision was based on several considerations, although I would suggest that none of them was finally relevant to the instant case. One factor weighed very carefully by the court was the protection of physicians against malpractice and criminal prosecutions. The Justices sought to provide a ruling that would liberate doctors "from contamination by self-interest and self-protection. . . ." However, the great weight of expert testimony in this case contained nary a suggestion that measures taken to continue Miss Quinlan's life would expose her doctors to such actions. Indeed, even in these litigious times, it would strain the credulity of a jury to argue that steps aimed at the preservation of life constituted malpractice! The Justices also several times alluded pointedly to the allegation that Miss Quinlan's condition was irreversible. But this is true of a large number of conditions—cerebral palsy, mongolism, diabetes, multiple sclerosis, blindness—and it has never served as a justification for denying or removing supportive or palliating therapy. There were also references in both the oral argument and the decision to a law that would require the patient "to endure the unendurable" where Miss Quinlan's choice is much like that made "by a competent patient, terminally ill, riddled by cancer and suffering great pain." Yet, there was never any evidence in *Quinlan* to suggest that the patient was enduring the unendurable or was in any pain at all. Her condition was frequently described as "chronic vegetative state," and such states are best thought of as untroubled, at least in regard to pain. On the religious side of the matter—although it is not clear that the court had any justification for addressing this—the Justices noted that a member of the Catholic clergy had instructed the Quinlans that the church does not require the use of "extreme measures" to defer imminent death, and that in ordering the removal of life-supporting equipment, the Quinlans would be guiltless in the eyes of the church. But the dispository court in this case was the secular and Supreme Court of New Jersey, not an ecclesiastical court in Rome. In any case, there is nothing "extreme" about either a tracheotomy or gastric feeding.

What ultimately counted most heavily of the various medical considerations was something dubbed "cognitive and sapient life":

> The evidence in this case convinces us that the focal point of decision should be the prognosis as to the reasonable possibility of return to cognitive and sapient life, as distinguished from the forced continuance of that biological vegetative existence to which Karen seems to be doomed.

I say "medical" considerations, although the "cognitive" and "sapient" features of life are, strictly speaking, matters for psychology and not medicine to determine. There is to a moral certainty, however, no chance of Miss Quinlan's restoration to the life she was living before the catastrophe halted it with such suddenness. That is, she will almost certainly never again be a "functional" member of society. In this respect, however, she is best considered as occupying an extreme position on that continuum of cognition and sapience along which the balance of the human race is distributed. Inevitably, then, the question of where one draws the dividing line must be raised. How much "functioning" constitutes a "cognitive and sapient" life?

All the easy answers to questions of this sort become ensnared in the facts of clinical neurology and the limitations of neurological and psychological diagnoses. It would be easy, for example to say that the line should be drawn in such a way as to confine all comatose patients on one side and all conscious ones on the other. But "consciousness" is not akin to blood type or core temperature. It cannot be measured or defined with precision. It does not necessarily remain at a given level for any significant period of time. Finally, in the patient whose condition renders overt behavior impossible, the usual signs of consciousness are absent, but it would be perilous to rely exclusively on such signs. We do not think of persons who are merely paralyzed as "unconscious." We do think of those under the influence of anaesthetics in these terms, but we recognize that the unconscious state is transitory—as it is in various stages of sleep. Furthermore, in cases such as *Quinlan*, simple criteria are frustrated by the frequent survival of primitive spinal reflexes. Indeed, Miss Quinlan—or at least her body—displayed reflex withdrawal of aversively stimulated extremities as well as incoherent but unmistakable vocalizations.

In *Quinlan*, the criterion of "brain death" was discussed at length, although both the state and the appellant agreed that the Harvard criteria of brain death were not satisfied in this case. Most salient among these criteria is the absence of recordable electrical activity in the patient's brain. Miss Quinlan's EEG, however, not only failed to meet this test but was unremarkable except for a degree of "slowing" that takes place in a number of neurological conditions, some of them not at all severe. Note, however, that any criterion grounded in a diagnostic instrument like the EEG is an arbitrary one. It is possible to obtain relatively normal EEGs from animals whose cortical hemispheres have been surgically removed, a fact that illustrates the failure of the measure to distinguish perfectly between cortical and noncortical neural processes. The electrical activity of the brain, when sampled at the surface of the skull, is generally at amplitudes varying between 50 and 100 millionths of a volt (microvolts). Much weaker signals will not be recordable, but this is not incontrovertible evidence that there is an inactive brain. Thus, the use of the EEG as a measure of brain death invites the same sorts of problems as those arising from the concept of fetal viability in the area of abortion. Both criteria may finally speak more directly to the state of the art in technology than to anything significantly true of the organs and beings under consideration.

In *Quinlan*, however, none of this figured, since the patient had regular heartbeats, a fairly strong EEG, and a number of vital signs. When I discussed the case in 1976,* I made the following observation:

> [C]linical experience leads most of the experts to conclude that the life Karen Quinlan now displays would not survive another year. In those cases where patients are similarly "chronically vegetative" and where, nevertheless, life is supported for as many as five years, the ability to breathe without mechanical assistance is the rule.

In winning declaratory relief from the New Jersey Supreme Court, the Quinlans were able to move their daughter to a different hospital where no mechanical respiration was initiated. At this point, however, Miss Quinlan began to breathe on her own and is, at the time of this writing, still alive. If the rationale of the court were to be followed, the mere fact of restored breathing still carries no promise of a return to "cognitive and sapient life," and therefore there should be no compelling reason to continue the nasogastric feeding. Although there is nothing "extreme" in either procedure, most qualified doctors would agree that such feeding is at least as "extreme" as artificial respiration. Why, then, continue the artificial feeding? The most direct answer here, again by

*Consult my *Introduction* to Vol. II of "In the Matter of Karen Quinlan: The Complete Briefs, Oral Arguments, and Opinion in the New Jersey Supreme Court." 1976, University Publications of America, Washington, D.C.

virtue of the court's ruling, is that the Quinlan family has not
ordered it stopped!*

In practice, the same considerations enter into the equally
publicized case of Joseph Saikewicz, the mentally retarded sixty-
seven-year old patient whose guardian refused the use of chemotherapy as a treatment for Mr. Saikewicz's leukemia.** As in *Quinlan*, there was no hope (or very little hope) of the patient surviving
the leukemia even after chemotherapy, and no hope whatever of
obtaining the patient's own informed consent. We have, then, the
combination of irreversible illness and a non-participating patient. Mr. Saikewicz died within months of the diagnosis of his
leukemia, but would not have been expected to live too much
longer even had chemotherapy been instituted, a therapy with
very unpleasant side-effects. In some respects, the decision in
Saikewicz is more portentous than that in *Quinlan* for at least two
reasons. There is first the fact that Mr. Saikewicz, though severely
retarded, was a conscious and active man, notwithstanding his
inability to speak or to communicate in any but a gestural way.
And then, too, there was the possibility—remote, but greater than
in the case of *Quinlan*—of a spontaneous recovery from the
leukemia. Such recovery would not, of course, have made the
patient any less retarded. It would only have prolonged the sort of
life he had been living for decades. But there is a difference in
principle between *Quinlan* and *Saikewicz* in that the Massachusetts Court was clearly skeptical of "quality of life" arguments and
grounded its decision primarily on Mr. Saikewicz's right not to be
exposed to painful therapies in return for an extra month of life.
What the Massachusetts Court was willing to weigh was the fact
that the State could not mandate such treatment in the case of a
competent patient and that such a patient, aware of the considerable cost in suffering and the marginal benefits in added time,
may well refuse the treatment. But on this very question of "What
would the competent patient decide?" every court may make one of
two mistakes. It may assume the patient would decline when, in
fact, he would not or that the patient would accept treatment when,
in fact, he would decline it. The first error speaks to the State's

---

*Mr. Jospeh Quinlan has recently and movingly told the press that he visits his
daughter on his way to and from work every day, and that he is grateful that she is
still "with us."

**Superintendent of Belchertown v. Saikewicz*, Mass. 370 N.E. 2d 417 (1977).

commitment to preserve life *whenever* there is doubt as to the wishes of the patient. The second speaks to the alleged right of persons to permit their own deaths when suffering is the alternative. The second error is the graver.

There was also in *Quinlan* occasional reference to *Roe* v. *Wade*, which the court took into consideration in framing this maxim:

> [T]he State's interest *contra* weakens and the individual's right to privacy grows as the degree of bodily invasion increases and prognosis dims.

But in this any parallel between *Quinlan* and *Roe* breaks down, for in the latter the state sought to proscribe "bodily invasion." It is the abortion, not the injunction, that is invasive. Moreover, how are we to measure "the degree of bodily invasion"? And does the maxim extend to "mental invasion"?

Some assistance might be sought from the United States Supreme Court in cases involving "bodily invasion," but in these our highest Court has preserved its delphic countenance. Some might have thought the matter was settled in *Rochin* v. *California* (1952), where the appellant had been forced to submit to a gastric lavage so that the arresting officers could recover the morphine tablets he had swallowed. The Court overturned the conviction against Rochin, Mr. Justice Frankfurter noting that such methods are "too close to the rack and the screw to permit of constitutional differentiation" (342 U.S. 165, 72 S. Ct.). But within five years, we would learn from *Breithaupt* v. *Abram* (1957) that the extraction of blood from an unconscious party involved in a fatal accident could provide evidence in a criminal case because, in the words of Mr. Justice Clark, the blood was extracted, "under the protective eye of a physician" and, after all, such procedures have "become routine in our everyday life" (352 U.S. 432, 77 S. Ct.). Both Rochin and Breithaupt were forced to give evidence against themselves, though not in the form of a verbal or written statement. Both bodies were "invaded." Together, the decisions suggest that our privacy rights extend to the viscera, but not the veins. We are not surprised, therefore, that the court in New Jersey tended to ignore Supreme Court rulings in the area of medical intervention. In the process, however, the justices in New Jersey laid down a somewhat epigrammatic standard that will permit and even encourage very wide interpretation. Let us note, for example, that the prognosis in severe cases of mental retardation is as dim as any we can find. It often becomes necessary in such cases to provide medical assistance as a result of the patient's proneness to disease and accident. And, of course, it is invariably the case that such patients are under the custodianship of parents or near relatives. How is the *Quinlan* ruling to be understood in these cases, in the event that the parent or other legal guardian instructs the physicians that lifesaving measures are not to be undertaken or continued? There is also a dim prognosis in cases of advanced senility, profound psychosis, and cancers of the brain—all of which may carry as consequences the elimination of "cognitive and sapient" signs. How is the New Jersey ruling to be applied when cases of this sort also come to need tracheotomies, nasogastric feeding, etc.? Suppose, for example, that in the deepest stages of senility, a person develops a diseased gall bladder, which is then surgically removed. It is necessary in such postoperative cases to drain the stomach through a Levine tube. What is the duty of a physician in New Jersey caring for such a patient when the legal guardian enters and forbids the insertion of the tube? What, that is, should the doctor construe from

> [T]he State's interest *contra* weakens and the individual's right
> to privacy grows as the degree of bodily invasion increases and
> prognosis dims.

We arrive at *Quinlan* circuitously, but the path remains that laid down by the psychosocial point of view. The most important factors in this case were psychosocial ones, not medical ones. On the medical side, we have a patient who is alive, who displays most vital signs, who has a steady heartbeat, a strong EEG, and a number of sensory-motor reflex chains. What she lacks are psychological attributes, and what she creates are psychological burdens.* She presents no evidence of pain or suffering. If her condition bears a resemblance to any larger class of disorders, she might be thought of as a mentally defective infant. The steps taken to continue her life are taken thousands of times every day throughout the world. What is "extreme" are not the measures,

---

*For a variety of reasons, all of them philanthropic, medical expense did not figure in this case, although it is not clear that the state's interest could have in any way been affected even if the financial costs had been great.

but her condition. At every stage of scientific and technical progress, however, methods become available that are "extreme" in the sense that they have not been used before. They move from the category of "extreme" to that of "standard" through use. For a court to bar their use is, effectively, to retain them within the category of "extreme measures" artificially and arbitrarily.

The Court in *Quinlan*, like the Court in *Roe* and *Doe*, could have said more by saying less. The New Jersey Supreme Court thought it had stumbled onto something decisive—"cognitive and sapient life"—but this, we see, is no more than a judicial rope of sand on which energies might be expended but no heights of sensibility scaled. The United States Supreme Court, with agnostic bravado, refused to specify the kind of life the state might have an interest in saving, except to insist that it must be postnatal. Thus in one case we discover the articulation of a criterion that is dangerous; in the other, a criterion that is groundless. In both, the *psychological* realities serve as the motive force. Miss Quinlan, like the fetus, is no longer troubled by the need to defer her education, by a reduced income, by the need to abandon career plans, or by the stigma of unwed motherhood. Like the fetus, she is not a "functioning unit" of the psychosocial machine. Again like the fetus, she is a weight on our "life style," a noncontributor, a disposable. I speak here not of the attitudes of Mr. and Mrs. Quinlan, for only they can know the pain and misery that parents in such a case endure. I refer instead to the courts, which increasingly examine the Fourteenth Amendment through a psychosocial rather than a moral or judicial prism. In *Roe*, the Court permitted destruction of life before it emerged as unequivocally "cognitive and sapient"; in *Quinlan*, just after it ceased to be "cognitive and sapient." Before the reign of psychosocial justice, the decisive fact was the fact of life itself, not its real or alleged or hypothesized psychological details. The state's interest is in safeguarding *life*. Here we have a principle both venerable and defensible. *The state's interest is in life.* Any qualification of whatever kind is a violation of this principle, and if only insensibly, the substitution of a different one: *The state's interest is in life of a certain quality.* I submit that this distinction, if it is ever to be made in any circumstance, is one to which the law must remain blind. The law teaches, and the lesson here pertains to, the value of life qua life. I am tempted to borrow the summoning phrase, "the sanctity of life," but I am addressing a principle that is best understood in nonreligious terms. It is first a *moral* principle that attaches protections to human life solely on the grounds of its existence. The protections are absolute in all instances in which the life at issue constitutes no threat to the life of an unoffending other. In the profession of medicine, this moral principle surfaces in the form of the maxim *Primum non nocere*—First, do no harm. It derives its binding power not from the Seventh Commandment, but from the appeal it makes directly to beings who are moral as such. It is, indeed, just this that gives the commandment its binding power. Thus, the basic right to life neither originates in nor requires as its justification any specific religious teaching or even a religious point of view. It is a *moral* right that moral beings honor through their laws. There is no higher right, none that is more fundamental. This is the sense in which it is not granted or even claimed. It simply *is*. I do not commit here one of those facile *ipse dixits* that punctuate so many ethical documents. The right to live is accorded primary status not by declaration but by the very logic of moral reasoning, for unless this right is taken as given and fundamental, the language of morals becomes incomprehensible. This is a language filled with such terms as promises, obligations, deserts, duties, and demands. Such terms are either neutral with respect to time or they are future-referential. But how can meaning attach to a promise when the life of the promisee is not covered by the very veil of morality that gently enfolds the promise itself?

It is as a result of the state's compelling interest in life that every citizen is, in principle and at law, protected from those who might harm him by design, by inadvertence, or by a genuine but misguided expression of Good Samaritanism. The practice of abortion places mother and fetus in what must be construed as an adversarial relationship. If not the state, who speaks for the fetus? In *Quinlan,* too, a similar relationship prevailed between the family and the lingering life of Karen Quinlan. Who, if not the state, stands behind her? These are not questions to be weighed against the shifting variables of life style, career opportunities, education, social stigmas, or *sapience*. They are moral questions first, legal ones by practical derivation, and not psychosocial ones at all. To find comfort in this new habit of the court which gives parity to the psychosocial criteria is a dangerous precedent.

3. Psychosurgery

The worrisome feature of *Donaldson* v. *O'Connor* is that it guarantees "treatment" for the involuntarily committed mental patient but does so at a time when there is a riot of therapeutic options. In principle, the potential recipient of therapy has the right of refusal, but in practice we must remain ever mindful of the implicitly coercive nature of life within an institution. Nor is it necessary to impute unwholesome motives to the professional staff in order to justify our vigilance. A doctor may intend no more than friendly persuasion, but he may be working with a patient and within a context such that this laudable intention effectively becomes coercion.

If we compare *Rochin* with *Breithaupt*, we are left with the conclusion that the factor likely to be decisive in constitutional tests of "bodily invasion" is the apparent wantonness of the invasion itself. Once questions of principle are forfeited in favor of purely empirical considerations, jurists have only their eyes to aid them. On the side of principle, it makes no difference whatever whether the medical procedure involves a blood sample, a gastric lavage, a Levine tube, or a blood pressure cuff. If the results of the examination or test are to be used as evidence in a criminal trial, the subject of these measures—if he is to be protected against involuntary self-incrimination—must have the right and the power to withhold his consent. Note that I am not taking a stand on the protection itself, for it is one that might benefit from an especially cautious moral analysis. Rather, I simply acknowledge that the protection exists and that, as a principle, it is necessarily indifferent to the purely technical aspects of those actions that violate it. But the modern courts now commonly become entangled in all sorts of technical, scientific, and quasi-scientific considerations and are thus forced to find technical and quasi-scientific ways out of them. Thus, the blood test in *Breithaupt* stands. Why? Because a physician was in attendance and because such tests have become routine!

What is portentous here is not only the retreat from principle, but a retreat that occurs at a time when the genius of technology is rapidly perfecting essentially bloodless forms of "bodily invasion" and visually unremarkable approaches to the monitoring and the control of biological and mental processes. Psychosurgery, even in its currently primitive state, is illustrative. If we look back only ten or twenty years, neurosurgical approaches to mental illness involved such radical assaults on the brain as prefrontal lobotomies. This procedure called for the severing of fibrous connections within the prefrontal cortex and generally produced a postoperative patient with significantly reduced emotionality and sometimes with equally reduced intellect, attentiveness, and social conduct. One did not have to be an expert to spot such patients in a crowd, and one surely did not have to think twice about whether the procedure involved a high degree of "bodily invasion."

Today's psychosurgeon drills a small hole through the cranium, using nothing more terrifying than a dental drill. A stimulating electrode of very small diameter is then carefully inserted to a given depth where it will permit the activation of only a small population of cells in the brain. It is even possible to conceal the tiny wire protruding from the skull simply by allowing hair to grow over it. Moreover, through telemetry, the probe can be activated at a distance without the need to connect the patient physically to the source of stimulation. And, finally, we can avoid the issue of "consent," we are told, because once the probe has been placed in position, it is the patient himself who determines when and how intensely his brain is thus stimulated.

As surgical procedures go, this one would trouble the squeamish far less than would an appendectomy, a tonsilectomy, or even a root-canal. In purely visual terms, it would fall somewhere between acupuncture and arterial catheterization. Ultimately, we may expect the same results to be achieved without any surgery at all; e.g., by the use of focused ultrasonic stimulation or the use of pharmacological agents acting on specific centers. The future aside, however, it would be fair to say that current psychosurgical operations would pass the test in *Breithaupt* except for their relative infrequency. I don't mean to suggest that the court would allow such operations for the purpose of extracting confessions; only that the procedure would not offend the senses the way a gastric lavage apparently did in *Rochin*.

The conditions that have been treated with the new psychosurgery are diverse. One of the leaders in the field, working at Tulane, is particularly proud of the results achieved with a pa-

tient who was described as "a knight of the open road; an inveterate homosexual." The approach in this case included the pair-
ing of stimulation delivered to a subcortical region associated
with sexual excitement with the showing of a "stag" film. The
therapy here was a form of conditioning by which sexual feelings
were made coextensive with heterosexual eroticism. This phase
completed, the medical staff then provided the patient with a
prostitute and noted that he "performed very well."

In this case, the patient had been repeatedly arrested both for
vagrancy and for homosexuality. He was finally committed to the
psychiatric ward at Tulane, where he was likely to spend many
months, even years. Orthodox approaches to his "problem" had
all failed. He was advised that the psychosurgical procedure offered no guarantees, but that any number of experiments had
confirmed the possibility of significant results. In all formal
respects, then, the patient consented to the operation. His options, however, were so constricted that the coercive element in
his "consent" cannot be denied. He would either spend a substantial fraction of his life in one psychiatric ward or another, or
he would avail himself of a possible "cure." Since his commitment to Tulane's hospital was involuntary, he would be covered
by the ruling in *Donaldson*. Thus, the bold initiative taken by the
physician in this case ten years ago could now be construed as
mandated. But this is to condemn neither *Donaldson* nor the
doctor. Who would deny the involuntarily committed patient the
right to treatment? And who would ask of a physician anything
less than what he judges to be in the best interests of his patient?
The fundamental problem is that the person in this case ever
became a "patient" in the first place. The American Psychiatric
Association, years later, would take a vote and thereupon decide
that homosexuality was not a disease. It is not clear whether this
vote is binding on the minority, but in any event the vote had not
been taken at the time of the Tulane case. The attending physician was of the opinion that the patient's homosexuality warranted treatment, as did his vagrancy, so that he could be restored
as a "functioning" member of society. But again, how did this
fellow find his way into a hospital in the first instance?

The answer is not difficult to find. Some judge, hearing the
clarion call of psychosocial jurisprudence, decided that it was

pointless to deliver such a person into the hands of a hardened community of prisoners who would exploit his homosexuality and do nothing constructive for his character. As the victim of his own perversity, he surely cannot be considered responsible for what he does. He is not a criminal, but a sick man to be shielded from punishment through the solicitude of competent physicians.

The State of Louisiana has statutes forbidding homosexuality. The person in question was found in violation of these statutes. The responsibility of the court in such instances is a determination of guilt and the noting of relevant extenuating circumstances. The former is dictated by the principles of justice, the latter by considerations of mercy. The latter, however, was intended to make penalties fit the crime, not to serve as the basis of exoneration. Without knowing it, the dispositive court in this case effectively sentenced a homosexual vagrant to psychosurgery. And it certainly sentenced him for an indeterminate term to a psychiatric facility.

What makes psychosurgery important in these regards is not that it is frequently practiced but that it stands as one of the starker possibilities when the psychosocial point of view conspires with *Donaldson* in an age of technical innovation. It is through the psychosocial perspective that many who have violated criminal statutes—or who have only been found guilty of misdemeanors—find themselves in hospitals rather than prisons. As involuntarily committed inmates, they now have the "right" to treatment. In some instances, treatment is the only means by which their indeterminate sentences might come to an end. And, increasingly, the available treatments are profound, radical in their effects, benign in their appearance, and largely experimental in their character. It is an abiding bromide that there is no minor neurosurgery, only minor neurosurgeons, but in these cases it is not so much a question of lethal risk as it is a matter of complete success. On the assumption that the surgeon cannot predict with any accuracy what the outcome will be, such cases are purely *experimental*. On the assumption that the outcome can be predicted with high accuracy, and on the further assumption that the patient's personality, perspective on life, sources of pleasure, and basic sensibilities will be surgically manipulated, such procedures clearly collide with Constitutional safeguards.

4. Persons

Although sometimes used to sentimental excess, the symbol of justice as a blindfolded goddess holding balanced scales aloft depicts with near perfection what our genuinely moral desires have as their aim. There is in this symbol not only the obvious recognition that justice is suitably distinterested, but that every judicial undertaking involves the balancing of facts, conditions, interests, and rights. Society would not have had to invent courts in order to decide on unequivocal matters. A court is a luxury in doubtless cases, but a necessity in doubtful ones. There is doubt where there is disagreement, so it is inevitable that a just court will hand down unpopular decisions. This, of course, is simply one more of the irrelevant consequences to which justice is blind on principle.

Where an action is brought in behalf of a fetus or a Karen Quinlan, or in those causes in which someone has broken the law but seems to be psychologically troubled, what the judiciary faces—or, as it happens, generally fails to face—is the metaphysical problem of "persons." It is doubtful that a prosperous businessman, a pillar of the community, who happened to be involved in a homosexual relationship, would have undergone psychosurgery. The difference here is not in the act, but in the relative (psychosocial) standing of the businessman and the patient at Tulane. In this I am not referring to the privileges of wealth or a "class" system, or any of the other tired clichés invented by Marxists to explain the success of capitalism. My point is not one of politics, but one of perspective. The psychosocial perspective is one that finds us defining and recognizing persons nearly exclusively in terms of their groupings. It is a perspective that takes individual differences as possible signs of non-personhood rather than as one of the marks of personhood. It makes it easier for us to think of the patient in Louisiana as "a knight of the open road; an inveterate homosexual," instead of as a *person.* And we permit ourselves, through the state, to do many things to "a knight of the open road" that we would not think of doing to a person—certainly what we would not allow to be done to *our* persons.

The burdens, accordingly, become great on those who cannot be easily typed and affiliated—those who are neither "minorities," nor "women," nor "establishment," nor "gay," nor "professional," nor "working class," nor "moderates, conservatives, or liberals." The heaviest burden falls on the mentally incompetent, such as fetuses and Karen Quinlan, but nearly as heavy a burden soon comes to rest on those who are impoverished or eccentric or defective. The task of justice thus is the traditional one of drawing lines; or, to return to the symbol, one of weighting the scales according to the developed morality of the human race.

In doubtful cases, the morality of our actions must be determined by the relative consequences attaching to an error on either side. It is already clear that the remarkable strides made in medical instrumentation can only increase the number and the range of doubtful cases of personhood, and it is already clear that judiciaries have not been able to find a standard. It is not enough to say that any such standard will be arbitrary, for it is in the very nature of adjudication that doubt must be dealt with. In *Roe*, for example, the first trimester of pregnancy was accorded special status on grounds that were arbitrary. The fault in this decision, however, is not that the standard was arbitrary, but that it entirely vitiated the most fundamental right of the doubtful person in honoring what can only be considered the derived right of the undoubted one. Similarly, in *Quinlan*, the fault lay not so much in the arbitrariness of the "cognitive and sapient" standard, but in the application of that standard in such a manner as to justify the death of the doubtful person in the interest of the alleged guardian rights of the appellant.

We see, then, that the question of standards is one that must be addressed in terms of the gravity of the potential or real injury that will result to the doubtful person. To invoke the criteria of intellect and moral reasoning where the finding of non-personhood will result, for example, in being denied the right to vote or to possess a driver's license or to serve in the armed forces, is to risk an injustice of lesser gravity than the use of these same criteria where the continued existence of the party at issue hangs in the balance.

There are only two classes of attributes, as I have noted, that can be applied to settle questions of personhood; those that are physical and those that are psychological. It has occasionally been proposed by philosophers that a "person" is any being in possession of at least one attribute from each class. Thus, if the physical attributes are taken as M-predicates (material properties) and the psychological ones as P-predicates, a *person* is any being possessing at least one M-predicate and at least one P-predicate. This is, however, a very generous guide to the classification of beings as persons, in that most advanced species share a number of M- and P-predicates with human beings and would, therefore, qualify as persons. Yet as I have noted often, we do have a number of laws designed to protect animals from cruelty and abuse, and our support of these laws is based at least implicitly on our judgment that the protected animals are enough like persons to suffer under some of the conditions persons would describe as insufferable. Still, most will find this particular classification to be insufficiently discriminating. It may be tightened in either or both of two ways: by choosing M-predicates that are possessed only by human beings and (or) by choosing P-predicates that are also unique to human beings. The only M-predicate that would qualify here is the genetic one, in that only human genotypes are identifiable as coming from the gene pool of *Homo sapiens*. In selecting this criterion, we would not of course declare open season on any and all non-persons, but we would reserve to all who satisfy this one criterion all the protections that attach to undoubted persons.

The advantage here comes largely by default. If instead we attempt to specify unique P-predicates, we will unfailingly either include many nonhuman beings or exclude staggering numbers of human beings, including all infants, most young children, and some adults. Yet, the psychosocial perspective urges just such a standard, which is at the core of such notions as "functioning," "adjusting to the demands of society," and "coping."

Notes

For an argument defending the one M-predicate, one P-predicate criterion of personhood, see Strawson's *Individuals: An Essay in Descriptive Metaphysics* (London, 1959). On psychosurgery and other approaches to altering personality, see my *Therapies: A Clear and Present Danger* (*American Psychologist*, 1973, *28*, 129–133).

7 Epilogue: Some Modest Proposals

What I have attempted to criticize in the foregoing chapters is the subtle effect the psychosocial perspective has had on a large number of jural matters and the dramatic effect it has had on several. It has not been my aim to discredit social scientists who study individual and social behavior or therapists who do the best they can with very limited professional resources. I would not even go so far as to say that such specialists have no place within judicial settings. Quite the contrary is the case. In many instances where questions of *fact* are involved, experts drawn from the social sciences may be able to provide invaluable assistance. We may, for example, need to know how quickly most persons can react to a visual or auditory signal; how complete our recollections are minutes, hours, or days after a novel occurrence; how the human faculties tend to be affected by various kinds of medication; how a particular admissions examination correlates with on-the-job performance; how most members of a community interpret a particular ordinance or perceive the mission of the police or estimate the value of a local or federal program. There are surely dozens of questions that might crop up in the course of litigation that would be most competently addressed by specialists in psychology, psychiatry, sociology, engineering, medicine, or even Romance languages. Accordingly, it would be folly to bar such testimony merely because it is given by an expert, or because the expert happened to be a social scientist. In this connection, there would seem to be a central role for such specialists in studying the very institution of justice—courts, juries, patterns of sentences, latent biases, prejudicial attributions. This is all useful and commendable, but it falls well beyond the perimeter of the arguments and assessments of this book. Justice must weigh facts, and it cannot be partial in the admission of facts. To the extent that a social scientist has facts to contribute to a cause, he must be welcome in any court of justice.

But what is a "fact"? In cases of criminal insanity, juries are routinely instructed to count psychiatric testimony as *evidence*. What sort of evidence is forthcoming? Is it factual, or hearsay, or merely opinion dressed up in the robes of fact, its true nature camouflaged by jargon? Thus:

> I have examined the accused, tested him on a battery of personality measures, interviewed him at length, and examined his family and social background. It is my finding that, at the time he committed the crime, he did not understand the nature of the act and lacked the power to conform his behavior to the laws of this state.

What, in all of this, is the fact? The only fact is that the testifying doctor gave some tests and arrived at an opinion. It is surely not a fact that the accused did not know what he was doing, but an inference based on tests and talk. Moreover, it is (usually) an inference not drawn by the experts for the prosecution. The most a reasonable and disinterested party would be willing to make of such comments is that they speak broadly to the "character" of the accused. Here, then, the "expert" can only be something of a character witness, not an unimpeachable truth teller. And let us be mindful that a life hangs in the balance only on the rarest occasion. Studies of insanity pleas in New York over a period of a dozen years indicate that 53 percent of the cases involve homicides. The rest run the gamut from simple assault to bank robbery! Additionally, with the decline of the death penalty—a penalty whose only justification would appear to be Biblical—it is again seldom apt to say that lives hang in the balance in any but a handful of cases. In any event, if we seek grounds on which to spare the life of a murderer, we can find broader and more principled ones than any yielded by the hocus-pocus of psychiatry. To the extent that society can protect itself by locking away the murderer for all the days of his life, it loses the self-defense argument for capital punishment and is left with little more than "an eye for an eye."

How, therefore, are we to treat psychiatric and psychological testimony? I would offer the following recommendations:

1. All statements regarding the mental state of the accused or of any party to litigation are to be treated as statements of belief or opinion. They are not to be accorded the status of evidence, are not to be admitted in evidence, and juries are to be specifically instructed not to take them as evidence.

2. Where eye witnesses are able to provide a consistent and noncontradictory account of the behavior of the accused or a party to litigation at the time of the acts in question, psychiatric or psychological testimony may be taken as evidence *only* when it is confined to statistical or epidemiological reports of the correlation between conduct of the sort described and the conduct of physically diseased persons.

3. In all cases in which psychiatric or psychological testimony is to the effect that the party at issue is diseased, the testimony must be accompanied by relevant biochemical or neurological findings. For purposes of justice, the term *disease* refers to a discernible pathological process in the tissues or organs of the body. The term "mental disease" is to be taken as a metaphor, not as a diagnostic specification.

4. In cases of testamentary capacity, the only evidence that is to be taken by the jury (or the court) is that which might sustain the charge of fraud or of physical threats perpetrated against the testator. Specifically rejected as evidence are all statements, beliefs, and opinions as to the testator's "state of mind" at the time the testament was made.

5. In cases of alleged injury, damage, or grievance of a "psychological" nature, the social science "expert" may offer an opinion as to the possible injuries suffered by some persons exposed to the conditions faced by the appellant, but this opinion is not to count as evidence. That some children are misled by television; that some persons are embarrassed by racial epithets; that some people will do immoral things in the act of obeying authorities— these and all other trends and tendencies observed in large (or small) experimental samples are to be taken as irrelevant to the

instant case, since it is not possible to determine whether the *appellant* actually has been injured merely by showing that *others* might have been.

6. In cases that carry the burden of involuntary commitment to a mental hospital, the testifying psychiatrist or psychologist must again restrict testimony to statistical summaries of the frequency with which a brain-damaged or otherwise medically diseased population yields conduct of the sort with which the accused is charged. What counts as *fact*, however, is the statistics. That the accused is drawn statistically from such a population must be established by other and *medical* facts.

7. In cases that carry the burden of involuntary commitment in a mental hospital, the *maximum* assigned time of hospitalization cannot exceed the time that would have been served had the defendant been found guilty under criminal statute. The *minimum* assigned period of hospitalization must be at least as long as the minimum sentence set by criminal statute. For practical purposes, it may be advisable—in the event the prisoner is "cured" during his time in the hospital—to have the balance of his sentence served in a prison. Nonetheless, the sentencing power is the court's, not the psychiatrist's, and the sentence is proportioned to the crime, not to some opinion about the mental state of the defendant at the time he committed it.

8. The involuntarily committed prisoner-patient is to be exempt from any and every therapeutic procedure that has not been validated through use with a noninstitutionalized consenting population of comparable cases. For purposes of justice, *no* involuntarily institutionalized person may be thought of as capable of a valid and informed consent.

9. Any therapeutic procedure failing to satisfy the above condition is, for purposes of justice, defined as *experimental*.

10. In all cases carrying the burden of involuntary commitment to a mental hospital, one dissenting opinion voiced by any examining physician or psychologist appointed by the state is sufficient to preclude the option.

11. For purposes of justice, a defendant who has been found mentally incompetent as regards his offense is taken also to be incompetent as regards the choice of hospitalization over imprisonment. Effectively, this provision establishes all such com-

mitments as *prima facie* involuntary, and affords to the committed those special protections that attach to the protesting patient.

12. The release of patients by psychiatrists on the grounds that such patients are no longer dangerous to themselves or to society carries with it certain civil liabilities in the event that said patients do imperil others. It is expected that such actions brought against the discharging physician would bear the same burdens as those ordinarily associated with malpractice litigation. In any event, justice requires accountability as well as remedies for negligence.

13. In any cause in which death is either the penalty or the most likely consequence of a ruling, the party at risk is judged to be a person if (a) there is any discernible sign of physical life and if (b) the party qualifies genetically as *Homo sapiens.* The principle here is one that forbids the state to order the death of innocent parties, parties guilty of neither crime nor malfeasance of any sort.

14. The state's interest in the protection of life is, for purposes of justice, to be taken as *compelling* whenever it is asserted. Such an interest extends to, but is not limited to, attempted suicide, abortion, and euthanasia.

15. With respect to the continuation of life, the state's interest is taken to be higher than that of any guardian whose decisions are likely to end or abbreviate life.

16. In all cases of the sort comprehended by (14) and (15), biological survival is taken to be more fundamental than psychological or social considerations.

17. Where a competent person, fully cognizant of his condition and its likely course, informs his physicians that his treatments are to cease, and when these physicians are convinced that the factors responsible for this decision cannot be removed or diminished, compliance with the patient's wishes does not expose the physicians to criminal prosecution or professional liability. In all other cases, *Primum non nocere* has the force of law, and "to let die" is taken to be one form of *"Nocere."*

Eminent and articulate spokesmen are already on record as opposing all of these recommendations. I need only mention Judge David Bazelon in this connection, a jurist who has done so much not only to restore psychiatry's flagging confidence in the courtroom but to alert the citizenry to the psychosocial problems that lurk behind many an offense. If I were to address Judge Bazelon directly, I would not attempt to refute his theories of criminal conduct or even deny his court the power to treat these theories as if they were facts. Rather, I would simply point out that every action has a predisposing cause, if only the will of the actor himself. Criminal actions, too, are caused, and every system of justice not grounded in muddy superstition has acknowledged as much. Thus, the issue is not one dividing "determinists" from "voluntarists"—though that too is an interesting issue—but one that divides *psychosocial* theories of justice from what might best be called *covenant* theories. The law, on the former reckoning, is an agency of society to be used in a manner that accords with general sentiments regarding what is right and wrong, desirable and unwanted, forgivable and unpardonable. On the latter construction, law is a promise that rational beings make to themselves in their most rational and disinterested moments. It promises the bounty of civilized life to those who honor it, and the threatened removal of this to those who don't. Centuries ago, and in a ruthlessly macabre caricature of this thesis, an English jurist said to the hopeless defendant, "I hang you not because you stole a chicken, but so that chickens not be stolen." This, of course, is the perverted extreme of covenant theories of justice. But it is not always apt to test a principle by seeing its effect in extremis. Justice itself is a balancing device, and what must be struck is a balance between the ruthless rejection of all varieties of mitigation and the equally ruthless rejection of all varieties of personal responsibility. Justice is not served by—as they said in the nineteenth century—hanging a lunatic, but it is also not served by the collection of non sequiturs that results in exoneration simply on the finding of a predisposing "cause." Such exoneration not only teaches bad lessons and violates basic covenants, but it does little for its intended beneficiary. If he is a fraud, it repays his fraud. If he is not, it reinforces what is already a diminished capacity for self-control, a capacity which, like all the rest, grows with exercise. Some, of course, are beyond all such remedies, but these—at least for purposes of justice—must qualify as *"furiosus, non compos mentis and fanaticus"* in the ancient sense.

On the matter of the right to life, I am enough in the present world to know how many sensibilities are likely to be offended by my proposals. In such a circumstance, I suppose I am obliged to say that I do not hope to see pregant women killed by illegal abortions, that I am not in favor of children being reared in loveless or in fatherless homes, and that I do not long to see any religious group impose its laws on an otherwise secular society. But none of this finally has anything to do with the issue of killing fetuses. The problem will not go away by insisting that it is a Catholic conspiracy or a vote against the poor or a disregard of women. The problem will remain riveted to every developed conscience as long as human beings of whatever nature or quality or age or stage of development or achievement are destroyed through anything short of an act of war. There are simply too many among us with no more mental or sensitive equipment than that possessed by Karen Quinlan; too many who, in all relevant psychological respects, are essentially and functionally "fetal." When the signboards and slogans are all put away for the night, and when the thoughtful citizen addresses his own sense of justice, he will realize that any law that does not protect Karen Quinlan, any decision that permits willy-nilly the destruction of inchoate humanity, is a law that has surrendered a principle to a program. The unwanted pregnancy, the vegetating daughter, the terminally ill loved one—these are cases in which misery is inevitable, but I can find no justification for employing homicide as a palliative.

It is sometimes forgotten, as we review the glories and the infamies of the human experience, that civilization is a relatively episodic phenomenon in our history. The Hellenic achievement came and went in a matter of only two centuries. The best of Rome lasted perhaps a century longer. Even in the vaunted Elizabethan epoch, there were more than 150 separate offenses that carried the penalty of death. Witches were still being burned on the Continent as John Locke was writing on civil government. My point, of course, is that civilization, as our most complex creation, is our most fragile possession. Every individual has moments when he would choose to discard it, and every age sooner or later becomes frustrated by its demands. It is chiefly the specter of its alternative that keeps majorities loyal to it.

Not only do we conveniently forget the ephemeral nature of civilized life; we also tend to underestimate the part played by written and interpreted law in this life. This is the special vulnerability of those privileged to live in just states. For them, the law, like oxygen, sustains life and health without ever being sensed. Only when it is removed or reduced do the alarming symptoms awaken them to its essence and essentiality. But under the ordinary conditions of life in a just state, the citizen thinks of law as a device to be used for personal advantage or as a measure his government may adopt for the purpose of securing compliance. Both of these, of course, are aspects of law, but they are only incidental to its fundamental mission in a just state. The real work of law is the nurturance of the human imagination. It creates and maintains a climate in which the flight of mind is boundless, and it does this in a striking variety of ways. It frees us from what is both unpredictable and unprincipled. That is, it secures our safety. It imposes upon daily life that degree of stability that makes planning both possible and realistic. Indeed, in the absence of law, every goal is largely restricted to the horizons of sight. The law guarantees that there will be a future and even the sort of future it will be. And it is just this that frees the mind to speculate, to long for, to aspire, to hope, and otherwise to escape from the narrow channels of mere survival.

To the extent that every civilization begins to collapse first from within—and this is only partly true—the earliest signs of internal weakness are institutional, for it is institutions that give a civilization its defining properties. In this regard, none is more basic than the institution of law, for none speaks more directly and diffusely to the people at large. The civilizations that have earned our respect *and* our love are those in which the laws were not only just—for this can happen as a result of fear or rebellion or habit or even accident—but were *intended* to be just. They reveal their intentions to us by their devotion to principle and their resistance to unreasoning clamor. Aristotle spoke for one of these civilizations when he wrote,

> He therefore that recommends that the law shall govern seems to recommend that God and reason alone shall govern, but he that would have man govern adds a wild animal also; for appetite is like a wild animal, and also passion warps the rule even of the best men. Therefore, the law is wisdom without passion.

Notes

The mounting doubts and frustrations surrounding the insanity defense are illustrated by the recent actions of several state legislatures. In Michigan, for example, statutes passed since 1974 effectively limit psychiatric testimony to matters of clinical diagnosis. More recently, both Illinois and New York have drafted bills that would essentially eliminate the insanity defense but they are wrapped in the curious language of "diminished capacity," "culpable but mentally disabled," "guilty but mentally ill." Thus, although the signs of restlessness are vivid, it is equally clear that legislators cannot confidently draw those boundaries that might preclude unwarranted psycho-social forays into jural domains.

The initiatives in Michigan were triggered by the *McQuillan* ruling of that state's Supreme Court: a ruling that called for the release of all "criminally insane" patients, indefinitely confined, who could not be shown to be mentally ill. (The ruling resulted in the release of more than 200 such patients then quartered in State-operated hospitals). It is, however, too early to discern a pattern in those scattered decisions handed down by the courts of the various states. Serving their ageless mission, legislatures are seeking the words that make laws useful, fair, and intelligible. Their continuing difficulties in the area of insanity are due in large measure to the diffuse influences of the psychosocial perspective on language itself.

Legal Citations

English Cases

Arnold (The Trial of) 16 Howell's State Trials 695

Banks v. *Goodfellow*, 5 English Law Reports 549

Bellingham (The Trial of), 1 Collinson on Lunacy 636

Cartwright v. *Cartwright et al.* 161 English Law Reports 923

Dew v. *Clark and Clark*, 162 English Reports 410

Ferrers (The Trial of), 19 Howell's State Trials 885

Hadfield (The Trial of), 27 Howell's State Trials 1281

M'Naghten (The Trial of), Vol. VII, English Reports 718

Smith v. *Tebbitt*, 1 Law Reports 398 (Probate and Divorce)

Waring v. *Waring*, 13 English Reports 715

United States Cases

Addington v. *Texas*, 99 S. Ct Reporter, 1804

Albermarle Paper Co., v. *Moody*, 422 U.S. 404

Alto v. *Alaska*, Alaska 565 P. 2d 492

Boardman v. *Woodward*, 47 New Hampshire 120

Bolling v. *State*, 54 Arkansas 588

Breithaupt v. *Abram*, 352 U.S. 432

Brown v. *Board of Education*, 347 U.S. 483

Doe v. *Bolton*, 410 U.S. 179

Donaldson v. *O'Connor*, 493 F. 2d 507

Graham v. *Darnell*, 538 S.W. 2d 690

Griggs v. *Duke Power and Light Co.*, 401 U.S. 424

In Re Alexander, 336 F. Supp. 1305

In Re Kaplan, 50 App. Div. Repts., New York 2d Series

In Re Quinlan, N. J. S. Ct., Sept. Term, 1975

Jackson v. *Indiana*, 406 U.S. 715

Michigan v. *McQuillan*, 392 Michigan 511

O'Connor v. *Donaldson*, 422 U.S. 563

Regents of the University of California v. *Bakke*, 438 U.S. 265

Rochin v. *California*, 342 U.S. 165

Roe v. *Wade*, 410 U.S. 113

Rogers: "The Trial of Abner Rogers," G. T. Bigelow and G. Bemis, Boston, Little Brown, 1844

State v. *Jones*, 50 New Hampshire 369

State v. *Ortiz*, 114 Arizona 282

State v. *Schmidt*, 216 New York 324

Stevens v. *Indiana*, 31 Indiana 485

Superintendent of Belchertown v. *Saikewicz*, Mass. 370 N.E. 2d 417 (1977)

U.S. v. *Cooper*, 465 F. 2d 451

U.S. v. *Ingman*, 426 F. 2d 973, 976

U.S. v. *McGraw*, 515 F. 2d 758

U.S. v. *Shackelford*, 494 F. 2d 67, 70

Wade v. *U.S.*, 426 F. 2d 64

Bibliography

Arkes, H. "The Problem of Kenneth Clark." *Commentary*, December 1974.

Binet, A. and Simon, T. *The Development of Intelligence in Children*. E. S. Kite, translator. Baltimore: Williams & Wilkins, 1916.

Collingwood, R. G. *The Idea of History*. Oxford: Oxford University Press, 1943.

Dworkin, R. *Taking Rights Seriously*. London: Duckworth, 1977.

Feinberg, J. *Doing and Deserving*. New Jersey: Princeton University Press, 1970.

Finkel, N. *Mental Illness and Health*. New York: Macmillan, 1976.

Hall, V. A. and Turner, R. R. "The validity of the 'different language explanation' for poor scholastic performance by black students." *Review of Educational Research*, 1974, *44*, 69–81.

Hart, H.L.A. *The Concept of Law*. Oxford: Clarendon Press, 1961.

Hegel, G.W.F. *Reason in History*. R. S. Hartman, translator. Indianapolis: Bobbs-Merrill, 1953.

Hempel, C. *Aspects of Scientific Explanation*. New York: The Free Press, 1965.

Hunter, C. *Adult Illiteracy in the United States*. New York: The Ford Foundation, 1979.

Jensen, A. "How Much Can We Boost I.Q. and Scholastic Achievement?" *Harvard Educational Review*, Winter 1969.

Laing, R. D. *The Politics of the Family and Other Essays*. New York: Vintage, 1972.

Paul, G. "Chronic mental patients: Current status—future direction." *Psychological Bulletin*, 1969, *71*, 81–94.

Robinson, D. N. (ed.) *Significant Contributions to the History of Psychology* (in fifty volumes). Series F: *Insanity and Jurisprudence* (in six volumes). Washington, D. C.: University Publications of America, 1978–1980.

Robinson, D. N. "Therapies: A Clear and Present Danger." *American Psychologist*, 1973, *28*,129–133.

Ross, W. D. *The Right and the Good.* Oxford: Oxford University Press, 1930.

Strawson, P. *Individuals: An Essay in Descriptive Metaphysics.* London: Methuen, 1959.

Szasz, T. S. *The Myth of Mental Illness.* New York: Harper & Row, 1961.

Winch, P. *The Idea of a Social Science and Its Relation to Philosophy.* London: Routledge & Kegan Paul, 1958.

Index

Abbott, Chief Justice, 41–42, 44
Abortion, 27, 32, 178–87, 193, 196, 209, 211. *See also Doe* v. *Bolton*; *Roe* v. *Wade*
  personhood of fetus, 180–84, 186–187
  protection of fetus, 185–86, 201–2
  rights of fetus, 184, 195
  viability of fetus, 184–85, 191
  woman's right to privacy, 184, 186
Addington v. *Texas*, 137–38, 213
Affirmative Action, 164, 166
Affirmative Action Policy Statement, 164
Albermarle Paper Co. v. *Moody*, 167, 213
Alston, W. H., 128–29
Alto v. *Alaska*, 70–71, 73, 213
Anarchy, 174, *See also* Liberty, anarchy
Aristotle, 30, 114, 212
Arnold, 38–39, 41, 43, 94, 213

Banks v. *Goodfellow*, 95, 213
Bazelon, D., 209–10
Bell, G., 167
Bellingham, 44–45, 47, 50, 92–93, 213
Bentham, J., 74, 117
Binet, A., 143, 143*n*, 176
Binet-Simon Scale, 143
Boardman v. *Woodward*, 95–96, 213
Bolling v. *State*, 52, 213
Breithaupt v. *Abram*, 193, 197–98, 213

Brown v. *Board of Education*, 144, 162, 169, 176, 213
Burger, Chief Justice, 136
Burt, C., 157, 159

Cardozo, B., 32–33, 52
Cartwright v. *Cartwright*, 92, 94–96, 213
Categorical imperative, 8–9. *See also* Kant, I.
Clark, K., 144, 162, 176
Coercion, 111–15, 122. *See also* Consent
  in mental hospitals, 125, 197
  in prisons, 125
  psychosurgery and, 199
Coke, E., 37–42, 44, 46–47, 50, 54–55, 91, 94
Collingwood, R. G., 30
Commitment
  involuntary, 124, 126, 130–39, 197, 199–200, 208–9
  voluntary, 124–29.
Confinement, of mentally ill, 134–38, *See also* Commitment
Consciousness, 10, 190
  "brain-death," 190–91
  personhood, 187
Consent. *See also* Coercion
  rights and, 126–27
  treatment and, 126–27, 138, 192, 198–99, 208
Cox, A., 168–69

Criminal responsibility
    insanity, 32, 47, 66, 93, 132
    testamentary capacity, 93, 100

Death penalty, 27, 206–7, 211
Delusion. *See* Insanity, delusion
Desegregation, 27. *See also Brown* v.
    Board of Education;
    Segregation
Dew v. *Clark and Clark,* 93–94, 213
Discrimination
    justice, 152–56, 163–69
    morals, 152–55
    psychological tests, 156–57, 162, 167,
    171
Doe v. *Bolton,* 177, 180–81, 185–86, 195,
    213. *See also* Abortion
Donaldson v. *O'Connor,* 134–36, 138,
    197, 199–200, 213
Douglas, W. O., 181, 185–86
Draco, 34–35
Drugs
    abuse of, 27, 126
    therapy and, 137, 139, 198
Dworkin, R., 13

Educable mentally retarded (EMR),
    144–48. *See also Larry P.* v. *Riles;*
    Mental retardation
Educational Testing Service, 174
Eighth Amendment, 125
Environmentalism, 145–47
Equal Employment Opportunity
    Council, 164
Equalitarianism, 124, 155. *See also*
    Liberty, equality
Equality. *See* Equalitarianism; Liberty,
    equality
Erskine, T., 41–43, 46, 56, 74, 93
Euthanasia, 178, 209
"Expert" testimony. *See* Insanity, "ex-
    pert" testimony

Fanaticus. *See* Insanity, fanaticus
Ferrers, 40–43, 47, 50, 93, 213
First Amendment, 181
Fourteenth Amendment, 125, 134–35,
    180–81, 183–84, 186, 195
Furiosis. *See* Insanity, furiosis

George III, 40–43, 94
Goddard, H., 143, 143*n*, 176
Graham v. *Darnell,* 104–6, 213
Griggs v. *Duke Power and Light Co.,*
    166–67, 213

Hadfield, 40–44, 47, 50, 56, 74, 93–94,
    213
Hale, M., 39–42, 44, 46–47, 40
Happiness principle, 117–18
Hart, H. L. A., 12–13
Hereditarianism, 145–47
Holmes, O. W., 12, 17

Individuals
    responsibility of, 35–36, 122
    rights of, 119, 140, 176
In re Alexander, 131, 214
In re Gault, 132
In re Kaplan, 107–9, 214
In re Quinlan, 177, 187–96, 201–2, 211,
    214
    criterion of brain death, 190–191
    "expert" testimony, 189
Insane Offender's Bill, 40, 44
Insanity, 32, 36–38, 40–42, 51, 53–54, 56,
    64, 148. *See also* Insanity defense
    criminal responsibility, 32, 47, 66, 93,
    132
    delusion, 42–50, 56–57, 62, 68, 93–97,
    103, 105
    as disease, 50–54, 58–61, 94, 102, 108,
    207
    "expert" testimony, 60–63, 66, 69–72,
    96–109, 126, 128, 203–4, 205–8
    fanaticus, 36–37, 210
    furiosis, 36–40, 47, 55, 94, 102, 210
    irresistible impulse, 56, 62
    lunar theory of, 39, 43
    medical model, 43, 47–48, 128
    mental capacity of testator, 85–86, 88–
    90, 92–109, 207
    non compos mentis, 36–38, 46, 210
    partial, 39, 41, 62, 93–96
    temporary, 33, 39, 50, 56, 62
    "wild beast" standard, 38, 40, 42, 46,
    54–56, 58, 63, 65, 92, 109
Insanity defense, 32–34, 63–74, 131,
    203–4, 206. *See also* Insanity, "ex-
    pert" testimony

Insanity defense (*continued*)
  in America, 34, 49–51, 65–68, 70–72,
    203–4, 206
  in England, 34, 38–50, 74
  in Europe, 34
Intelligence Quotient (I.Q.), heritability of, 157–60. *See also* Tests, intelligence
Intention, 38–39, 92, 96
  criminal, 51–52, 59, 65, 69
  of law, 181
  morals and, 5, 10–11, 19, 152, 154
  reasons vs. causes, 25, 30
  of testator, 101, 103–4, 106

Jackson v. *Indiana*, 135, 214
Jefferson, T., 120–21
Jensen, A., 157–60
Jensen thesis, 158
Justice, 134, 140, 142, 152–54, 162, 170,
  195, 200–202, 206–12. *See also* Insanity, "expert" testimony; Insanity defense; Intention; Law
  American, 119–22
  civilization and, 211–12
  criminal, 32–33, 52
  discrimination, 152–56, 163–69
  injury, 166
  law, 15–19, 21, 30, 34, 64, 73–74
  legal positivism, 12–14, 17
  legal responsibility, 14
  logic, 11, 13, 15–16, 19–21, 27–31, 210
  morals, 4, 11–21, 27–31, 142, 201–2
  natural law, 13–14
  psychological tests, 156–57
  quotas, 169
  retributive punishment, 57–58, 74
  rule of recognition, 12–14
  social sciences and, 3, 21, 63, 90, 100,
    148, 177, 205–7
  welfarism, 124, 129

Kant, I., 8–9
Kenyon, L., 41, 43–44, 74

Laing, R. D., 138, 142
Larry P. v. *Riles*, 144–47
Law
  common, 17, 34, 64

  English common, 33–34
  justice, 15–19, 21, 30, 34, 64, 73–74
  natural, 13–14, 35
  Roman, 33–36, 64
Legal positivism, 12–14, 17
Libertarianism, 115–19, 124, 132, 134,
  140
Liberty, 115, 117–18, 137, 141–42
  anarchy, 141
  equality, 120–21, 133–34, 155
Locke, J., 38, 76, 80, 211

M'Naghten, 32, 40, 45–52, 94, 213
  Queen Victoria and, 45
M'Naghten Rule, 33, 46–49, 66
Maule, Justice, 45–48, 94
Medical model. *See* Insanity, medical
  model
Mens rea, 33, 36, 39, 52
Mental retardation, 147–48, 193. *See*
  also Superintendent of Belcher-
  town v. *Saikewicz*
  educable mentally retarded, 144–48
Michigan v. *McQuillan*, 204, 214
Mill, J. S., 8, 115–19, 121, 140
Morals, 27–31, 118, 140, 196, 202
  concept of "ought," 6–8, 13, 21, 27,
    29–30, 55, 79, 82, 141
  discrimination, 152–55
  feelings, 9, 17, 27
  intention, 5, 10–11, 19, 152, 154
  "just deserts," 152–53
  justice, 4, 11–21, 27–31, 142, 201–2
  moral beings, 179, 196
  moral sensibility, 56, 62, 78
  personhood, 178–79, 181
  universality of, 5–9, 14, 28–29

Natural right. *See* Rights, basic
Non compos mentis. *See* Insanity, non
  compos mentis

O'Connor v. *Donaldson*, 135–36, 214

Patients. *See* Rights, of patients
Peckham, R., 144–45, 147–48
Personhood. *See* Persons

Persons, 177, 180–81, 183, 201–3, 209.
  See also Consciousness
  personhood of fetus, 180–84, 186–87
  philosophical analysis of person-
    hood, 177–79, 184, 186–87, 202
  rights of, 177–79, 183–84
Psychiatry, 25–26, 52, 61, 72–73, 102,
  138, 205–6, 209. *See also* Social
    sciences
  psychological tests, 156
Psychology, 24–26, 52, 61, 73, 122, 190,
  205. *See also* Social sciences
  psychological tests, 156
  theories of, 37, 122
Psychosurgery, 178, 197–201, 203
  brain stimulation, 138
  consent and, 198–99
  lobotomy, 138, 198
Punishment, 58, 73–74, 112, 122, 125,
  128, 142, 152. *See also* Death pen-
    alty
  retributive, 57–58

Quia Emptores, 91–92

*Regents of the University of California
  v. Bakke*, 164, 166–68, 176, 214
Responsibility. *See also* Criminal re-
    sponsibility
  of individuals, 35–36, 122
  justice, 210
  legal, 14
  rights. 82–83, 141
Right to liberty, 76, 117–19, 133, 136.
  See also Confinement
Right to life, 76–79, 81, 83, 195–96, 210–
  11. *See also* Abortion: rights of
    fetus, viability of fetus; Euthana-
    sia; Rights, basic; Therapy, medi-
    cal
  and degree of dependency, 185, 195
  and state's interest, 195–96, 209
Right to privacy. *See also Breithaupt* v.
    Abram; Rochin v. *California*
  bodily invasion, 193–94, 197–98
  therapy, 193
  woman's, 184, 186
Right to property, 75–76, 80–84, 90–91,
  95, 100–101, 104, 109
  right to use, 80–81, 95, 99–100, 109–10

Right to treatment, 134–38, 199–200.
  See also Commitment; Confine-
    ment
Rights, 81–82, 140–41. *See also other
    rights*
  of animals, 184, 203
  basic, 31, 100–102, 104, 109–10, 132,
    141, 196, 202
  of beneficiaries, 109–10
  consent and, 126–27
  of criminals, 74
  derived, 76, 109–10, 202
  of fetus, 184, 195
  of individuals, 119, 140, 176
  obligations, 79, 114, 124, 131
  of patients, 132, 139, 192–93
  of persons, 177–79, 183–84
  powers, 77–79, 83
  privileges, 77–79, 82–83, 90, 109-10
  responsibility, 82–83, 141
  of testators, 82, 84, 90, 109
Rochin v. *California*, 193, 214
Roe v. *Wade*, 177, 180, 182–83, 185–86,
  193, 195, 202, 214. *See also* Abor-
    tion
Rogers, 49, 50–51, 214
Ross, W. D., 74
Rule of recognition, 12–14

Science, 21–26, 138. *See also* Scientific
    explanation
Scientific explanation, 22–25, 30, 215
  in social sciences, 24–27, 30, 123
Segregation, 162–63. *See also Brown* v.
    Board of Education; Desegregation
Self-incrimination, involuntary, 197.
  See also Breighaupt v. *Abram;*
    Rochin v. *California*
Shaw, Chief Justice, 49–50
Simon, T., 143, 176
Smith v. *Tebbitt*, 94–95, 213
Social sciences, 60–61, 63, 65, 69, 109,
  121, 123–24, 141, 180, 205. *See also*
    Insanity, "expert" testimony; Psy-
    chiatry; Psychology; Sociology
  justice and, 3, 21, 63, 90, 100, 148, 177,
    205–7
  psychological tests, 143, 156, 171
  scientific explanation in, 24–27, 30,
    123

Sociology, 26, 52, 61, 73, 149, 205. *See also* Social sciences
State v. *Jones*, 51-52, 214
State v. *Ortiz*, 71, 214
State v. *Schmidt*, 32-33, 52, 214
Stevens v. *Indiana*, 51, 214
Stoicism, 35-37. *See also* Law, natural
Strawson, P., 203
Superintendent of Belchertown v. *Saikewicz*, 192, 214
Szasz, T., 138, 142

Testamentary capacity. *See* Criminal responsibility; Wills, mental capacity of testator
Tests, intelligence, 143-49. *See also* Tests, psychological
  America culture and, 172-74
  assumptions behind, 149
  Binet-Simon Scale, 143
  cultural bias, 144-47, 171-72
  educable mentally retarded (EMR), 144-48
  environmentalism, 145-47
  hereditarianism, 145-47
  heritability of I.Q., 157-60
  Jensen thesis, 158
  special education, 143-47, 162
Tests, psychological, 144, 149, 153, 155-58, 161-64, 167, 170-71, 174-75, 203. *See also* Tests, intelligence
  assumptions behind, 149-51
  discrimination, 156-57, 162, 167, 171
  validity, 149-52
Therapy, medical, 124-25, 189. *See also* Euthanasia; *In re Quinlan*; Right to privacy; *Superintendent of Belchertown* v. *Saikewicz*
  consent, 192
  duties of physicians, 188, 194, 209
  primum non nocere, 196, 209

Therapy, psychological, 124-25, 127-28, 136-39, 142, 200, 209. *See also* Coercion; Commitment; Confinement; Right to treatment; Therapy, medical
  consent, 126-27, 138, 198-99, 208
  drugs, 137, 139, 198
  electroconvulsive shock, 138
  in mental hospitals, 125-29, 134, 136-37, 177, 208
  psychosurgery, 138, 178, 197-201, 203
  recidivism, 137, 142
Thirteenth Amendment, 29
Tindal, Chief Justice, 45-47
Tocqueville, A. de, 120-21, 155
Tracy, Justice, 38-42, 44, 50, 61
Treatment. *See* Therapy, medical; Therapy, psychological

United States v. *Cooper*, 70, 214
United States v. *Ingman*, 70, 214
United States v. *McGraw*, 66, 68, 214
United States v. *Schackleford*, 70, 214
Utilitarianism, 13, 31, 74, 115, 117-18, 124
  happiness principle, 117-18

Victoria, Queen. *See M'Naghten*

Wade v. *United States*, 66, 214
Waring v. *Waring*, 94-95, 213
Welfarism, 122, 132, 134, 175, 177, 186
  justice, 124, 129
"Wild beast" standard. *See* Insanity, "wild beast" standard
Wills, 84-110
  mental capacity of testator, 85-86, 88-90, 92-109, 207
  rights of beneficiaries, 109-10
  rights of testators, 82, 84, 90, 109